OVERRUN!

The Viet Cong clutched at the shoulder of my fatigues, squeezing and twisting with his clenched fist, screaming at me in shrill Vietnamese as he desperately clawed at my throat with his other hand.

I couldn't reach his eyes, so I grabbed his Adam's apple with my right hand and tried to tear the windpipe out of his scrawny neck. He started to gag and cough a foul, fish-smelling breath into my face. I felt something cut the side of my neck.

A knife! I thought. He's cutting my throat! I let go of his neck, grabbed his right arm with both hands, and pushed it away from my throat.

My God! His right hand had been shot off just above his wrist and a piece of sharp white bone extended out of the bloody stump. He was trying to drive the bone into my throat!

Whack! A deafening shot exploded a couple feet from my ear, and the enemy soldier flew off my chest and out of my hands as if he'd been hit with a wrecking ball. I turned and saw it was the wounded Cambodian who had fired the shot. . . .

By James C. Donahue:

MOBILE GUERRILLA FORCE: *With the Special Forces in War Zone D*
BLACKJACK-33: *With Special Forces in the Viet Cong Forbidden Zone*
BLACKJACK-34

BLACKJACK-34

James C. Donahue

(Previously titled *No Greater Love*)

BALLANTINE BOOKS • NEW YORK

A Ballantine Book
Published by The Ballantine Publishing Group
Copyright © 1998, 2000 by James C. Donahue

Originally published in slightly different form by Daring Books in 1988 under the title *No Greater Love*.

www.randomhouse.com/BB/

Library of Congress Catalog Card Number: 99-91746

ISBN 0-8041-1765-9

Manufactured in the United States of America

First Ballantine Edition: April 2000

10   9   8   7   6   5   4   3   2   1

To Sandi, Michael, and Sarah
and
to the Americans and Cambodians
who fought with the
Mobile Guerrilla Force,
5th Special Forces Group (Airborne)

Greater love hath no man than this,
that a man lay down his life for his friends.

John 15:13

ACKNOWLEDGMENTS

This book would not have been possible without the encouragement and assistance of my wife, Sandi, and my good friend John Truax. I would also like to acknowledge the contributions of the following friends and agencies:

B. Kimball Baker   Editor, *National AMVET*

Stephen Banko   Sergeant, D Company, 2d Battalion, 7th Cavalry, 1st Cavalry Division

Aloysius Bartel   AMVETS National Service Officer

Anthony Cardinale   *Buffalo News*

Robert Cole   Sergeant First Class, Mobile Guerrilla Force, 5th Special Forces Group (Airborne)

James Condon   First Lieutenant, Mobile Guerrilla Force, 5th Special Forces Group (Airborne)

Francis Hagey   Sergeant First Class, Mobile Guerrilla Force, 5th Special Forces Group (Airborne)

James Hartman   Sergeant, 6924th Security Squadron, U.S. Air Force

James Howard   Master Sergeant, Mobile Guerrilla Force, 5th Special Forces Group (Airborne)

Henry Humphreys   Specialist Fifth Class, 519th Military Intelligence Battalion, Gia Dinh

William Kindoll   Sergeant First Class, Mobile Guerrilla Force, 5th Special Forces Group (Airborne)

Acknowledgments

Warren Pochinski   Sergeant First Class, Duc Phong
      Special Forces Camp, 5th Special Forces Group
      (Airborne)

L. Brooks Rader   Staff Sergeant, Mobile Guerrilla
      Force, 5th Special Forces Group (Airborne)

Roger Smith   Staff Sergeant, Mobile Guerrilla Force,
      5th Special Forces Group (Airborne)

Ernest Snider   Sergeant First Class, Mobile Guerrilla
      Force, 5th Special Forces Group (Airborne)

Scott Whitting   Staff Sergeant, Nha Trang Mike Force,
      5th Special Forces Group (Airborne)

Steven Yedinak   Captain, Mobile Guerrilla Force, 5th
      Special Forces Group (Airborne). Author, *Hard
      to Forget*.

Department of the Army, Research Assistance Branch,
      Alexandria, Virginia

Headquarters, 1st Infantry Division, Fort Riley, Kansas

John F. Kennedy Center for Military Assistance, Fort
      Bragg, North Carolina

National Personnel Records Center, Saint Louis, Missouri

U.S. Army Center of Military History, Washington, D.C.

U.S. Army Military History Institute, Carlisle Barracks,
      Pennsylvania

FOREWORD

Southeast Asia is an ancient land of intense beauty that has been traversed for centuries by warring factions. It is a land whose appeal has been shattered repeatedly by moments of terror so brutal that its people have become like unwitting participants in a modern-day Greek tragedy. We Americans were also called upon to march through this mysterious land.

It has been several decades since our hasty exit from the troubled lands of Indochina. Since then, our society has attempted to come to grips with the nation's involvement in the costly war we conducted there. A number of today's artists have attempted to capture on film and in literature the "true" nature of the war in Vietnam. Their aim, to respond adequately to our overwhelming fascination with the many puzzles of Vietnam, may never be accomplished. In part, the war's legacy may be the crystallization of the perpetual conflict between soldier and citizen concerning "what it all meant."

Vietnam was a young man's war, fought in thousands of small-unit skirmishes across the country. It involved many cultures, their soldiers and civilians alike, locked in a valiant struggle. For many of the vanquished, there was only death; for the winner, only a promise of continued struggle until, perhaps, he too joined ranks with the vanquished dead. The war was experienced, interpreted, and stored in the depths of the soldier's mind, to be truly recalled and re-experienced only from his perception. *Blackjack-34* provides us with these perceptions—Vietnam as experienced by a soldier.

The common thread in this bloody environment, which is woven into the experiences of all participants and is brought out in this chronicle, is devotion, the attachment to one's comrades-in-arms, regardless of nationality. This deep-seated human response evolves from simple acts, such as drinking from the same canteen and witnessing a friend's self-sacrifice so that others may survive. Vietnam was a time of joy, of sadness, and of violence. Lillian Hellman said, "Most people coming out of war feel lost and resentful, what had been a minute-to-minute confrontation with yourself, your struggle with what courage you have against discomfort, at the least, and death at the other end, ties you to the people you knew in the war and makes for a time others seem alien and frivolous." The author of *Blackjack-34* vividly expresses these mixed emotions as he shares with us one day of his war.

I encourage the reader of *Blackjack-34* to approach this book slowly, to listen to the sounds of the jungle and the nervous chatter of soldiers as they engage with the enemy. Try to re-create the sensations that assault your senses as you crouch under fire with your fellows beside fallen comrades. Allow your adrenaline to flow in anticipation as the battle erupts around you. Only then can you develop an appreciation for what was endured by thousands of soldiers who fought in vain.

Robert L. Jones*
February 1988

*Bob Jones retired from the U.S. Army as a major. His experiences included two tours in Vietnam, and he was assigned to Airborne, Ranger, and Special Forces units throughout his career.

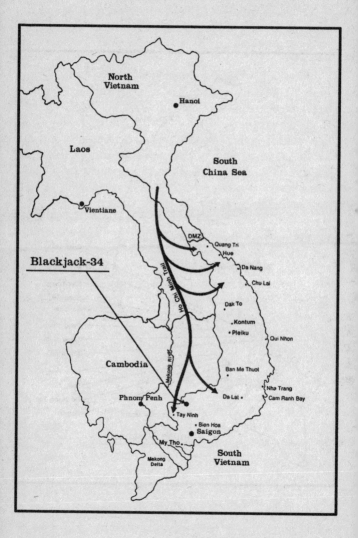

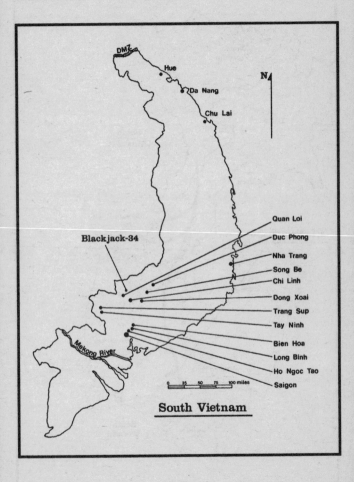

Quan Loi
Duc Phong
Nha Trang
Song Be
Chi Linh
Dong Xoai
Trang Sup
Tay Ninh
Bien Hoa
Long Binh
Ho Ngoc Tao
Saigon

DMZ
Hue
Da Nang
Chu Lai

N

Blackjack-34

Mekong River

0   25   50   75   100 miles

South Vietnam

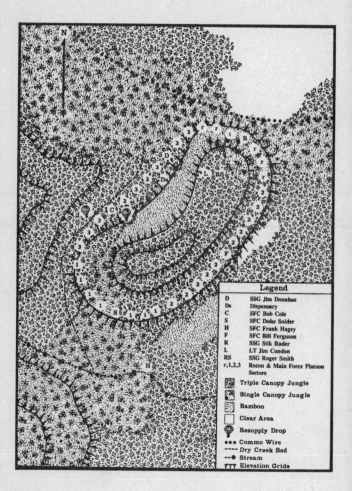

	Legend
D	SSG Jim Donahue
Ds	Dispensary
C	SFC Bob Cole
S	SFC Duke Snider
H	SFC Frank Hagey
F	SFC Bill Ferguson
R	SSG Stik Rader
L	LT Jim Condon
RS	SSG Roger Smith
r,1,2,3	Recon & Main Force Platoon Sectors

Triple Canopy Jungle

Single Canopy Jungle

Bamboo

Clear Area

Resupply Drop

••• Commo Wire
---- Dry Creek Bed
--• Stream
ᴛᴛᴛ Elevation Grids

INTRODUCTION

0430 Hours, 18 July 1967

High above our mist-shrouded ridge, a thunderhead had given birth to a predawn downpour. It was thirty minutes before first light when I awoke to a steady drumming of water on the poncho that was strung tight above my hammock. I was wet but managed to ward off a chill by wrapping myself in a piece of camouflaged parachute nylon.

Slowly unraveling from my nylon cocoon, I raised my head above the side of the hammock. The cool night air smelled of mold and rotting vegetation and was as black as tar. Except for an occasional snore or nocturnal grunt, there was little indication that 158 Cambodian guerrillas and 8 American Green Berets were camped within our small defensive perimeter astride a ridgeline six kilometers north of Quan Loi, South Vietnam. Our mission had been code-named Blackjack-34, and our objective was to locate large enemy units so that they could be engaged and destroyed by the 1st Infantry Division.

It was too early to get up, so I lay in silence, pondering the road that had brought me this far. My thoughts drifted back eighteen months to the day our twelve-member Special Forces A Team arrived at the coastal city of Nha Trang in January 1966.

* * *

When our C-130 rolled to a stop in front of the air terminal, we loaded our gear into waiting two-and-a-half-ton trucks and headed through Nha Trang. As we drove along the palm-lined streets, I was struck by the picturesque beauty of the city. Long strips of white sandy beaches separated the azure blues of the South China Sea and the emerald green mountains that overlooked this tropical paradise.

Breakers caressing the beach and the whitecaps glistening like sunlit crystals were a soothing sight to our flight-weary eyes.

Open-air restaurants, colorful storefronts, and white-plastered villas with wrought-iron balconies lined the main boulevard, reminding us of its French Colonial history.

Smells of sandalwood, bougainvillea, spicy oriental cooking, and the noxious stench of diesel fumes choked the stagnant street air. The narrow streets were congested with jeeps, cyclos, bicycles, Vespas, Lambrettas, military trucks, and an occasional vintage black Citroen, all jockeying for position as we negotiated the throng of pedestrians and vehicles. The raucous sounds of sputtering scooters, the cough of diesel engines, and the blare of impatient horns heralded our attempts to inch our way through the crowded intersections. It appeared to me that the sole traffic law was that the biggest vehicle had the right of way.

Upon arrival at the Special Forces compound, we moved our footlockers and rucksacks into a squad tent where we were greeted by a hobbled, gray-haired mamma-san with betel-nut-stained teeth and gums as black as piano keys. She wore the traditional white blouse, black silk pants, and conical hat, and continued sweeping the concrete slab as we unpacked our fatigues, underwear, and toilet articles. When we were finished, she dutifully carried off our dirty laundry, and everyone took showers.

With sixty men and their equipment packed into a C-130, the flight from North Carolina had been long and cramped. We had left Fort Bragg in the cold, early morning darkness, with a band playing the music of John Philip Sousa, and wives and girlfriends crying as they said what would be to some their last farewells. As our plane lifted off in the rain, most of the men quickly drifted off into a deep sleep. Some had partied heavily the night before, and the steel floor soon became slippery with vomit. After four days of flying with refueling stops in San Francisco, Guam, and the Philippines, we arrived, the relentless hum of the props still lingering in our ears.

The following morning, Col. William McKean, commander, 5th Special Forces Group (Airborne), welcomed us to Vietnam and assigned us the mission of constructing a new fighting camp near the small district capital of Duc Phong in Phuoc Long Province, about eighty miles northeast of Saigon. The camp would be located astride a major Viet Cong supply and infiltration route forking off the infamous Ho Chi Minh trail, which funneled men and materials south through Laos and Cambodia. From there, we were to conduct counterguerrilla operations against local Viet Cong units and interdict the movement of enemy personnel and equipment through the area.

After making an aerial reconnaissance of the area, we decided to construct our camp on a hill three kilometers southwest of Duc Phong. Half of the elevation was covered with bamboo and brush. The rest consisted of rows of evenly spaced rubber trees. A few weeks later, we choppered into the area and began construction.

Our assault forces consisted of our twelve-member A Team, a detachment of Vietnamese Special Forces, a Cambodian company that had been transferred to us from the Special Forces camp at Dong Xoai, a small contingent of navy Seabees to help clear the hill and build a runway, and two companies of Chinese Nungs from the Bien Hoa Mike Force. The Nungs were descendants of Kuomintang forces who had retreated into Indochina at the end of the Second World War. They were professional soldiers for whom the war had never ended. By aggressively patrolling the surrounding area, they kept the Viet Cong on the defensive while we were engaged in the initial stages of construction. Once our concertina wire was strung, our trenches dug, and our runway cleared, the Nungs returned to their home base at Bien Hoa.

Because enemy battalion- and regimental-size units were suspected of operating in the Duc Phong area, we concluded that we would need more than one Cambodian company to carry out our mission. In an effort to increase our manpower we established contact with the chief of the local Stieng montagnards, one of the primitive hill tribes that inhabited the convoluted highlands of Vietnam.

There was no love lost between the montagnards and the Vietnamese lowlanders. The montagnards had been victimized by the Vietnamese from both sides, so they mistrusted the government of South Vietnam as well as the Viet Cong. However, they reserved a special hatred for the Communists. Because their remote mountain villages often straddled enemy infiltration routes, they were repeatedly subjected to Communist terror—their village chiefs executed, rice confiscated, and young men forcibly conscripted. Many villages had packed up and fled, but others refused to leave their ancestral homelands and embraced the help we offered.

Not only were the Vietnamese and montagnards longstanding enemies, but they were ethnically different as well. Unlike the Vietnamese, who were slight of frame, delicate, thin-boned, and amber brown, the montagnards were hard and compressed, tough and wiry, with a reddish, nut-brown tint to their skin. The Vietnamese had almond-shaped eyes; those of the montagnards were more round without the oriental fold of skin in the corners. The sound of their language also differed; Vietnamese had a singsong sound, almost melodic; the montagnards' was a mixture of singsong and guttural tones which had a "clippity-clop" quality.

My introduction to the local chief was like an introduction to primitive man. He was gnarled and ancient with leathery skin and black, shoulder-length hair. Large pieces of elephant tusk pierced his earlobes, a beaded necklace hung around his neck, a dozen brass bracelets jangled on his wrists, and a loincloth was bound around his waist. He looked more Comanche than Asian. While we talked, he puffed on a homemade cigar that smelled like burning hemp. When our discussion ended, he tossed it on the ground and crushed its burning glow under his thick, callused heel.

With his assistance, we were able to recruit, arm, and train a force of four hundred montagnard light infantry. When the recruits arrived in camp, they wore nothing more than red-and-black loincloths and carried crude spears and crossbows.

At first, they appeared to possess an innocence that would be no match for the Viet Cong. However, as time and training progressed, we grew to admire the innate qualities that made them tenacious warriors. That, combined with their extensive knowledge of the surrounding terrain and people, enabled us to mold them into an effective fighting force.

While at Duc Phong, I served as an adviser to a montagnard light infantry company and was planning to rotate back to Fort Bragg in December 1966. However, in early

October, we received a coded message that our new group commander, Col. Francis "Blackjack" Kelly, was looking for volunteers to form and command a Mobile Guerrilla Force. Kelly's plan to introduce American-led guerrillas into the conflict represented a significant shift in strategy. From the beginning of our involvement in the war, Special Forces had been primarily employed as advisers to the Vietnamese Special Forces who, in turn, commanded montagnard, Cambodian, Chinese Nung, and ethnic Vietnamese from the Cao Dai and Hoa Hao religious sects in the conduct of counterguerrilla operations.

I considered the use of an American-commanded unit to press guerrilla operations against the Viet Cong and North Vietnamese forces a challenging concept; I had always thought that the policy of limiting Special Forces to static counterguerrilla advisory roles was a tragic waste of combat skills and training. I was convinced that the best way to beat the enemy was to out-guerrilla him. By employing irregulars who were better equipped and better trained, we could beat the enemy at his own game.

Following a discussion with my A-Team commander, I decided to notify our headquarters in Nha Trang that I would be willing to extend my tour in Vietnam for another six months in return for reassignment to the Mobile Guerrilla Force. It was a decision laced with mixed emotions. I wouldn't miss the endless steel-gray skies, torrential rains, and boot-sucking mud of the monsoon season, the daily stench of diesel fuel burning the contents of the camp's four-hole latrines, or our French-trained cook who threw cinnamon on everything he dished up, but I would miss my friends and comrades. I suppose what I most regretted leaving was the holding of sick call in remote montagnard villages. It gave me pleasure and a rewarding sense of accomplishment to aid people who wouldn't otherwise have been helped.

Within two weeks, I boarded a C-123 aircraft and was on my way to Bien Hoa with orders to report to Capt. James G. Gritz.

When we landed at the air force base, I picked up a couple cheeseburgers and a chocolate milk shake at the post exchange, then hitched a jeep ride the short distance through town to the Special Forces compound. Bien Hoa seemed especially hot, dry, and dusty that day; the air was thick with the smell of exhaust fumes and human waste. Throngs of American and Vietnamese soldiers, peddlers, prostitutes, and money changers crowded the narrow sidewalks as we sped past the shantytown shacks, sleazy bars, souvenir shops, and whorehouses. In our wake, we left still another layer of red dust, the consistency of fine flour. After arriving at the compound, I checked in with the sergeant major and moved my gear into a room.

Before reporting to Gritz, I got a whitewall haircut at a Vietnamese barber shop, spit-shined my jump boots, took a hot shower, and slipped into a set of heavily starched jungle fatigues. I was nervous about the meeting, not knowing what to expect. As I waited to see the captain, I found myself repeatedly wiping my sweaty palms on my trousers.

When I finally got to meet him, I was greeted by a man who stood five foot nine inches with sandy brown hair and piercing blue eyes. He welcomed me with a warm smile and handshake and told me he was glad to have me on board. For about thirty minutes, we sat in a very relaxed atmosphere and discussed the Mobile Guerrilla Force and the role I would play.

As we spoke, I could see he was an original, a professional soldier, but an unconventional thinker; a leader, but not a pompous elitist. Probably the single thing that impressed me most was the fact that he was very open to ideas. When we finished our preliminary talk we passed into another room where I met the other members of the team. All of them were career Special Forces soldiers who had come from A Teams located in the III Corps Tactical Zone. I hadn't known any of them before, but if my gut instincts were right, we had the makings of one hell of a team.

In order to gather our indigenous force, we relied on an underground Cambodian organization known as Khmer Serei. They had been selected from among the other ethnic groups because of their inherent discipline, physical strength, stamina, good-naturedness, tactical prowess, ability to execute silent operations, and intense hatred for the Vietnamese. Through a chain of contact whose links extended throughout the III and IV Corps Tactical Zones, the Khmer Serei raised a force of two hundred of its best men.

On 10 November 1966, we completed our recruitment phase in Bien Hoa and trucked everyone the short distance to the Special Forces camp at Ho Ngoc Tao. The camp was located on the Bien Hoa to Saigon Highway, a few miles north of the capital. The flat, sandy terrain was in stark contrast to the verdant green jungles of Duc Phong.

The morning following our arrival, the Cambodians were broken down into four platoon-size units as a languid morning sun broke free from a mist-layered horizon. From their motley appearance, they looked like anything but an effective fighting force that day. Some had gray beards, while others weren't old enough to shave. Many wore black pajamas and tire-tread sandals. A few displayed red, green, black, or maroon berets with an odd assortment of medals on their chests from the United States, France, South Vietnam, and the Viet Minh. Even though they appeared to be a ragtag bunch, I could sense that they were something more. When the platoon sergeants barked orders calling them to attention, their lines snapped straight as rulers. Silence reigned, and no one budged. These were soldiers in every sense of the word. The Khmer Serei had done its job well.

From 13 November to 15 December, we trained sixteen hours a day, seven days a week. Our typical working day began in the predawn darkness, about two hours before breakfast, with a long run, followed by calisthenics. After eating, we trained the Cambodians in such basic skills as marksmanship, hand-to-hand combat, and first aid. Because the unit was to be engaged in unconventional operations, mining, booby-trapping, sniping, special weapons, and use of other devices were also taught. After dinner, we practiced such skills as night-firing techniques, movement at night, light-and-noise discipline, and setting up night ambushes. Whenever we had a few hours off, everyone enjoyed playing volleyball or a game similar to Italian bocce. The volleyball games were pretty even; the Americans were taller, but the Bodes were more agile.

While at Ho Ngoc Tao, we organized a headquarters section, a reconnaissance platoon, and three main-force platoons. The headquarters section consisted of the mobile guerrilla force commander, an American radio operator with a PRC-74 radio, which would be used to communicate with Bien Hoa by Morse code, a Cambodian company medic with a major surgical kit, a Cambodian interpreter, and a ten-member headquarters security section. The reconnaissance and the three main-force platoons had American commanders and deputy commanders. Each of these consisted of approximately thirty Cambodians, including a Cambodian platoon sergeant and three Cambodian squad leaders. In addition to command responsibilities, each American was also assigned duties as a specialist in one or more areas: operations and intelligence, communications, medical, light weapons, heavy weapons, or demolitions.

On 15 December, we completed our training and flew to Duc Phong Special Forces Camp to field-test the guerrilla tactics developed at Ho Ngoc Tao. Our return was a pleasant change since it afforded me the opportunity to see old friends. We spent the first two days in the rolling green hills south of camp practicing tactics and aerial resupply methods. While at Ho Ngoc Tao, we had initially planned to resupply our operations by parachute-dropped supplies and ammunition from Air Commando–flown C-123 or C-130 aircraft, but we soon concluded that large, slow-flying aircraft would compromise our location. As a solution to the problem, we tested a method in which A-1E fighter aircraft dropped supply-filled napalm containers rigged with T-7A reserve parachutes. We saw that resupply methods resembling fighter bombing runs would alert no one to our presence.

Our first practice drop that day overshot the clearing by about fifty yards, and the chutes snagged in the congested canopy. On the second pass, we developed a system where the pilot released his load over an orange ground panel on command from Captain Gritz. The olive drab parachutes opened at one hundred feet, and the chutes, with their silver napalm containers attached, drifted like silver seed pods into the center of the clearing, landing with a dull thud. Once on the ground, the napalm containers, tied shut with nylon parachute line, were cut open and their supplies distributed to the troops.

A few days after our arrival at Duc Phong, we were informed that Colonel Kelly had volunteered the Mobile Guerrilla Force to conduct an on-the-ground search for a downed U-2 spy plane and its top-secret electronic countermeasure System 13A black box. We later learned that the black box's state-of-the-art technology fooled enemy radar into thinking that the U-2 was somewhere it wasn't. Unlike those electronic countermeasure systems that filled enemy radar screens with clutter, the System 13A device gave no indication to the enemy that the information displayed on his radar screen was false.

The Dragon Lady, CIA designation for the U-2, had broken up at an altitude of twenty-six thousand feet and crashed somewhere south of the provincial capital of Song Be. Because it had been calculated that the U-2 could have crashed anywhere within a 440-square-mile cone-shaped area of enemy-controlled jungle, our mission was compared to finding the proverbial needle in a haystack. After four days and numerous skirmishes with Viet Cong units, a Cambodian from the 2d Platoon hit pay dirt when he found the missing footlocker-size instrument intact and uncompromised.

On 4 January 1967, the Mobile Guerrilla Force began its ground infiltration of War Zone D. The mission was code-named Blackjack-31, and during the month-long operation, we fought fifty-one engagements, called in tactical air strikes against twenty-seven targets, and raided fifteen company- and battalion-size base camps.

One of the lessons learned from Blackjack-31 was that American-led guerrilla units were capable of conducting unconventional operations in Viet Cong–controlled areas and secret zones for extended periods of time.

On 7 February, we were extracted by choppers from War Zone D and ferried back to Duc Phong, and later that day to Bien Hoa, where all of the Americans were decorated by Colonel Kelly and the Cambodians given a welcome leave. When the Cambodians returned from their leave, the company was trucked west to our new base of operations at Trang Sup Special Forces Camp.

Following a thirty-day leave in Buffalo, I returned to Bien Hoa where I talked a chopper pilot into giving me a hop to Trang Sup. Arriving there, I found that the company had established itself in an abandoned French-built compound next to the Special Forces Camp. Its crumbling stucco walls, pockmarked by bullets and time, and the rusted coils of concertina wire were haunting reminders of another war. Our new home was situated six kilometers northwest of Tay Ninh City, not far from the foot of Nui Ba Den, or Black Virgin Mountain as it was known to many Americans.

The camp was surrounded by jade-colored rice paddies, a few scattered palm clusters, and dusty red roads rising a couple feet above the paddy waters. The lone mountain, which I assumed to be an extinct volcano, seemed perpetually brushed by clouds.

Over the next few months, the camp at Trang Sup served as a base to launch a number of major operations. On 2 May, we were inserted by choppers into War Zone D southeast of Cao Song Be Special Forces Camp where part of the company was immediately surrounded by elements of the 271st and 273d Viet Cong Main Force Regiments. During the day-long battle, the unit was nearly overrun by repeated human-wave attacks from fully uniformed Viet Cong as well as khaki-clad Chinese mercenaries. But, for some inexplicable reason, the enemy eventually broke off the attack and melted back into the jungle.

As I lay in the morning stillness listening to the muffled patter of droplets splashing against broad leaves and my hammock, it felt good to be alive. My experience of Vietnam was a mental scrapbook of mingled joys and tragedies. Indeed, there had been times of brain-numbing monotony and gut-wrenching carnage, but there were also special times when it seemed that everything within me simply savored the essence of life because I had lived so close to death.

My last trip to Nha Trang had been that way. It had all seemed so out of place. I had bought a six-pack of Coca-Cola, a pair of swimming trunks, and a bottle of Coppertone at the post exchange and caught a ride down to the beach.

The scent of salt air blowing off the bay, the sound of palms ruffling in the wind, and the pleasant sensation of warm sand squeezing between my toes were a refreshing contrast to grueling weeks in the bush. I spread my camouflage poncho liner a few yards from the pounding surf, then ran into the backwash, diving headfirst into a large wave. The warm saltwater cleansed my scrapes and cuts, and for thirty minutes, I lost all track of the war as I bodysurfed the rolling breakers. Finally, after one too many mouthfuls of saltwater, I retired to my liner, where I sat, rubbing Coppertone over my body and soaking up the sun.

In a restaurant down the beach, the Beach Boys were blaring from a loudspeaker. A torrent of nostalgic memories played upon my emotions as the words, "I wish they all could be California girls . . ." drifted across the sands. It seemed strange how certain songs conjured up different times and places. It was also odd that war could have so many moods, so many haunting realities. One day you were knee-deep in leech-infested slime or brooding over the bloodied bodies of your friends, and the next day you were relaxing on a tropical beach, sipping Coke and fantasizing with the Beach Boys. Vietnam was like that. It could be so brutally real and yet so very unreal at the same time, like one of those recurring dreams that never seem to end.

The here and now reasserted itself as the annoying whine of a hungry mosquito about my ear snapped me back to the present. I squinted and yawned, then took a measured look at the hands on my watch. It was about that time. . . .

News Clippings

The American Forces total 466,000 men.
Buffalo Evening News, July 18, 1967

The polls had given Lyndon Johnson a long cold winter and a dampening spring, but with summer his popularity burgeoned and his sudden rise in the polls induced such a state of ebullience and playfulness in the President that he took up bicycle-riding at his ranch.
Life, July 21, 1967

The nationwide rail strike disrupted the country's economy yesterday, crippling the movement of people, mail and food supplies.
The New York Times, July 18, 1967

In the first five months of 1967, the South Vietnamese suffered 3,681 battlefield deaths. The Americans lost 2,853.
Buffalo Evening News, July 18, 1967

Three war protesters were carried out of the Pentagon in wheelchairs today as defense officials laid down a policy of prohibiting announced demonstrators from expressing their dissent inside the building.
The New York Times, July 18, 1967

Joe Namath, the New York Jets star quarterback, headed the 51 holdovers who reported to training camps today at Peekskill Military Academy.
The New York Times, July 18, 1967

James Lee Barrett is a script writer from Hollywood who likes realism. In order to gather material for the John Wayne movie "The Green Berets," he went on a tour of Special Forces camps throughout Vietnam.
Army Digest, July 1967

The all-night curfew in Newark was eliminated as New Jersey's Gov. Hughes said that "the rioting and looting are apparently over and the violence has ceased."
The Wall Street Journal, July 18, 1967

Gemini: Your ability to cooperate will be tested, and collaboration will succeed where independent action would be of no avail.
Buffalo Evening News, July 17, 1967

1

0500 HOURS

In our world beneath the canopy, the predawn smells of wet foliage, rotting humus, and moist earth hung heavily in the air. The sky above the trees was beginning to glow with the first hints of dawn, and the jungle was alive with the chirping of birds and the hooting of monkeys.

I sat up tentatively in my hammock and dangled my bare feet over the side only to be shocked by the sensation of cold mud beneath my soles. Balancing in my suspended perch, I reached into my rucksack to remove a can of foot powder. A little powder between the toes was one of the few pleasures the jungle permitted. I picked up my boots, turned them upside down, and gave them a vigorous shake to dislodge any creatures that might have sought shelter from the downpour. I didn't need any surprises that early in the morning.

After lacing up my wet boots, I stood and did a few toe touches to stretch my cramped back muscles. Sleeping in a hammock had the disadvantage that you couldn't roll over and so fought a constant battle to get comfortable. There was only one position, and that was flat on your back.

Though my morning stretch had brought my system to life, I was in no mood for a breakfast of cold ham and lima beans, so I dug out a package of lightweight, dehydrated

16

Vietnamese rations. In spite of ingenious recipes and in-the-field concoctions, it was a rare troop who savored the taste of C rations. Still, most of my team members didn't relish the taste of dehydrated rice rations either. I was an exception. They had the advantage of being a lot lighter than C rations, and after more than a year of experimenting with them, I had come up with a number of variants, including: rice with instant cream and sugar, rice with cocoa mix, rice with dried carrots, rice with hot peppers, rice with instant soup, rice with dried minnows, rice with dried shrimp, rice with dried spinach, and rice with Tabasco sauce. That morning I selected rice with dried minnows. After adding a half canteen of water and a few minnows to the plastic bag the meal came in, I tied off the top with a rubber band and set it on a nearby stump. In fifteen minutes, the water would be fully absorbed by the rice.

I glanced to my left and saw the silhouette of SFC Bob Cole rolling out of his hammock. Well over six feet tall, Bob was a huge black man who reminded me of James Earl Jones. I could never quite figure out how someone his size could sleep in a small Vietnamese hammock. To the Bodes, he was affectionately known as *Trung si Camau.* They were awed by the fact that the chocolate brown color of his skin was as dark as their own, yet he was so large in comparison to their slight frames. Bob was an operations sergeant who came to the Mobile Guerrilla Force from one of the Special Forces camps in Tay Ninh Province. He had been assigned to the 3d Platoon after George Ovsak was killed at Trang Sup.

"Sleep okay?" I asked in a hushed voice.

"Yeah, not bad. Got up around two-thirty," he yawned as he laced up his boots. "Checked the guard and went back to sleep."

"Looks like the storm moved east," I said.

"Yeah, it's breakin' up," he said while staring up at the sky. Through holes in the canopy, we could see a few stars in the early morning sky.

"Hope so," I mused. "My toes look like bleached prunes."

As Bob and I talked, the grays were quickly turning to dull shades of green, yellow, and brown, and high in the canopy a few monkeys cried *hoot, hoot, hoot* as they scurried from branch to branch.

His boots laced, Bob took a couple of steps to where I was pulling the quick releases on my hammock.

"Hear those explosions?" he whispered.

"Yeah, around three-thirty. Sounded like a Sky Spot going in a few klicks north of here."

"Think the lieutenant called 'em in?"

"May have," I said.

"It's amazing how they can bomb a target in the middle of the night."

"I think it's all done with computers," I whispered. "We radio the coordinates of the target back to the air liaison officer in Bien Hoa. The ALO phones 'em down to the III Corps Direct Air Support Center at Tan Son Nhut, and thirty minutes later, good night Charlie. From thirty thousand feet below, ya can't even hear the plane."

"It's all computerized?" he asked.

I guess we were all amazed by some of the state-of-the-art wizardry and sophisticated electronics being tested.

"Think so," I said. "I'm not sure how it works, but from what I've heard, the coordinates are fed into a computer, the aircraft locks onto a radar beam, and the computer calculates the bomb release point."

"How accurate are they?"

"The air force won't let ya call 'em in any closer than

six hundred meters," I said. "But when it's gotten tight, we've lied about our coordinates and brought 'em in a lot closer."

"Better be damn sure of your coordinates," Bob chuckled. "If you're wrong, you're history."

"You got it," I said. "On Blackjack-31, I almost shit my pants."

"What happened?" Bob asked as drops continued to filter through the canopy.

I explained that one night one of our listening posts reported a large enemy unit on the next hill. We contacted Bien Hoa and requested that a Sky Spot be brought in on the target. About thirty minutes later, the air was filled with the soft whistle of bombs falling through the blackness. As the whistle grew louder, we all hit the ground. I could feel my heart pounding faster and faster. Then the jungle lit up like an enormous flash bulb had gone off, and the ground buckled and heaved from the concussions with such force that it seemed as if someone was literally shaking the jungle floor beneath us.

"Betcha a lot of prayers were going up to Buddha," Bob whispered.

"Better believe it. Every Bode had his Buddha crammed in his mouth," I said. "The problem in the Dong Nai Valley was that the terrain looked like a thousand green balls on a pool table. It all looks pretty much the same whether you're humpin' through it or flyin' over it."

As we talked, Thach, our Cambodian platoon sergeant, could be heard checking the men. Since the Viet Cong often attacked at dawn, he made it a practice to have everyone saddled up and ready to move before first light. Bending over beside my rucksack, I opened the side pocket and removed a toothbrush and toothpaste. A splash of water on my face and the sweet smell of Colgate Dental

Creme were a real treat. Even though my body was covered with layers of dried sweat, mosquito repellent, and grime from the previous day, the morning ritual somehow made me feel clean.

In the lower levels of the canopy, hundreds of small lime green birds chirped as they fluttered from branch to branch. High in the trees, a thin layer of mist glowed white, and a few monkeys sat watching our every move. Mornings were always the best time of day.

I removed my T-shirt and slipped into my damp camouflage fatigue jacket as Bob squatted beside me and switched on our PRC-25 radio.

"I'd better check in," he said matter-of-factly. "Our primary still 42.70?"

"Yeah, 42.70," I said after checking my commo pad.

"Fox Control, this is Fox Three. Over," Bob whispered into his radio handset.

"Fox Three, this is Fox Control. Over," Lt. Jim Condon responded from his position near the center of our perimeter.

"Control, this is Three. This is a commo check. How d'ya read me? Over."

"Three, this is Control. I read you five by five. How me? Over."

"Control, this is Three. I read you same. Out."

"Better change that battery," I said as I stuffed my wet poncho in my rucksack.

"Yeah," he said. "I'll booby-trap it."

"Trackers'll pick it up," I whispered. "They got a way of rechargin' 'em."

"I'll rig it for instant detonation."

We found that if we didn't rig fragmentation hand-grenade booby traps for instant detonation, the normal four-second delay gave the enemy plenty of time to jump clear of the explosion.

Looking up through isolated holes in the blanket of vegetation, we saw welcome patches of blue begin to appear. It was going to be a clear day. As I listened to the radio, I heard Recon and the 1st and 2d platoons making commo checks with Lieutenant Condon. The familiar sound of their voices was reassuring.

"Bac-si," a hushed voice called to me. Anticipating a serious problem, I felt my heart rate accelerate. When I neared the source, I saw that it was Danh, our silent weapons specialist.

"What's wrong?" I whispered.

"Bac-si, Rinh have thing on mouth. You look."

I followed Danh, and a few meters away, we found Rinh sitting in his hammock. With his mouth wide open, he had a blood-filled, brown leech attached to the end of his tongue.

"Told ya not to sleep with your mouth open," I joked with a sense of relief.

Although smoking was not permitted, I told Danh to light up a cigarette. That was risky because the telltale scent of tobacco could be detected far downwind. When Danh handed me the cigarette, I carefully touched the sluglike sucker with the glowing tip of the cigarette. In a few seconds, it released its hold and dropped off, enabling me to squish it into the mud with the heel of my boot. Rinh stood there, spitting.

"Numba ten," Danh grunted in disgust as I removed a canteen from Rinh's rucksack and crushed a few salt tablets in a cup of water.

"Wash your mouth out," I said as I handed him the cup.

After gargling and spitting for a few more minutes, he flashed me a toothy grin.

"Feel better?" I asked.

"Yes, Donahue. Thank you."

I gave him a pat on the back and headed back to where Bob and Thach were sitting on a fallen tree, eating breakfast. Thach was the oldest man in the platoon, somewhere around forty. He had the typical Cambodian build, lean and sinewy; a compressed little man with a yellow-brown tint who stood about chest-high. Thach had a friendly face with a disarming smile, which concealed a fierce hatred for the Vietnamese and intense loyalty to us and his men. He had served as a squad leader but took over as the platoon sergeant when his predecessor was shot in the stomach near Phuoc Vinh. The wound was very serious, and the man was still recovering at the 24th Evacuation Hospital in Long Binh. Thach had survived more firefights than anyone could count and was one of the best soldiers I'd known. His military experience and knowledge of the jungle were an indispensable asset to our team.

Thach was also a man of contrasting personalities. During off-duty hours, he was a very easygoing person who had a fatherly relationship with the younger men in the platoon, but during an operation, he was a hardened warrior who tolerated nothing less than instant, willing obedience. He knew that discipline was one of the keys to survival. A unit that fought as a group of individuals wouldn't last long, but a unit that fought as one could slug it out with anyone. On more than one occasion, I had seen him sink his boot in someone's butt. But he never hurt any of the men, just scared the hell out of them so that they feared him more than the enemy.

The still morning air was filled with the chirping of birds, the hooting of monkeys, and an occasional screech. Overhead, a few patchy clouds scudded away to the east. It was one of those Vietnam mornings I both loved and hated. I loved it because the air was refreshing and the sky resplendent with color; I hated it because the rising sun would soon turn the jungle into a steam bath.

As the jungle colored in, I was overwhelmed by its beauty and variety. Towering, brown-black trees supported a canopy of green foliage like the four-story pillars of an ancient temple. In the lower levels of the canopy, gnarled brown vines twisted in all directions or dangled like limp tentacles from the branches. Occasionally, vines ensnared the trunks of trees as if struggling to strangle them in some quiet death grip. Here and there, stands of bamboo stood clumped together like bundles of lime green poles.

"Everything squared away?" Bob asked.

"Yeah," I said, as I removed a can of peaches from my rucksack and sat on the fallen tree. "Rinh had a leech on his tongue."

"A leech?"

"Yeah." I smiled. "I've seen 'em get into ears and noses."

"Yuk." Bob shook his head.

"You know Rinh long time?" Thach inquired as he ate his rice with a plastic C-ration spoon.

"Over a year," I said, thinking how long a year really was to know someone in Vietnam. With men constantly being transferred, wounded, or killed, relationships generally didn't last long, even though they were often some of the most intimate of friendships, friendships forged in the crucible of war. Rinh was one of the survivors: someone who, through luck or skill, had managed to stay alive.

"He's a good man," Bob said as he used his metal canteen cup to mix up a batch of cocoa.

"That he is." I worked open the lid of my peaches.

About a week after reporting to the Mobile Guerrilla Force, I went back to Duc Phong and smuggled him and a few others out on an Air America plane that was ferrying up a load of pigs from Saigon. I had to sneak them out because the Vietnamese Special Forces—the *Luc Luong Dac Biet*—had turned down their request to go with me. The Vietnamese were madder than hell when they found out, and were still looking for them.

"Yeah," Bob said, taking a sip of his cocoa with a grimace. "The Bodes are number one, but this cold cocoa is number ten."

"Old Rinh still hasn't recovered from the wounds he got when we hit that POW camp near Cao Song Be," I said. "The Vietnamese hospital in Tay Ninh didn't even treat 'im because the Viets don't like the Bodes," I said as I enjoyed my peaches.

"Vietnam want kill all Cambodian," Thach added with contempt.

"Didn't ya take 'im to the American hospital?" Bob asked.

"Yeah, as soon as I got back."

When I returned to Trang Sup, about three days after Rinh got hit, I drove to the hospital to see how he was doing. I found him lying on the floor, still covered with dirt and dried blood. After telling the Vietnamese administrator what I thought of his hospital, I carried Rinh to my jeep and drove him to the 196th Light Infantry Brigade's MASH Hospital.

"They take care of 'im?" Bob asked.

"Are you kidding? He was the only patient in an air-conditioned ward. He had three or four American nurses takin' care of 'im."

"Think he was gettin' any?" Bob laughed.

"Tell ya one thing. He didn't wanna leave." I laughed. "You guys want some peaches?" I passed the half-full can to Thach.

"*Bac-si,* you and *Trung si* Cole come Kampuchea when we go?" Thach asked.

"Cambodia?" Bob said.

"In Vietnam, government and VC want kill all Cambodians," Thach said. "In Kampuchea, Sihanouk *sau lam,* so, we go Kampuchea, kick out numba ten Sihanouk, and all Khmer people live in peace."

"We'll have to check that one out with Colonel Kelly," Bob said, trying to act serious.

"Sounds like somethin' Blackjack would go for," I added.

"Looks like your rice is ready," Bob told me.

I grabbed the by then bulging bag of rice from the stump. As we ate, Bob broke out his acetate-covered map and spread it on the ground in front of us.

"Rice tastes flat," I said. "Got some hot sauce?"

He reached into his rucksack.

"Here ya go," he said as he handed me a bottle of Tabasco sauce.

"You lift this from that French restaurant in Nha Trang?"

"You know I wouldn't do that," he said with feigned innocence as I sprinkled some on my rice.

"How can ya eat cold Cs this early in the mornin'?" I asked.

"They're not bad," he said as he sunk his fork into a can of ham and eggs.

"I'll tell ya what," I said. "I'll trade ya a can of ham and lima beans for a bag of rice."

"You got it."

"Speaking of food—what d'ya say you, Thach, and I head down to Saigon for a couple of days when we get back?" I asked.

"Great," Bob said. "We'll stay at the villa on Pasteur."

I always looked forward to staying at the Special Forces

villa for a night or two, a stately old French mansion on a palm-tree-lined avenue. I especially liked the smell of clean sheets on the beds, and bacon and eggs for breakfast.

"We'll stop at the USO," I added. "They got great cheeseburgers and milk shakes."

Whenever I got down to Saigon, I always found time to stop at the USO. While filling up on cheeseburgers and chocolate milk shakes, I always caught up on what was going on in the rest of the world by browsing through their collection of current newspapers and magazines.

"What about it?" Bob asked Thach. "You like burgers?"

"What burger?" Thach shrugged. "If we go Saigon, you and *Bac-si* come stay my family in Cholon."

"It's a deal," I said. "When we get back to Trang Sup, we'll head out as soon as we get the troops squared away."

Thach removed a wallet from his pocket, carefully took out a waterproof plastic bag, and proudly displayed a picture of his wife.

"She good cook." Thach smiled. "She make burger."

"What's our route of march?" I asked as I chewed on a few minnows.

"Let's see." Bob used his finger to point to the terrain features on his map. "We're on this ridgeline, with the creek off to the east, and, ah, we're gonna head north up toward the Loc Ninh–An Loc border."

"Terrain doesn't look bad," I said. "Shouldn't have any trouble makin' fifteen or sixteen klicks."

"Good area for operation," Thach added. "Mountain not big. Much water."

Thach was right. The area had many features that made it ideal for mobile guerrilla operations. Being light infantry and highly mobile, we could move cross-country much quicker than larger, more heavily armed units. In the low area, we would navigate around the swamps and mangroves and move quickly through bamboo thickets. Except for the ridgelines, growth was usually thicker at the higher elevations. If we had to move over high ground and couldn't travel the ridgelines, our movement could be slowed to two to three hundred meters an hour. If there were elephants in the area, we could also use their zigzag trails if they coincided with our route of march.

Because of the area's favorable conditions, it was also an ideal location for enemy base camps. Whatever was advantageous to us was also advantageous to Charlie. Experience had taught me that if an area had overhead cover, high-speed trails, and an abundant water supply, there was a very real possibility it also concealed enemy base camps.

"Better keep to the west of those swampy areas," I said, pointing to them on Bob's map. "They can be bad news."

"Got a lotta rubber up there." Bob pointed. "Probably owned by that asshole we ran into back at Quan Loi."

When we had landed on the airstrip in Quan Loi, a Frenchman driving a black Citroen and dressed in a white suit and pith helmet screeched to a halt in front of our formation. With a heavy French accent, he had threatened to sue the United States government if we damaged any of his rubber trees.

"He must be playin' both sides of the fence," I said. "Payin' off the VC and sellin' rubber to the States."

Whoomph, whoomph, whoomph. What sounded like artillery exploded far to the south.

"Hien wanted to booby-trap his Citroen." Bob laughed. "But you're right. Here he is livin' in a big house with hundreds of plantation workers and servants, and the Cong hasn't greased his ass. Something ain't right."

"You don't think he knows anything about our mission, do ya?"

"Hope not," Bob said. "Ya know damn well he'd sell us out."

"If we make contact, we'll call in a B-52 strike on his rubber," I joked.

Bob looked at the map with a mischievous smile. "Three strikes'll take out the whole plantation," he mused as SFC Duke Snider walked up to where we were sitting.

"Move out in three-zero minutes. Two columns," Duke told us. "Third Herd's got point on the left. Recon on the right."

"Okay," Bob said as he folded his map and slipped it back into his pocket.

"You'd better do somethin' about that bald head," I said to Duke. "You can spot it a mile away," I added as he laughed and headed toward the 2d Platoon's sector of our perimeter.

"*Trung si* Cole not need camouflage." Thach smiled. "You and *Trung si* Snider too white to hide in jungle."

"Won't argue with that one," I laughed.

"Duke's something else. Probably the best demo man in country," Bob said. "On Blackjack-33, his booby traps saved our ass."

"Yeah, those trackers were on our trail."

"They were mad as hell about us hitting that base camp. Remember Fergy's platoon killin' all those guys in the bleachers?" Bob asked. "Think it was a map-reading class."

"How could I forget?" Kim Lai, the platoon sergeant, told me that when the Viet Cong instructor saw the platoon standing on line a short distance from his podium, his face turned white and his jaw dropped, just as one of the Bodes hit him in the chest with a burst of three.

"Caught 'em with their pants down," Bob added.

"VC not have guard," Thach said.

"Ya know my hair still hasn't grown back where that

bullet gave me a new part," Bob said as he rubbed his head. "Felt like someone hit me with a baseball bat."

"Your lucky day," I said. "If that round had been a hair lower you'd be dead."

While attacking the base camp, Bob and I had been pinned down behind a large anthill. A burst of machine-gun fire shot off his hat, and when I checked his head, I found that the bullet had creased his scalp. There was some bleeding but nothing serious. After we broke contact with the enemy, I asked him if he was going back to look for his hat. He didn't think it was funny, and I often reminded him that he had no sense of humor.

I scooped a small hole in the jungle floor with Thach's entrenching tool and buried our meager scraps of garbage, a couple of plastic rice bags and a few crushed C-ration cans.

"Make sure they bury everything," Bob told Thach.

"Okay, *Trung si*," Thach said as he stood up.

"A few other things," I said to Thach as he was about to leave.

"Yes, *Bac-si*."

"Yesterday Lieu had his selector switch on automatic," I said while removing my rifle-cleaning kit from my rucksack. "Gotta make sure the squad leaders check every weapon every mornin'. That means a round in the chamber and the selector switch on safe."

"Okay, *Bac-si*," he said as I passed him my silicone cloth.

"Don't want any accidental discharges," Bob added. "Jim, gimme your chamber brush." I passed it to him, still reflecting on his last words.

Bob was right. As a light infantry guerrilla force, we wanted to select the time, place, and circumstances of all contacts with the enemy.

"Another thing," I added. "Last night, some of the guys

didn't clean their weapons. Every night, every weapon in the platoon has to be broken down, scrubbed with solvent, and oiled."

"Break 'em down into twos as soon as the claymores and LPs are out," Bob said. "One man cleans, and the other stands guard. Then they switch."

"Okay, *Trung si*."

I was concerned about the ammunition and the weapons. Every time we made heavy contact, some of our M-16s jammed. I suspected that it was due to high-carbon-content ammunition and poor workmanship on the M-16s.

We also had problems with our Japanese-made indigenous rucksacks and World War II–vintage Browning automatic rifle belts. The rucksacks required constant maintenance and often tore out at the strap connectors. When the Browning automatic rifle belts were fully loaded with ammunition, they frequently tore out at the eyelets. Our camouflage fatigues weren't much better. After a couple of weeks in the jungle, the crotch had a tendency to tear. The Bodes wore Japanese-made boots that often came apart at the soles.

"Got the green tape?" I asked as Thach finished wiping down his rifle.

"Yes, *Bac-si*," he said, pointing to his rucksack.

"Make sure the safety pins on the grenades are taped down; that means HE, gas, and smoke."

"Don't want 'em catchin' on branches," Bob said. "Use that tape to secure anything that makes noise, and remember, no slings on the weapons and tape down the swivels."

Voicing my own concern with a practical sense of seriousness, I said, "Thach, ya gotta keep on the squad leaders' asses. You can't do it all yourself."

"Gotta kick ass," Bob added.

"I know, *Trung si*. You know I fight at Dien Bien Phu with 5th Vietnam Parachute," he said with emotion. His leathery, weathered face proudly portrayed the scars of countless battles.

"I understand, my friend," I conceded, "but if ya want 'em to live, you'd better tighten up." I looked into his brown bloodshot eyes and put my hand on his shoulder. He smiled, revealing a set of gold-capped teeth covered with rice.

"Okay, *Bac-si*."

"One other thing," Bob added as he pinned a wet pair of socks to the outside of his rucksack. "Yesterday, a few of 'em looked like they were out for a stroll at the Saigon Zoo. They can't be daydreaming. That means their thumb on the selector switch, finger on the trigger, and eyes open."

"Today I keep machine gun behind me. Okay, *Trung si*?" Thach said.

"Good," Bob said as he adjusted the webbing of his ammunition harness. "Make sure he maintains visual contact with you. No fallin' behind."

Our M-60 was the most effective weapon in the platoon. Its rate of fire and killing power was coveted by all grunts. In the event of enemy contact, it was critical that we be able to deploy it to the point of contact. If that proved possible, we could often gain fire superiority and overrun the enemy before he could deploy on line. It was similar to crossing the *T* in naval warfare.

"Yeah, and tell Danh we put that silencer on his Sten so we can take prisoners. That means arm and shoulder shots, nothin' to the head or chest," I added as I checked the twenty-five ammunition-filled magazines in my ammunition belt.

"No leg shots," Bob added. "Don't wanna carry anyone."

It took six to eight men to carry a wounded man any distance. The Bodes would carry an American or fellow

Cambodian until they dropped from heat exhaustion, but they weren't all that enthusiastic about carrying a wounded enemy soldier.

"Okay, *Trung si*," Thach said. "I talk squad leader."

"Keep an eye on Lieu," I said. "This is his first operation."

Thach nodded and then headed for the perimeter. After Thach left, I told Bob that I was concerned about Lieu because I had a feeling he didn't have what it took to be a member of the Mobile Guerrilla Force. As a possible weak link, he could jeopardize the lives of others.

A couple of weeks earlier, I had taken him down to Saigon with me on my monthly Budweiser and Coca-Cola run. After hitchhiking from Trang Sup to Saigon, we found that there weren't any two-and-a-half-ton trucks available at the Special Forces compound on Cong Ly Street or at the villa on Avenue de Pasteur.

As a last resort, we caught a taxi out to the Cholon exchange. Once there, we stood near the front entrance, waiting for someone to park a truck. Fifteen minutes later, a soldier from the 1st Logistical Command drove up in a new two-and-a-half-ton truck and parked about fifty meters down the street. As soon as he entered the exchange, we jumped into the cab. Lieu was too nervous to drive, so I drove it to a nearby body shop that was owned by the family of a Chinese Nung from the Mike Force in Bien Hoa. He quickly painted out the 1st Logistical Command's numerals and replaced them with A-303 and USSF.

From there we drove to the Saigon beer and soft drink distribution center to requisition a truckload. It was as large as a city block, and stacked inside its barbed-wire fence were thousands of cases of every conceivable brand of beer and soft drink, warming in the open. It was very busy that day as trucks from all over III Corps were being loaded by forklifts.

After a forklift driver loaded pallets of Budweiser and Coca-Cola onto our truck, we drove to the front gate where we were stopped by a Vietnamese guard. I pulled a receipt out of my briefcase and showed it to him. After comparing it with our cargo, he returned the receipt and waved us through the gate.

A block away I pulled the truck over and showed Lieu the receipt. The date on it was over a year old, and I had managed to keep it in mint condition by storing it in my briefcase. After I explained that we'd been using the same bogus receipt over and over without paying for anything in almost a year, he turned white. He was convinced that the White Mice—the Vietnamese police—were going to arrest us.

On our drive back to Trang Sup, we hoped to pick up a convoy at Cu Chi, but no one else was on the road that day. The road from Cu Chi to Trang Sup was especially dangerous because the enemy often mined it or set up ambushes. Rather than return to Saigon, we decided to go it alone. With Lieu riding shotgun, armed with my Swedish-K submachine gun, I put the truck into high gear and drove down the center of the road as fast as it could go.

When we finally pulled in the front gate at Trang Sup, we parked in front of the team house and downed the first two cans of beer. It was warm and nasty, but we thoroughly enjoyed the spoils of war.

Nothing was simple in Vietnam. Even something as seemingly easy as picking up some beer and soft drinks could become complicated. Every time you assumed that everyone knew everything they were supposed to know, or would do everything they were supposed to do, it could cost you lives. Nothing was routine. Because we had suffered so many dead and seriously wounded in recent months, that problem had become more acute than ever before. It was further complicated by the fact that our early departure from Trang Sup reduced the amount of time we could devote to training replacements.

We had to move out more than a week earlier than planned because a few Bodes had beaten the hell out of a high-ranking ARVN officer in a Tay Ninh barbershop and stolen his silver-plated pistol. When we refused to conduct a search for the guilty Bodes, the White Mice, and a Vietnamese armored unit threatened an all-out attack on our camp. In order to avoid a potentially explosive situation, we flew out as soon as we could issue food and ammunition.

"I'm gonna take a crap," I told Bob as I grabbed our entrenching tool and headed into the dense brush. I walked to a spot ten meters outside the perimeter where I encountered a solid wall of thorn-covered brushes, dug a small hole, and squatted.

No sooner had I dropped my trousers than a malevolent cloud of hungry mosquitoes swarmed over my exposed buttocks. Trying to maintain my balance, I batted them away with my hand as they dove and darted. Squatting over my makeshift latrine, I was pleased that I had something as basic as toilet paper. On Blackjack-31, I'd run out of paper and had to use green leaves instead. I'd never forget the day I used poison ivy leaves by mistake.

Whack-whack-whack. Whump-whump-whump. My thoughts were interrupted by an exchange of M-16 and AK-47 fire.

Damn! Of all things to be doing during an attack, I said to myself as I yanked up my pants and grabbed my M-16.

"Wetsu!" I yelled as I ran in the direction the perimeter. Wetsu—"we eat this shit up"—was used as our running password when quick identification was required. Reentering the perimeter, I felt a great sense of relief that I wasn't shot by my own men: you definitely didn't want to get caught outside the perimeter during a firefight. As I approached Bob, I saw that he was down on one knee with the radio handset pressed to his ear.

"What's goin' on?" I asked as he monitored radio transmissions.

"Second Platoon made contact with two VC," Bob said. "Black pajamas and soft hats."

"Rucksacks?" I asked, trying to determine who we were up against.

"No."

"Everyone okay?"

"Yeah," he said. "Let's get the troops ready to move. They could be back with a regiment."

Running into a few Viet Cong in the middle of the jungle was significant because the enemy generally didn't move cross-country. When possible, he traveled on established trails, roads, or animal tracks. They might have been trackers, but if that was the case, they surely would have detonated one of the many booby traps Duke Snider had left along our back trail.

In our area of War Zone D, the Viet Cong were organized into six- to twelve-man cells. For the most part, they were responsible for maintaining base camps, serving as guides for Main Force Viet Cong and North Vietnamese Army units moving through the area, and providing security for their base camps. Since the two men seen wore black uniforms and weren't carrying rucksacks, I had to assume that they were part of a local security unit. They were either on patrol from a nearby base camp or were part of an outpost that had been set up to guard the most likely avenues of approach to a base camp.

That they got away was bad news. The contact probably meant that we had forfeited the crucial element of surprise;

they knew we had penetrated the area, and they were probably on their way to inform their superiors.

If the two were from a base camp that was occupied by a large unit, their next move would probably be to deploy against us. If they were a Main Force Viet Cong unit, they would likely be one of the regiments of the 9th Viet Cong Division, the same regiments we had tangled with a few weeks earlier during Blackjack-33. If they were a North Vietnamese Army unit, they could be the crack 101st, 141st, or 250th Regiments. There was also a possibility that regiments from the Viet Cong's 7th Division had moved into the area. We also knew that the enemy could mobilize a number of local Viet Cong platoon- and company-size units against us. Those were under the command of the Viet Cong province committee and were usually difficult to deal with because of their extensive knowledge of the local terrain.

Our early morning contact was ominous and predicted a long, hot day.

As I surveyed the platoon area, I saw that everyone was on their feet, rucksacks on their backs and weapons at the ready. Some of the Bodes were fidgeting nervously with their weapons while others kept a watchful eye on the surroundings, eyes darting purposefully in nervous anticipation.

Bob helped Ly, the 3d Platoon radio operator, get his PRC-25 radio and the rest of his gear secured on his back. The load was heavy and cumbersome, but Ly was strong and resilient and never complained. Once he got the rucksack on, he bounced a few times to settle the load. He was a lot like Bob, a quiet person who exuded an inner strength that engendered confidence.

"Okay, *Bac-si*." Ly smiled as he adjusted two pieces of foam rubber he had attached to the inside of his shoulder straps to keep them from tearing the skin off his protruding clavicles.

"Stay close to *Trung si* Cole," I said as I slipped into my harness and buckled the ends of my ammunition belt.

"Like stink on shit," Bob quipped.

The PRC-25 radio was our only voice contact with the forward air control aircraft that was our great equalizer. We used the small single-engine Cessna to give us six-digit fixes on our location, call in air strikes, direct re-supply aircraft to our drop zones every four days, and at times, to serve as a communications relay back to our forward operations base.

Early every morning, the forward air controller made a flyover of the area to see if he could detect any enemy activity. If we made heavy contact during the day, he would assist us in directing air strikes against the enemy. When we set up our night defensive perimeter, he often supplied us with a critical six-digit fix on our location so that, if necessary, we could call in Sky Spots or artillery fire during the night.

Normally we made contact with the forward air controller by PRC-25 radio when we first heard the faint drone of his engine. After we established radio contact, we gave him a compass heading to our position, and once there, we used an air force White Dot signal mirror or an orange ground panel to give him our exact location. If we were under a thick canopy and not visible from the air, we gave him a heading and then a "now" when he was directly over our position. When we were locked in a fire-fight and weren't concerned about giving ourselves away, we marked our position with colored smoke or flares.

I lifted my rucksack by the straps, swung it around to my backside, and got the straps up as far as my elbows, struggling with its awkward weight.

"Damn thing's heavy," I said, as I bounced a few times to work the straps up to my shoulders. Once secured, it didn't feel bad at all. In fact, I'd reached the point where I felt out of place without it.

"Look, Ly," Bob said, pointing to his breast pocket. "My commo pad's right here. If I'm hit, get it and the radio to someone who speaks good English. Those FAC pilots don't speak broken Bode." Ly nodded that he understood.

"If you or *Bac-si* die, I eat your heart," he said.

I turned to see if he was joking, but one look at his face, and I knew that he wasn't. He was dead serious.

"What's that?" I asked.

"If soldier die, his friend eat heart," Ly said. "Is great honor."

I'd heard of the practice but didn't quite know what to say. Not wanting to offend him, but at the same time wanting to discourage the idea, I fought for an answer.

"Ly, it's an old American custom that a soldier must be buried with his heart if he is to be with his ancestors."

"Oh," he said with a disappointed look.

I stood there adjusting my scarf and compass that hung around my neck, hoping that he got the message. Bob smiled, half winking, and gave me a nudge in the ribs.

As we waited for word to move out, Bob rigged a grenade for instant detonation. He first disassembled it and removed the four-second timing device. Then he re-assembled it, pulled the safety pin, and placed it in a small hole with the safety lever facing up. Finally, he carefully placed the used PRC-25 radio battery on top of the safety lever. The next person to touch the battery would be a dead man. As I waited, I felt a tug on my rucksack and turned to see who it was.

"Rinh, my friend, *sak sa bai*?" I smiled.

"I am fine," he said as he grabbed my arm and shook my

hand. He smelled as though he had just put on a lot of mosquito repellent. Evidently he was determined not to have any more problems with leeches.

Rinh, our senior Cambodian medic, spoke excellent English and was a very good friend. With his well-combed, jet-black hair and spare frame, he looked more like a schoolteacher than a guerrilla. No matter how long we stayed in the jungle, he always looked clean, which might have had something to do with the fact that the Bodes didn't generally have facial hair. Most of them retained a boyish look well into their thirties.

I first met him at Duc Phong when we were building our dispensary. Initially, progress was slow because none of the montagnards or Cambodians assigned spoke a word of English or knew anything about medicine. My assistant at the time was a young montagnard named Yen. After three days of first-aid training, he changed it to Doctor Yen. When a Vietnamese woman came to the hospital with a headache, he took two aspirins out of a bottle and, using surgical tape, attached one to each temple. One of the Americans complained that Dr. Yen had tried to put an Ace bandage around his neck when he complained of a sore throat. Needless to say, I had to keep a close eye on "the doc."

A couple of weeks after we opened the dispensary, Rinh walked in and, in perfect English, told me that he was a medic, and that he wanted to work with me. Without hesitation, I agreed and put him to work. That same day, Rinh came in with one of the local montagnard village chiefs. The old bandy-legged chief said he was in much pain and kept pointing to his loincloth-clad rear end. When I asked Rinh what the chief's problem was, he told me that he wanted an injection, preferably something in red if we had it. Rather than waste any valuable medicine, Rinh suggested we give him a shot of sterile water. Well, we gave him the injection, he recovered almost immediately, and in deep gratitude invited me to his longhouse for dinner. I'll never forget his gaping pomegranate grin of betel-nut gums, lips, and toothy snags.

That night, at a tribal ceremony, I was made a member of the Stieng tribe and was presented with a red-and-black loincloth and the traditional brass bracelet of brotherhood. During the ritual everyone took turns drinking homemade rice wine from a thirty-gallon earthenware vat. We drank through a three-foot bamboo straw that, after a few rounds, became covered with betel nut and drool. When my head began to spin from the potent brew, I tried to fake drinking but failed to do so because the straw was notched. Every time it was my turn, I had to drink the wine down to the next lower notch. I guess it was a montagnard version of chugalug.

The following morning, I woke up with the dry heaves and the world's worst hangover. I felt like a construction crew was working the inside of my head over with jackhammers. I had nothing on but my loincloth and couldn't remember how I got back to camp. From that day on, Rinh and I worked together, and we grew to be close friends.

"Any problems?" I asked him.

"Just two," he said. "A bad cough and a possible case of malaria."

The cough worried me. On a still day, the sound could carry for quite a distance.

"Give 'em anything?" I asked.

"Yes, terpin hydrate and Cepacol lozenges."

"If that doesn't work, give 'im some codeine," I said. "Keep an eye on the other guy's temperature and ask Thach to have someone carry his gear."

"I will keep an eye on him."

"Everyone takin' their malaria pills?"

He nodded.

"Good. What about halazone?" I knew the Bodes didn't like the taste of the water purification tablets.

"I can't be sure," he shrugged.

"The medics straight on morphine?" Bob inquired.

"Yes," Rinh said. "Empty syrettes will be attached to the patient's collar."

On Blackjack-31, one of the Bodes had been shot in the arm and was given morphine by three different medics. A short time later, he died of an overdose.

As Rinh and I talked, I turned and saw Kien, a rifleman in the second squad, limping toward us. He didn't speak much English, so Rinh asked him a few questions in Cambodian.

"What's wrong?" I asked.

"His foot is bleeding," Rinh said. "He needs some moleskin."

"Better do it quick," I said. "We're about ready to move."

"Right," Rinh said as he grabbed Kien by the arm and escorted him back to his position.

Kien was a short, stocky Bode who was a great soldier but had a tendency to steal anything he could get his hands on. He always started an operation with the lightest rucksack in the platoon and finished with one weighing over a hundred pounds. With everything under the sun tied to the outside of his rucksack, he often resembled a traveling junk man.

On Blackjack-31, we'd captured a couple of rucksacks, and one contained what looked like a large bear skin. Before moving out, we placed the rucksacks along the edge of a well-used trail and booby-trapped them with a claymore mine attached to a pull device. We also buried an

M-14 "toe popper" mine next to the rucksacks. When we lined up to move out, we passed the word down the line that they were booby-trapped. But Kien just had to have that bear skin. A couple of minutes later, there was a muffled explosion. When I got to him, I found that the toepopper had blown off a few of his toes and peppered his genitals with shrapnel. As we bandaged his wounds, he seemed more embarrassed than concerned about his wounds. I guess it was a loss of face for him.

As the 3d Platoon lined up to move out, Danh was on point, followed by me with a map and compass. Bob was third, followed by Ly with the PRC-25 radio. Thach was the fifth man in the column, then Son with the M-60 and the rest of the 3d Herd in tow.

Danh was a sixteen-year-old who had been with the unit since it was formed at Ho Ngoc Tao in October 1966. He stood five foot three, was well built, had black wavy hair, and possessed a great sense of humor. He was also very intelligent and agile, two qualities that made him the best volleyball player and the best point man in the platoon.

"Ready, partner?" I asked.

"Ready, *Bac-si*." He smiled as he stood with his rucksack on his back, machete in his right hand, and silencer-equipped MK-II British Sten gun resting on the left side of his ammunition belt.

"Put that machete away," I said.

"Not use?"

"No, not unless ya have to," I said. It leaves a trail a blind man can follow.

"Yeah," Bob added. "Too much noise. Can hear it a mile away."

Danh slid the razor-edged machete back into its sheath, and Bob handed him a pair of leather work gloves that would protect his hands from the thorns.

"*Bac-si,* you have?" Danh asked, pointing to the Buddha cloth he had tied around his neck.

"Better believe it," I said as I took a small plastic bag out of my jacket pocket and removed a white cloth the size of a handkerchief.

As I uncovered the cloth, you could see that it was covered with skillfully drawn Buddhist designs and symbols. When we were at Ho Ngoc Tao, Danh spent many days preparing the cloth and presented it to me just before the black-box mission. Although I wasn't a Buddhist, it was one of my most valued possessions, and I carried it everywhere.

"I got mine," Bob said. "When ya operate in Buddha's territory, ya treat the guy right." He turned to Thach. "Pass the word not to touch that booby-trapped battery." He pointed at it.

Thach turned to Son and passed the word down the line.

"Fox Three, this is Fox Control. Over," Lieutenant Condon radioed.

Ly passed the radio handset to Bob.

"Fox Control, this is Fox Three. Over," he responded.

"Three, this is Control. Let's get the show on the road. We're burning daylight. Over."

"Roger, Control. Three, out."

News Clippings

Adm. U.S. Grant Sharp, commander of the American forces in the Pacific, said yesterday the North Vietnamese underestimate the determination of the United States to win the war in Vietnam.
Honolulu Star Bulletin, July 18, 1967

Brand New '67 Mustang—$2,249
Courier Express (Buffalo), July 18, 1967

Mr. Ellsworth Bunker, the American Ambassador, told Vietnamese newsmen Saturday that successful elections in September will not by any means mark the completion of the progression toward representative government and full participation of the citizenry in the politics of the nation. *Saigon Daily News,* July 18, 1967

Tel Aviv—After an unexplained delay of 30 hours, U.N. ceasefire observers formally began their operations along the quiet banks of the Suez Canal at 6 p.m. Monday. *Los Angeles Times,* July 18, 1967

Yaz, 'Old' at 27, Heads Boston's Kids
The Atlanta Journal, July 18, 1967

Mrs. Minh appealed to the National Assembly to allow her husband to return to campaign. General Minh, better known as "Big Minh," has been in exile in Thailand for several years as ambassador-at-large and is trying to return to Vietnam to run for President in the September 3 elections. The nation's ruling generals, however, have declared that he cannot return for "security reasons."
The Saigon Post, July 18, 1967

The effects of the strike on the Vietnam war effort were also noted, company officials said. Norris Industries Inc., Los Angeles, said five rail carloads of "various types of ordnance" failed to meet a delivery schedule yesterday. *The Wall Street Journal,* July 18, 1967

There is a catch, too, in the polls on Richard Nixon. Long the favorite of the Republicans high and low, he has consistently led the other Republicans in the polls and gets up to 46% of all the votes.
Life, July 21, 1967

Rock 'n' roll radio stations are programming more and more albums. Not just the Beatles, the Rolling Stones, but groups including the Jefferson Airplane, Grateful Dead, the Moby Grape, the Fifth Dimension, Country Joe and the Fish, the Grass Roots, Bob Dylan, the Doors, the Who, the Cream, the Hearts and Flowers, Donovan.

Billboard, July 22, 1967

2

Only rarely did splinters of sunlight pierce the world of shadows beneath the jungle canopy. The few that did glowed a translucent white when they touched the mist on the jungle floor.

As our columns threaded their way through the thick tangle, they resembled two long snakes slithering through the undergrowth. With a catlike grace, Danh crept forward on point, pausing every few paces to scrutinize every color, every contour for any irregularity before resuming his quiet footfalls. His eyes cautiously surveying the jungle for trip wires suspended tautly a few inches above the jungle floor, a section of black claymore wire trailing off through the rotting leaves, or punji pits. His senses were tuned to near perfection as his brain sorted every

shred of stimuli for possible danger—the gentle rustling
of palm fronds, the subtle crack of a twig, the smell of
Vietnamese cooking. When on point, a soldier's primal instincts are electrified. It was a raw game whose outcome
depended upon every thought, every reflex, every nerve
being alert and poised for fight or flight.

As we proceeded, the column followed the pace set by
Danh, tentatively moving forward when he moved, halting
when he halted, then releasing itself once more in har-
mony with his signals.

I followed five to ten meters behind him, helping him
navigate with my map and compass. To keep him on a
northerly azimuth, I adjusted his heading every fifty to one
hundred meters. When necessary, I used hand-and-arm
signals to adjust his course to the right or left. We had
played our parts often and worked well together.

For at least an hour, we would have a ridgeline to the
west and a stream a couple hundred meters to the east;
navigation wouldn't be a problem. A seasoned point man,
Danh moved slowly and deliberately. He knew that if he
moved too fast, the column would expand and contract
like a giant rubber band. Those near the front would have
no trouble keeping up, but those near the tail end would be
run into the ground. If the column got strung out, it would
be impossible for each man to maintain visual contact
with the person in front of him. That would affect our
ability to react quickly if we made contact with the enemy.

Duty in Vietnam usually consisted of extended periods
of peaceful silence or intense boredom occasionally interrupted by violent convulsions of high intensity. The
unit able to move the quickest and shoot the straightest
when contact was made normally came out on top. Back at
Trang Sup, we had spent days practicing immediate-
action drills based on enemy contact from every possible

direction. We grew expert at it, and I felt confident that we could slug it out with the best of them.

As the sun inched higher in the pale blue sky, we pressed forward through a dripping tangle of leaves and vines. Except for the hooting of monkeys, the chirping of birds, the soft rustling of broad leaves, and the brittle *clackety-clack* of bamboo from an occasional breeze, everything was still. High in the canopy, leaves fluttered in the sighing breezes, reflecting light like a million tiny mirrors. Every now and then, I'd glimpse a few monkeys scampering from tree to tree. But there were no signs of the enemy.

The foliage began to thin as we moved north, and I could soon see for ten to twenty meters in all directions. The only things slowing us down were the moss-encrusted remains of large fallen trees and hanging wait-a-minute vines whose sharp, needlelike thorns stabbed and slashed the exposed flesh of hands, face, and ears. Whenever someone got hooked, he had to stop to remove the thorns from his skin.

After moving for thirty minutes, Danh stopped and motioned me forward.

"What's up?" I whispered. He pointed to what appeared to be a fresh trail. Judging by its size, I figured it had been made by a large enemy force moving cross-country.

Bob, Thach, and Ly moved to where we were standing.

"Trail," I said softly.

"Not VC," Thach chuckled. "Phant."

"What?" Bob wanted to know.

"Big phant," Danh said, making exaggerated stomping motions with his feet.

"Elephants?" I offered.

"El'phant, *Bac-si*," Thach said as Danh squatted and examined one of the impressions in the spongy floor. "El'phant come here."

"Charlie usin' 'em to carry equipment?" Bob asked.

"No," he said. "El'phant live in jungle."

"You're right," I said. "If they were usin' 'em, they'd stick to the trails."

"Why should they bust brush?" Bob mused. "Let's keep movin'."

Resuming our march, I felt a bit embarrassed that I hadn't recognized it as an elephant trail. I had seen them before, particularly south of Duc Phong in War Zone D. The animals always seemed to be afraid of us and fled whenever we got near. A couple of times, the terrifying sound of them crashing through dried bamboo thickets in the middle of the night had scared the hell out of me. With a little imagination, they sounded like a thousand Viet Cong.

As we continued, my eyes darted back and forth, scanning for signs of the enemy. Since I'd arrived in Vietnam, my sensitivity to smells had developed to a point where I could often detect enemy troops and base camps long before contact was made. Sometimes it was the distinctive smell of Vietnamese cigarettes, but on occasion it was the moldy smell of troops who had lived for weeks, months, and sometimes years in the jungle. More than anything else, it was the smell of woodsmoke or Vietnamese cooking that gave them away. When I thought about it, I realized that the only thing that got me through my first few months in Vietnam was a lot of luck. I had made some stupid mistakes but was still living to talk about them. Five years of Marine Corps and Special Forces training had taught me the mechanics of soldiering, but time proved there was no substitute for experience. It was a combination of training and experience that enabled me to develop a "skin feeling" for things, a kind of sixth sense that often meant the difference between life and death.

I also noticed that the longer an operation lasted, the closer I grew to nature. During the first few days, my back ached from my rucksack, I drank a lot of water, our rations tasted terrible, and I was comparatively insensitive to my physical environment. But as time passed, the pains disappeared, I drank less water, the food seemed to improve, and my senses grew keen. I became more and more like an animal bred to survive in the jungle. On a few of the longer operations, I was actually disappointed when they ended.

We had been humping for about an hour when we arrived at the bank of a clear, slow-moving stream that sparkled as it flowed around moss-covered boulders. Large gray cypress trees and chest-high ferns grew to both banks, and the still morning air was filled with the croaking of frogs. Looking at my map, I saw that the stream flowed east to the stream that we had been moving parallel to. Having worked up a good sweat, I was longing for a drink. The taste of salt on my lips only added to my thirst.

Bob radioed Lieutenant Condon and was told to take a break after we forded the stream. As I stood on the bank looking at the sparkling water, I daydreamed of big fish swimming just below the surface; a panfried trout would really hit the spot.

"Let's get across," Bob whispered.

"Right." First Danh, then I, slid down the slick mud bank. As we sank calf-deep in cool water, our feet stirred up clouds of silt, sending a light brown current of muddy water downstream.

"Better fill up," I advised Danh. "No tellin' how long it'll be before we hit water again."

The surface gulped and bubbled as we submerged our canteens. When we finished, Bob, Thach, and Ly slid down the muddy bank.

"Water good," Thach said as he cupped his hand to drink.

"Better use your halazone tablets," I said.

"No sweat, *Bac-si*. Water not have shit."

Convincing the Bodes to use halazone tablets was a constant contest of wills. They realized that a canteen of contaminated water could disable a man for days, but at the same time, they really hated the taste of the tablets. Maybe, in our after-action report, I'd recommend that they start making them in Kool-Aid flavors. After helping Danh replace his canteens in his rucksack, we dug the toes of our boots into the soft mud on the opposite bank, grabbed a few small saplings, and pulled our way up the slope.

We waited for Bob, Thach, and Ly to finish filling up, then moved to a position seventy-five meters north of the stream.

"Take ten," I whispered to Danh as I lowered my rucksack to the ground among waist-high ferns at the base of a five-story cypress tree. While I waited with my rifle at the ready, Danh positioned a claymore mine ten meters north of where I had dropped my rucksack. Since the ground was wet and yielding, we left a trail that the rest of the company would have no trouble following to close the gap.

"That mosquito repellent you brewed doesn't wash off," Bob whispered as we stood waiting for Danh to return.

"Yeah; mixed it with lanolin," I said. "Got a couple of extra bottles if ya need any."

"I'm good," he said.

"Use it around the tops of your boots and waistline," I said softly. "It'll keep the leeches off."

"Okay, *Bac-si*," Danh whispered as he returned and lowered his rucksack to the ground.

"Let's take a walk down the line," Bob told Thach.

"Okay, *Trung si*."

Before leaving, Bob and Thach positioned two-man flank-security teams twenty meters to the left and right of our route of march. With security in place, Ly, Danh, and I sat among the ferns with our backs against our rucksacks.

Although still early morning, the temperature had already soared into the nineties. Looking up through a hole in the canopy, I saw large white butterflies and hundreds of insects drifting in and out of a brilliant shaft of sunlight that penetrated to the jungle floor. On the branches above our heads, a few blue-and-white birds chirped as they fluttered from branch to branch. After downing two salt tablets with a long drink of water, I felt refreshed.

As I sat leaning against my rucksack, I could feel a bubble rising on my gum just above my front teeth. One of my front teeth had been shot out months earlier, and it was abscessing again.

Damn, I said to myself as I ran my finger over the raised area. Something always happens at the worst possible time.

While Danh and Ly finished what rice remained from their morning meal, I punctured the bubble with a twenty-gauge needle and pushed the pus out onto the ground.

"Numba ten, *Bac-si*," Danh said with obvious concern on his face.

"Tried to get it fixed," I said. "The dentist at Nha Trang said I had to wait 'til I got back to the States. Shoulda got it fixed at the VA when I was home on leave."

"Make you sick." He shook his head.

Looking at Danh, I found myself wondering what would become of him after I left Vietnam.

"What ya gonna do when the war's over?" I whispered.

"I fight to I die, *Bac-si*."

"That's no way to look at it," I said, trying to seem as convincing as possible. Still, in my heart I knew that Indochina had been ravaged by war for centuries. The Chinese, Burmese, Cambodians, Japanese, Vietnamese, French, and Americans had all taken their turns, and there was no reason to expect anything would change in the foreseeable future.

"Maybe I go America with you." He grinned. "I be engineer."

"We'll go to the University of Buffalo. You'd freeze your balls off." I laughed. But, it would be great if I could figure out a way to take Danh and Rinh with me back to the States. Danh had the ability to become an engineer, and I felt Rinh had what it took to become a doctor. If they remained there, the war would catch up with them sooner or later. No matter how good you were, statistics and the fortunes of war dictated that your head and a bullet would eventually meet at the same place and the same time.

"Everyone's across," Bob said as he and Thach returned to sit on the ground beside their rucksacks.

"How they holdin' up?" I asked.

"Good." He took a long swig of water and used his scarf to wipe the sweat from his face.

"I was just tellin' Danh we'll take him back to the States," I said.

"Good idea." Bob smiled.

"You still thinkin' about retiring?" I asked.

"Naw, I'm good for another five."

"Got any plans for when ya get back to Bragg?"

"Maybe I'll find me a quiet job in a warehouse," he mused.

"Who you tryin' to kid? You eat this shit up. You thrive on it. You've been living on the edge too long to just let go."

"You're probably right," Bob said as I got up and extended my hand to help Danh to his feet. He held out his four-fingered right hand. His thumb had been shot off a few months earlier and only a short red stump remained. I clasped him by his wrist and pulled him up. As soon as we got the rucksacks on our backs, we were ready to move out on the same northerly azimuth.

"Keep it slow," I told him. "Give 'em a chance to close up."

"Okay, *Bac-si,*" he responded.

Thinking about his thumb, I wondered how he managed to fire his Sten with any accuracy. I remembered the day he lost it, south of Dong Xoai Special Forces Camp. That morning, the 3d Platoon had been assigned to conduct a day-long search for the enemy in an area measuring about twenty-five square kilometers.

That day, we had spent the morning hours moving through stretches of scrub brush and six-foot elephant grass without detecting a sign of the enemy. In the afternoon we had hit a large stream and began moving parallel to it. Later that afternoon, we were moving through a bamboo thicket, about two hundred meters south of the creek, when we hit a well-used north-south trail.

It had been one of those long, hot days. We needed water for our evening meal, so we left a two-man ambush on the trail and followed it north to the stream. The water was clear and slow moving, with four-foot-high mud banks, and measuring about ten meters across. Sliding down the bank into the cool, knee-deep water was a welcome relief from the heat.

I had just finished filling my empty canteens when Kien ran to the edge of the stream and told us that an undetermined number of Viet Cong was coming down the trail in our direction.

Bob hurriedly got the platoon across the creek and set

up an ambush along its bank while I radioed our coordinates to Captain Gritz, requesting a forward air control aircraft. By the time I finished relaying the information, Bob had the platoon deployed. He, Danh, the radio operator, and I took up a position behind a large fallen tree. As we waited, I ran a claymore mine out to the bank in front of our position while Bob passed the word not to fire until we blew the claymore.

Seconds later, I began hearing laughter and the sing-song chatter of Vietnamese voices. The voices grew louder as they moved down the trail. When their point man neared the creek, I saw that he was carrying his weapon almost nonchalantly on his shoulder. I assumed they had no idea we were in the area. I was surprised that they hadn't picked up the distinct footprints of our American-made jungle boots.

The second enemy soldier stopped at the edge of the bank and stared at the water. His facial muscles suddenly tensed; something was wrong, and he knew it. He must have noticed that the water upstream was crystal clear while the water downstream was clouded with mud. It looked as though he was about to say something to his comrades when Bob blew the claymore, and the rest of the platoon opened up. For a few seconds, a hailstorm of automatic rifle fire and explosions filled the air, followed by silence. The first enemy soldier bobbed like a cork in the shallow water, and the second lay dead on the bank.

I slipped a fresh magazine into my M-16 and picked up the radio handset to relay news of the ambush to headquarters. Bob and Danh were about to reenter the water when a tremendous volley of fire erupted on the far side of the creek. The first shot pierced the heart of our radio operator, dropping him at my feet.

Bob, Danh, and I hit the ground behind the same fallen

tree. Looking to my left and right, I saw enemy troops firing and moving into position along the opposite bank. As Bob and Danh returned fire, I made contact with the forward air controller who was by then circling overhead. I told him that we had ambushed the point element of a large force and that we were in heavy contact. He said that fast movers were in flight, so I popped a yellow smoke canister to give him an exact fix on our location.

My conversation with the forward air controller was interrupted by a tap on the shoulder. I turned and saw that it was Danh pointing to his hand. His thumb had been shot off. I gave the radio handset to Bob and applied a dressing over the stump. He didn't have any signs of shock or pain, so I withheld the morphine. The body has a built-in defense mechanism that sometimes reduces bleeding and pain when a person is first wounded. I'd seen it many times, and I knew that he would be in a lot of pain when it wore off.

As soon as I finished covering his dressing with an Ace bandage, we both resumed firing. The forward air controller was already in contact with fast movers screaming in from the east. With engines howling, the Phantoms swooped down in strafing runs, opening up with the buzzsaw *burrrrr* of 20mm cannons. The firing kicked up a string of explosions as they worked their deadly swaths closer and closer to our position. After a few minutes of the murderous pounding from the air, I felt a second tap on my shoulder. It was Danh. He was pointing to his shoulder. He'd been hit again. I checked his wound and was relieved to see that even though it was a deep flesh wound there was no bone involvement. While I was working on his second wound, we received word that large numbers of enemy troops were crossing the creek up and downstream from our position. Since they couldn't launch a frontal assault across the creek, they had decided to try a flanking move to sandwich us in a cross fire with our backs pinned against the stream, then cut us to pieces.

Rather than risk encirclement, we decided to break contact. In an attempt to slow their advance, I called in bombing runs on the Viet Cong who were crossing the creek. We, in turn, filled the creek bed with a noxious cloud of CS gas and made a hasty retreat out of the pocket. Moving down the trail at a fast clip, we continued to call in air strikes to cover our rear. We had to move as quickly as possible because we didn't want to give the enemy on our flanks the opportunity to move ahead and block our withdrawal with an ambush.

A short distance north of the stream, we cut back into the jungle and pushed northeast. The last rays of daylight were fading fast as the rumble of an approaching thunderstorm preceded a curtain of darkness. The slate gray cloudburst finally broke with a clap of thunder, releasing torrents of rain that came down so hard I couldn't make out the man in front of me.

By holding on to the back of the next man's rucksack, we were able to keep everyone together as we felt our way through the bush. It was slow going as we slopped our way through the pelting downpour, pausing every few seconds to wait for a flash of lightning to illuminate the jungle before groping a few feet farther. The whole experience was nerve-racking as we stumbled forward through the inky blackness, nearly blinded by the elements.

After what seemed like hours, we stopped in a bamboo thicket and set up a small defensive perimeter. It was a cold, wet, miserable night, one that left us chilled to the core. To conserve body heat, the Bodes slept back to back. As soon as everyone was settled in, I contacted Captain Gritz and, using him as a relay, began calling in 175mm artillery strikes on suspected enemy positions. We spent a nearly sleepless night, shivering, while the locomotive sound of projectiles passing overhead rent the air with deafening concussions.

At first light, we broke camp and headed north. A few hours later we linked up with the rest of the company at a clearing and were able to call in a chopper to evacuate the dead and wounded.

As Danh lifted off in the chopper that morning, he waved to me with a big smile on his face. When we returned to Trang Sup after the operation, we found him standing on the airstrip waiting for us with that same warm smile.

"Hey, Jimmy, wait one," a voice interrupted my thoughts.

It was SFC Frank Hagey. He and SFC Bill "Fergy" Ferguson were the two Americans assigned to the 2d Platoon. At thirty-seven, Frank was the oldest American in the unit, something like gramps to many of us. He had a wife and eight kids back at Fort Bragg and had joined the Mobile Guerrilla Force in March. He had previously been assigned to Trai Bi, a small Special Forces camp in Tay Ninh Province just a few klicks from the Cambodian border. I was worried about Frank's health. He looked a lot thinner than he did when I first met him. His face was gaunt, and he had trouble hiding a subtle limp; I could tell that his back was bothering him. Although he wouldn't admit it, I knew that he was in a lot of pain. A couple of months earlier, he'd been driving a load of supplies from Saigon to Trang Sup when his truck hit an antitank mine near Cu Chi. The explosion blew him over thirty feet through the air and dropped him on his head in a rice paddy.

Medevacked to Saigon, where the doctors sewed him up, he discovered he was paralyzed from the waist down.

But within weeks, he had regained movement and somehow managed to convince our C Team headquarters in Bien Hoa to allow him to return to full duty.

"Got a couple meprobamate tablets?" he whispered in my ear.

"You okay?"

"I'm in great shape," he said, beaming unconvincingly. "My lower back gets a little tight. But other than that, I'm a hundred percent."

"Bull, Frank, you're lyin' like a rug."

"I'll be okay, Jimmy. Just need a little somethin' to loosen up my muscles."

"Okay. Tell Rinh to give ya a couple tablets," I said. "Get back to me if it doesn't help."

"God and country." He gave me a thumbs-up, turned, and moved back down the line.

"Tell Fergy to keep an eye on 'im," Bob said as we began moving on our northerly azimuth.

"Right," I said. "Might have to carry his gear."

Whoomph! a muffled explosion sounded to our rear. I wheeled and used my compass to get an azimuth on the explosion.

"Two hundred degrees," I said to Bob. "A perfect back azimuth."

"The booby-trapped battery!" He smiled.

"Trackers."

As we slipped past stalks of yellow, green, and brown bamboo, I thought about the trackers. If we were lucky, booby traps and stay-behind ambushes would slow them down. However, if they were able to get a fix on us, the enemy commander would likely deploy all available units against us.

Looking at my map as I walked, I saw that we were passing within a couple hundred meters of a large open area that we'd like to keep well to the west of. A kilometer to the east of the clearing were the evenly spaced dots of another rubber plantation. If the war ever ended, Vietnam might realize its potential: rubber, minerals, lumber, oil, not to mention tourism. Places like Nha Trang and Vung Tau had some of the best beaches in the world. Maybe, after the war, I'd come back and get involved in the country's reconstruction.

Without warning, Danh suddenly stopped and sank to one knee, raising his left arm to halt the column. I relayed the signal to Bob as Danh slipped out of his rucksack and crawled forward. As I waited, my eyes scanned our left flank. Although I was drained from the hump, I now felt full of energy as adrenaline surged into my system. After what seemed like a long minute, Danh came trotting back to my position.

"*Bac-si,* big trail," he whispered. I turned and motioned Bob forward.

"What's up?" he said softly.

"Trail," I told him as I double-checked my map.

"Many VC use," Danh said.

"Let's have a look-see," Bob said as we removed our rucksacks. Bob, Danh, and I moved ahead until we hit a wall of densely compacted brush. Using our hands to separate the leaves and vines, we quietly inched forward. As we parted the leaves, we were surprised to find the jungle suddenly dissected by a trail which measured a good five meters across. With my head poking through the wall of vegetation at the trail's edge, I saw that vehicles had worn two parallel strips of muddy, water-filled ruts. They extended for about fifty meters in both directions before disappearing into the green.

"The Lincoln Tunnel," Bob commented.

The enemy had cut away the brush and small trees and

left the branches and leaves of the big trees to form a trellised tunnel, overhung with tangled vines, interwoven branches, and thick foliage.

"Never spot it from the air, and it ain't on the map," I said. "Closest trail is supposed to be northwest of here."

Whoomph! Something exploded far to the west.

"Looks like they run convoys down it," Bob hissed.

"Must be part of the Ho Chi Minh trail," I said.

"Trung si," Danh said, pointing to our left. Thirty meters down the trail to our left was what appeared to be a two-and-a-half-ton truck. It was parked to the side of the trail and was well camouflaged with branches and leaves.

"Front tire's gone," I noticed. "Probably got a flat."

"Yeah, it's jacked up on logs," Bob said. "We'll check it after we get security in place."

"Okay," I agreed.

We left Danh at the trail's edge and crept back to where Thach and Ly were waiting. They were both down on one knee, their weapons pointed toward our left flank. I squatted next to Thach and briefed him on the situation while Bob took the handset and radioed the lieutenant.

"Fox Control, this is Fox Three. Over."

"Three, this is Control. What's the holdup? Over."

"Control, this is Three. We've hit an east-west trail. Got an abandoned deuce-and-a-half parked off to one side. Over."

"Roger, Three. Let me know when you're ready to move. Control, out."

Bob turned to Thach.

"Get two men up the trail." He pointed west.

"At least seventy-five meters," I said. "We don't want any unannounced company."

He sent two Bodes up the trail, and Stik Rader radioed

that he was sending two men down the trail to the east. As soon as both outposts were in place, it would be safe to cross. If an enemy unit came rolling down the trail, we wanted as much advance notice as possible so we could organize an appropriate reception. If they were too many, we would let them pass and attempt to call in tac air or a B-52 strike on them. A single B-52 strike covered an area measuring one thousand meters wide and three thousand meters long, with evenly spaced craters pockmarking the impact zone. Nothing could live through it. If they were a small unit, we would have time to set up a hasty ambush.

"Get security on the other side," I said to Thach.

He motioned two men forward. They moved to the edge of the trail, looked left and right, then darted across and disappeared into the foliage.

"I think we make contact," Thach whispered.

"You've got a sixth sense," I said softly.

It was true; I had seen it many times before. Whenever the enemy was near, the Bodes could sense their presence long before we made contact. Whenever I saw them with their jade Buddhas in their mouths, I knew that contact was imminent. They believed that by placing Buddha in their mouths, they were closer to him and had nothing to fear. I had the same feeling that large enemy units were operating in the area. The elements were all there: a triple-canopy jungle, an excellent water supply, and a major trail, all the necessary requirements for an enemy base camp.

"If the shit hits the fan, reinforcements are only a few minutes away," Bob said as we waited for security to radio that they were in position.

"The cavalry doesn't always come when ya need 'em," I added.

"You got that right," Bob said. "Remember Cao Song Be?"

"How could I forget?" An American division was supposed to have been standing by to reinforce us when we locked horns with a couple of Main Force regiments from the 9th Viet Cong Division. Only no one showed up.

"Many Cambodian die," Thach said. "My son fifteen." His eyes were welling with water, and he turned away in embarrassment, wiping his face with his sleeve.

I'd never forget the plane ride back to Trang Sup after the battle. I was in the troop compartment of a C-123 aircraft with wall-to-wall bodies. It was over 120 degrees inside, and there weren't any body bags. Whenever the plane banked, a pool of blood flowed from one side to the other.

Gazing at the disfigured remains of the dead, I found it hard to believe that so many good friends had died. Only in the heat of war could such meaningful relationships form so quickly or end so abruptly. There were naïve moments when I had bought the delusion of invincibility and convinced myself that I couldn't be killed. Maybe it stemmed from mythical illusions of immortality so coveted by youthful men, but that planeload of bodies was a grim reminder of how mortal we really are. Still, I couldn't bring myself to let go of that unspoken bond, even in the presence of death.

"I'll never forget the wives cryin'." Bob lowered his head. "A sad time."

"Yeah, you could smell the incense and hear the wailing for days," I said.

"Ever get the feelin' those conventional types are out to shaft us?" Bob asked.

"Feeling, hell! They don't like Special Forces, and they don't give a damn what happens to the Bodes."

"You're probably right," Bob said.

I remembered when we formed the Mobile Guerilla Force in October 1966. We had to trade, steal, or scrounge everything from weapons and ammunition to cots and food. When they wanted to arm us with World War II carbines, one of the guys went up to an arms supply depot and traded his tape recorder for two hundred new M-16s. When we needed food, I had a few Viet Cong flags made from red, blue, and yellow cargo parachutes at a tailor shop in Bien Hoa. Then I took them to the 25th Division at Cu Chi where a lieutenant at the supply depot agreed to give me anything and everything for a real Viet Cong flag. I even shot a few holes in them so they'd look like the real McCoy. Needless to say, the Bodes ate well at Ho Ngoc Tao. All of their meat came from the general staff's food locker.

My thoughts were interrupted by a Cambodian voice on the HT-1 radio.

"It Kien," Thach said as he squatted with the radio pressed to his ear. "He one hundred meter up trail."

"Tell 'im to hold his position 'til everyone's across," Bob said.

"Okay, *Trung si*."

Seconds later, Thach sprang to his feet.

"Kien say one VC come," he whispered.

"Tell 'im to let 'im pass," Bob ordered. "Let us know if there's any more."

"I'll have Danh take 'im out with the Sten," I said.

The silencer-equipped British Sten would allow us to knock him down without killing him. I hoped to take him prisoner without alerting the entire area.

"If he's a point man, let 'im pass," Bob said as I turned to move back to Danh's position along the trail.

"One VC," I whispered, pointing down the trail to our left. "Go for a shoulder shot, we need a prisoner."

Danh nodded. I was excited. If we could take a prisoner and convince him to help us, it could save a lot of lives. If he wasn't an officer or political cadre, there was a good chance that we could quickly convince him to reveal the size and location of enemy units operating in the area. Once convinced the Bodes weren't going to kill them, enemy enlisted men often became very cooperative. On the black-box operation, one volunteered to serve as a guide.

We backed off about a meter and positioned ourselves behind a large cypress tree. Danh lay on the right side, closer to the trail; I took the left. A few birds were chirping on the branches above us and a woodpecker was tapping on a nearby tree. As Danh parted a clump of ferns so that he could have a clear field of fire, I brushed aside a tangle of dead branches and settled into a comfortable prone position. I soon saw what appeared to be a face moving toward us. In the direct sunlight it appeared white as it danced in and out of the patches of mottled greens and browns of jungle growth.

Glancing back to my right, I saw that Danh was ready: his finger nervously caressing the trigger of his weapon, his front sight blade slowly tracking the enemy soldier. Just a couple of ounces of pressure on the trigger, and the bolt would slam home.

I checked the selector switch on my M-16 and cautiously moved it from safe to automatic. The dull click sounded unusually loud in the silence. Even though I didn't want to fire an unsilenced weapon, I would be ready just in case anything went wrong.

Twenty-five meters down the trail, I saw that the approaching soldier was wearing a blue uniform and a pith helmet. A brown rucksack was on his back, and he was carrying an AK-47 cradled under his left arm. This could be close, I thought. If he had a round in the chamber, it would only take him a split second to get off a burst. I sensed movement on the tree next to my head.

Oh no, I said to myself, fire ants!

At fifteen meters, I saw what looked like a red and gold star embossed on the front of his helmet. The swarm of red ants was crawling over my left sleeve and onto my hand. The soldier's rifle was pointing our way. It seemed as if he was looking right at us.

I took in a deep breath, let half of it out, and took up the slack on my trigger. The top of my front sight blade was aimed at the middle of his chest. The ants began to dig their fiery mandibles into my skin. Each bite burned like a white-hot needle. I could hear my heart pounding, but in spite of the pain, I couldn't afford to move.

At five meters, the man in the pith helmet saw us. A look of terror suddenly flashed on his face.

Chunk! Before the enemy soldier could react, the bolt on Danh's silenced Sten slammed home. The bullet hit him with such force he looked like he had run into an invisible wall. His arms flew upward, and he landed on his back with a dull thud.

We jumped to our feet, and Danh moved cautiously forward with his gun trained on the body. I quickly brushed away the ants, noticing red welts on the back of my hand. The enemy soldier was lying on the trail with his body quivering and his mouth and left eye wide open.

Danh and I each grabbed an arm and began dragging him off the trail. Bob and Thach came running up and picked up his rifle and pith helmet.

"He alive?" Bob wanted to know.

"Can't say," I said, as we dragged him back to where Ly was waiting with the radio.

"Looks dead," Bob said. I squatted next to the now motionless body to check for vital signs.

"Let me check his pulse." Squatting at his side, I found that he didn't have a pulse.

"He's dead," I said.

My left hand burned from the ant bites. I looked at the back of my hand and wrist and noticed that the welts were quickly growing larger and felt warm to the touch.

"He see us, *Bac-si,*" Danh responded with a trace of apprehension in his voice. He was obviously concerned how I would react. "I have to kill."

"I know," I said. "Where the hell did ya hit 'im?"

"Wait a minute," Bob said, leaning over. His thumb pried open the dead man's right eye. Red and white jelly filling the socket was all that was left.

"Right in the eye," I said.

Looking closer, I saw that the bullet had entered the socket and somehow veered downward through the roof of his mouth, evidently lodging somewhere in his trunk. Thach patted Danh on the back. Thach seemed relieved by the gesture and returned to his position on the trail.

As I stared into the dead man's face, I was surprised to see that it bore the same expression he had shown the split second before Danh squeezed the trigger. The look of wide-eyed terror was frozen. He must have died instantly. In a way, he was fortunate. Dying is easy, I thought, it's the getting there that can be rough. I once saw a man with a smile on his lips looking up at the sky through maggot-filled eyes. Maybe he knew something we didn't.

"He VC message man," Thach said after searching through his wallet and pockets, "271st Regiment."

"The 271st!" Bob said. "The same unit we fought near Cao Song Be."

"Yeah, one of the regiments of the 9th VC Division," I said.

Maybe it's our lucky day, I thought. We may just have

nailed the courier who was carrying the news of our presence. Maybe the Frenchman in Quan Loi wasn't working for the enemy. Maybe the Viet Cong we made contact with earlier hadn't passed the word that we were in the area. There were a lot of maybes but no for sures.

The fact that the courier was alone on the trail was probably a good sign. I had learned from experience that whenever the enemy was unaware of our presence, they weren't security conscious.

But even if we had been compromised, there was still a good chance we could accomplish our mission. Although enemy troops in the area greatly outnumbered us, they were handicapped by poor communications. They had radios at the regimental and possibly the battalion levels but nothing at the company, platoon, or squad levels. At the lower levels, they had to rely on runners to carry messages, so they often found it difficult to respond quickly to targets of opportunity. Even if they knew we were there, we could conceivably pinpoint the location of their larger units and be out of the area before they could do anything about it.

Estimating the strength, capabilities, and what action the enemy might take was no simple matter. If you overestimated him, you became overly cautious and failed to accomplish the mission; if you underestimated him, you became careless and suffered the consequences. The one thing I knew for sure was that in the past few months, there had been a major shift in the enemy's strategy; he appeared willing to accept heavy losses in order to achieve limited objectives. On several occasions, he tried to surround and overrun elements of the Mobile Guerrilla Force and took heavy casualties in the process.

With Thach squatting next to me, I noticed that he was

carrying a new pistol: a chrome-plated 9mm Browning automatic with hand-carved ivory grips.

"Nice pistol," I said. He paused for a moment.

"Yes, *Bac-si*. Very good."

"Pick it up in a Tay Ninh barbershop?" I asked with mock surprise in my voice.

"Yes, *Bac-si*." He knew that I knew that it was the same pistol taken from the ARVN officer a few days earlier.

"Look here." Bob removed a plastic bag from the dead man's rucksack. "The mail's gonna be late."

"Might be some valuable stuff in there," I said, as Bob continued to rummage through the rucksack, finding a box of cookies from a Saigon bakery. He gave the box to Thach and told him to pass them out to the troops.

"Better update the lieutenant," Bob said. When Ly handed him the handset, Bob informed Condon that we would be moving out as soon as we checked out the truck.

"Booby-trap that rucksack," I told Thach. "Bob and I'll check the truck."

"Okay, *Bac-si*."

Bob and I moved back to the trail. As we drew near, I saw Danh sitting on his rucksack next to the same cypress.

"Let's check the truck," I told him. As the three of us walked down the trail, we moved through a cloud of mosquitoes. Although it was only a few meters to the truck, I felt naked and exposed; anyone who set foot on a trail was inviting sudden death.

"Looks like a freeway," Bob whispered.

"Yeah, probably runs all the way to Hanoi."

In the dry area at the center of the trail, bicycle and rubber-sandal tracks had been pressed into the hard surface.

"Chinese and Russian bring supply Kampuchea in boat," Danh told us. "Then VC bring Vietnam in truck."

"You could be right," I said.

When we reached the truck, we found that it had been unloaded so that a tire could be removed. A large canvas-draped pile stood near the rear.

"Check the load," Bob said. "I'll get the truck."

Danh kept a watchful eye on the trail while Bob climbed into the cab and I pulled the canvas cover from the pile.

"Russian," Bob said, as he checked out the bed of the truck. "There's a plate on the dash with Russian on it."

"Take a look at this," I said in amazement. "I can't believe it! More fifty-pound bags of rice from the Continental Grain Company of New York."

During Blackjack-33, we found twenty tons of rice from the same company.

"You shittin' me?" Bob grunted as he jumped to the ground. "Why the hell is New York sendin' rice to Vietnam?"

"Got me." I shrugged. "I didn't know we grew rice in New York."

"Got any time pencils?" Bob asked.

"Yeah, two," I said. "Eight-hour delays."

The copper and brass devices were shaped like a pencil. Each had a glass vial of acid and a fuse at one end. Once the vial was crushed—with five pounds of pressure—it would take eight hours for the acid to eat through the restraining wire. The striker would then hit and detonate the percussion cap and the grenade.

"Great, we'll bury 'em in the rice."

I handed him the two time pencils. While he used a crimping pliers to attach a blasting cap to each of the time pencils, I used my knife to cut three-inch slits along the seams of two of the bags. The musty smell of the burlap reminded me of a barn on a hot summer day. When I finished rolling up my right sleeve, he handed me the first grenade.

"She's ready to go," he said.

I took the grenade and attached time pencil and slowly worked it deep into the fifty-pound bag. When he finished attaching a time pencil to the second grenade, I repeated the process with the other sack.

"That'll do it," I said, as we pulled the tarp back over the pile.

In eight hours, the time pencils would detonate the grenades and blow the rice all over the area.

"What about the truck?" I asked. "Looks new."

"Yeah," Bob said as he turned to Danh. "Gimme a grenade."

Danh removed a fragmentation grenade from his harness and tossed it to Bob.

"Keep an eye on the trail," Bob said. "I'll hook this up to the engine."

Danh and I moved to a sunny area several meters down the trail from the truck and stood guard. As we waited, I noticed that the grass at both edges of the trail was pressed flat to the ground—some to the east and some to the west. When grass was stepped on, it generally returned to an upright position in less than twenty-four hours. The fact that it remained pressed to the ground was a good indication that the enemy had recently used the trail. I also saw that some of the branches that grew to the edge of the trail had been broken in recent days.

"Dry heat feels good," I said as I removed my hat, closed my eyes and faced the sun.

"It warm." The small ruby on Danh's front tooth sparkled in the sunlight.

If it had been a different time and place, I would have hung my sweat-soaked fatigues on a branch to dry and stretched out to absorb a few rays.

Looking at my left hand I saw that it was taut and

swollen from the ant stings. The back of it was as smooth as a balloon, and my fingers felt fat.

"All set," Bob said as he closed the hood on the truck and jumped to the ground.

When we got back to the platoon, we found Thach placing a fragmentation hand grenade under the enemy rucksack. The grenade's pin had been removed, and it was rigged for instant detonation. He had also dragged the corpse to a spot that could be seen from the trail and rigged a claymore mine attached to a trip wire. If the wild pigs didn't eat the body, his friends would have no trouble spotting him.

While I gave the area a once-over, Ly finished booby-trapping a few rounds of the dead man's ammunition. Using a pliers, he removed the projectiles from their shell casings. He then dumped out the powder, replaced it with detonating cord, and reassembled the bullets. If anyone fired the ammunition, his weapon would blow up in his face.

Bob briefed Lieutenant Condon, then we crossed the trail and moved north for a hundred meters. While we waited for the rest of the company to cross the trail, I rubbed some cortisone ointment into my hand, hoping it would relieve the swelling. I didn't want to take any Benadryl because it made me drowsy.

"Everyone's across," Bob said. "Let's move."

Glancing to my right, I saw that the Recon Platoon was in position. Their lead man was twenty meters to my right and a few meters to the rear.

I checked my map, took a quick azimuth with my compass, and pointed Danh in the right direction. He gave me a thumbs-up, and we continued north in two parallel columns.

News Clippings

Saigon . . . . . . 8AM   95°

The New York Times, July 18, 1967

Optimism of Robert McNamara, Defense Secretary, over progress in the Vietnam war, following a few days' visit to that country, is described by very well-informed military men on the scene as "phony." It is considered the standard operating "line" put out for political consumption.

U.S. News & World Report, July 21, 1967

Born: To Sen. and Mrs. Edward M. Kennedy, an 8-pound 7-ounce son, their third child; in Boston, July 14. Will he run for President? "He'll have to clear that with his uncle," quipped Teddy. "Bobby thinks every baby is his."

Newsweek, July 24, 1967

The war in Vietnam cannot be won by the U.S. It can only be won by the South Vietnamese. If South Vietnam refuses to raise enough troops to win the war, why should the U.S. continue to pour troops into the war?

The Miami Herald, July 18, 1967

Your voluminous Vietnam issue accomplished three things: it convinced the doves that the hawks were flying into disaster, encouraged the hawks to try harder and left the majority of us sparrows circulating around in confusion as usual.

Diana Wahmann, Coventry, Conn.
Newsweek, July 24, 1967

Best Sellers
Fiction
    1. *The Arrangement,* Kazan
Nonfiction
    1. *The Death of a President,* Manchester
U.S. News & World Report, July 21, 1967

With the war budget up $5 billion (to $27 billion a year), a tax increase on the way and the Presidential campaign already rumbling into low gear, Mr. Johnson could neither accept the strategic and political risks of stopping the war on Hanoi's present terms nor the even wider risks of greatly enlarging it.

Newsweek, July 24, 1967

Mr. AIKEN. Mr. President, on Thursday, July 13, in announcing the decision to send more troops to Vietnam President Johnson told the American people that—

We are generally pleased with the progress we have made militarily. We are very sure that we are on the right track.

Congressional Record—Senate, July 18, 1967

3

1015 Hours

The midmorning heat was stifling as we threaded through a steamy tangle of vines and leaves. Rivulets of sweat coursed through oily insect repellent, stinging my eyes and blurring my vision, but so far, no more enemy had been sighted.

I checked my army-issue Seiko. It was 1015 hours. I had a Rolex back at Trang Sup but always left it in my foot-locker when I went out on operations because I didn't want the enemy to get it if I was killed or captured.

The 3d Platoon continued to set the direction and pace while the Recon Platoon determined the distance between our two columns. In thick foliage, the columns closed the gap, and when it thinned, we moved farther apart. At times, the tangle was so compacted, it was nearly claustrophobic. At other times, it melted away so that we could see for thirty meters or more.

Following Recon in the column on the right was the headquarters section with Lt. Jim Condon and his radio operator S.Sgt. Roger "Ranger" Smith. The headquarters section was followed by SFC Bill "Fergy" Ferguson, SFC Frank Hagey, and the rest of the 2d Platoon. On the left, the 3d Herd was followed by SFC Ernest "Duke" Snider's 1st Platoon. In all we were 166 men.

Ten meters to my right, I saw the green scarves of the Recon Platoon. Each platoon's scarves were different colors, so we could more easily identify and control them when we made contact with the enemy. The 3d wore red, the 2d yellow, and the 1st blue. Watching Recon move parallel to us, I saw that S.Sgt. Larry Brooks "Stik" Rader was on point. Stik was incredibly agile. Like Danh, he had that feline grace that enabled him to slip almost imperceptibly through the thickest tangle. He was our light-weapons specialist and, prior to volunteering for the Mobile Guerrilla Force, served with the A Team at Dong Xoai. He stood five feet nine inches tall, with brown hair and sharp, distinct features. He was by far the thinnest American on the team, but resilient and tough. His friends affectionately referred to him as Stik. He knew his business and had a hard-earned reputation for being one of the best small-unit leaders in Vietnam.

As we continued on our northerly azimuth, the terrain changed from a dark, triple-canopy jungle to a bright, single-canopy area consisting mostly of two-story saplings, bamboo thickets, and clumps of banana plants with large drooping leaves. Green bananas hung from the plants, and small brown monkeys with yellow eyes cried *ka, ka, ka* as they scurried across the ground.

While moving through a thicket of green, yellow, and brown bamboo, I spotted what appeared to be a thatch roof. I had no way of knowing whether it was the edge of an enemy base camp or a farmer's hut. Until it was checked out, I had to assume the worst.

"Psst," I signaled Danh. When he turned, I pointed my M-16 to our left flank. He immediately went down on one knee, and Bob came up and squatted beside me.

"What d'ya got?" he whispered.

"Looks like a hootch." I pointed.

"Any movement?"

"No."

"Let's check it out."

Bob radioed the situation to the lieutenant while I relayed the word down the line that we would be moving out on our left flank.

Bob and I then lowered our rucksacks to the ground and moved in a low crouch with our M-16s at the ready. Weaving through the bamboo, we were careful not to step on one of the mold-covered stalks that littered the ground; a crunch would be heard for a hundred meters. The monkeys watched our every move as if they were spectators to a mysterious event. Some appeared frozen by fear while others fled our unwelcome intrusion.

It took us a minute to work our way around to the side of the hootch. Once there, I saw that it was a three-sided lean-to, about four feet high in the front. It had a moldy thatch roof, and its sides were covered with banana leaves. From where we were standing, it looked empty, but one never knew. Bob and I slowly sank to one knee, our eyes and ears straining for the slightest movement or sound. Suddenly, the air filled with the rank odor of human feces. We looked down and saw that Bob's knee had landed in the middle of a fresh pile of human crap. He shot me a wounded "Why me?" look. I had to restrain myself to keep from laughing. No sounds were coming from the hootch, so we rose to our feet and began inching forward. When we neared its front, we both stopped. Bob gave me a nod, and we stepped in front of the hootch, our weapons pointed inside it. It was empty.

"Out post," Bob whispered as he bent down to pick up a small, soot-blackened aluminum pot from its bamboo floor.

"Musta left in a hurry," I said softly. "They wouldn't

leave a good pot." I crawled inside the hootch and found a canteen, two rolled-up bamboo mats, a green undershirt, and a khaki Viet Cong belt stored near the rear wall.

"Don't touch anything," Bob cautioned as he squatted and ran his fingers through a fire pit in front of the hootch. "Still warm."

"Keep your eyes open," I said. "I'll rig it."

While Bob stood with his M-16 resting on the roof, I knelt next to the pit and tied a piece of string around an M-26 fragmentation hand grenade that had been rigged for instant detonation. Using my knife, I dug a three-inch-deep hole in the middle of the pit.

"Must be a hundred monkeys," Bob commented as he watched for signs of the enemy.

"Waitin' for the bananas to ripen," I said as I pulled the safety pin from the grenade then carefully placed the grenade in the hole, the safety lever facing up. Once in place, I packed dirt around it and covered it with charcoal dust and small pieces of unburned wood. If someone started another fire, the string would burn, the safety lever would fly off the grenade, and the explosion would kill or wound anyone within ten meters.

"How's that look?" I asked, smoothing the surface.

"Good," he said as he used a stick to scrape the crap from his trousers. "Let's get back to the platoon."

I wiped my blackened hands on my trousers, picked up my M-16, and we moved back to where Stik was talking with Thach.

"What was it?" Stik asked.

"Two-man OP," Bob said as Ly handed him the radio handset.

"Used today," I told Stik as Bob radioed Lieutenant Condon. "Probably bugged out when they saw us."

"It face south?" Stik asked as Bob updated Condon.

"Yeah," I said. "Guardin' somethin' up north of here."

"A base camp," Stik offered.

I pulled out my map and opened it as Bob gave the handset back to Ly.

"Condon says to bootleg east for a few hundred meters and then head north again," Bob said.

"Okay," I said.

"We'll be skirtin' some of those open areas," Stik warned as he pointed to a location on my map. "Hate to get pinned up against one of 'em."

Stik was right. Mobility was one of the keys to our survival. If we made heavy contact on one flank and had an open area on the other, our ability to maneuver would be greatly reduced.

"I'll watch it," I said as I checked my map. "I'll follow forty-five degrees for a few hundred meters and then go back on our old azimuth."

Stik gave us a thumbs-up and headed back to his platoon. As soon as Bob and I got our rucksacks on our backs, I gave Danh the signal to move out. If we had been spotted by someone in the hootch, there was a good chance they were on their way to warn whoever was up ahead. If we stayed on the same azimuth, the enemy could easily anticipate our route of march and set up an ambush. If we walked into a battalion-size or larger horseshoe-shaped ambush, they could cut us to pieces. In our business, setting a pattern could be hazardous to the health.

We moved out on an azimuth of forty-five degrees and soon passed within a hundred meters of an open area on our right flank. Moving over relatively flat terrain, we found ourselves in a forest of four-story, gray-trunked trees, with little growth close to the ground.

While slipping past the great trees, we hit an east-west trail whose ruts were packed with six-inch blades of grass. There was no evidence that it had been used in recent days. The grass wasn't pressed to the ground, and there were no fresh prints in its spongy surface. A few minutes past the trail, we reached the bottom of the slope we had been descending and waded across a shallow stream whose stagnant water was covered with a crust of green algae.

After crossing the creek, we moved up a gradual incline. When we reached the top of a kidney-shaped hill, we changed direction and headed north once more. Looking at my map as I walked, I saw that we were on some of the highest terrain in the area. It wasn't much of a hill compared to those we'd encountered on other operations, but for that area it was the high ground.

As we moved down the north slope of the hill, Recon increased the distance between our columns to thirty meters.

"Jim," Bob whispered and I turned.

"Yeah?"

"Hold it up," he said as he walked with the radio handset pressed to his ear.

"Psst!" Danh glanced over his shoulder, and I signaled him to stop.

I turned to Bob.

"What's up?" I asked.

"Stik hit some commo wires," Bob said. "Take a look."

"Okay."

I moved to my right until I hit the Recon platoon and found most of the Bodes down on one knee watching for signs of the enemy. Looking to my right, I saw Lieutenant Condon and Duke Snider moving up the line in my direction. The lieutenant was a former enlisted man with extensive Special Forces experience. Before attending Officers Candidate School, he had served as an enlisted man with the 77th and 6th Special Forces Groups at Fort Bragg, the 1st on Okinawa, and the 10th in Germany. Prior to volunteering for the Mobile Guerrilla Force, he was assigned to one of the A Teams in Tay Ninh Province. He had only been with us for a short time, and it was his first mission as the unit commander. Although I hadn't known him long, I had a feeling he would do well.

"Mornin', sir," I said. "How ya doin', Duke?"

"Good morning, Jim," the lieutenant responded with a New England accent. "Where's Stik?"

"Up ahead, sir," I said, motioning with a nod of my head. We moved a short distance before we saw Stik, his radio operator, and platoon sergeant standing near the southern edge of a large open area. As we neared their position, I saw that the clearing measured two to three hundred meters across and extended far to the north. The area's sun-bleached, foot-long grass rippled gracefully in the morning breeze like a field of grain.

"Where are they?" the lieutenant asked Stik.

"Over here, sir," Stik said as he led us a few meters into the clearing, stopped, and pointed to the ground. "Eight multicolored wires runnin' east-west."

In the direct sunlight, the temperature was a good twenty degrees hotter, and my pores opened like faucets.

"Only battalions or larger use commo wire," I said.

"No shit," Duke responded sarcastically.

"Get on the horn and get Hagey up here," the lieutenant told Stik. "I want him to check it out before we make a decision."

"Yes, sir," Stik responded as his radio operator passed him the handset.

Kaw, kaw, kaw. A crow drifted on the thermals high above the clearing.

Looking out over the open area, I found that its serenity

exerted a mesmerizing effect upon me. But the postcard beauty couldn't counter reality for long.

"Let's get back in the wood line," Stik advised, snapping me out of my momentary daydream.

As I neared the tree line, one of the Bodes from the Recon Platoon pulled a machete from his scabbard and raised his hand to cut the wires.

"No!" Duke grabbed his arm. "You wanna get us killed? Cut those, and we'll be in deep shit."

Stik's platoon sergeant grabbed the young Bode, gave him a couple of firm shakes, and said something to him in harsh muffled tones.

"Look, sir, we'd better not hang around here too long," Stik advised.

"I know," the lieutenant said as we turned to see Frank Hagey approaching.

"Sir." Frank smiled.

"Frank, we've got eight commo wires." The lieutenant pointed. "Would ya check 'em out?"

"Yes, sir," Frank responded as he headed into the clearing and squatted next to the wires. After a minute or so, he returned to where we were waiting.

"What d'ya think?" Condon asked.

"Judging from the number of wires, I'd say we've got a regiment." Frank paused. "Maybe larger."

"That's what I thought," Condon responded.

"Ya know, there's been talk that COSVN may be in this area," Frank added.

"C'mon Frank, give us some slack," Stik said.

"Can ya tap 'em?" the lieutenant wanted to know.

"Yeah," Frank said. "But I don't have a wiretap device with me. Any chance of havin' an MS-1 dropped in?"

"No time," Condon said. "Gotta find out who's talkin' to who, and we gotta do it quick."

"Yup," Duke added.

"Okay, Stik, take your platoon and follow the wires west," Condon ordered. "The rest of ya return to your platoons and stand by."

"Better get a FAC up, sir," I said.

"Yeah, let's get movin'."

Frank and I headed back to our platoons while Duke, Stik, and the lieutenant spread a map on the ground and continued comparing notes. When I got back to the 3d Platoon, I found the Bodes down in firing positions. The tension was palpable. They had jade Buddhas in their mouths, a sure sign that they were expecting something big. The sight of them caused the knot in my stomach to tighten. Bob, Thach, and Ly were kneeling together, looking at Bob's map. I knelt next to Bob and picked up a small twig.

"How's it look?" Bob asked.

"Eight commo wires," I said while using the twig to point to their location on the map.

"Eight?" Bob inquired with an apprehensive look.

"Yeah, eight wires."

Thach sprung to his feet.

"I talk to squad leader," he said.

"Okay," Bob said. "Jim, what's the lieutenant gonna do?"

"Stik's gonna follow the wires west while we hang loose," I said. "Better pass the word that Recon'll be out on our flank."

"Yeah." Bob folded his map and rose to his feet.

"The Bodes look a little uptight," he added as he extended his hand to pull me to my feet. "Why don't ya take a walk down the line and calm 'em down?"

"Once the first shot's fired, they'll settle down," I said.

"A lot like a parachute jump," Bob added. "You're a

little nervous on board the aircraft, but once you're out the door, you lose any fear ya had."

Whack-whack-whack. The silence was shattered by M-16 fire coming from the direction of the clearing. As if on cue, everyone instinctively flung himself to the ground, weapon pointed outward. Seconds later, an ominous silence returned. I jumped to my feet and moved back to where Bob was monitoring radio transmissions.

"What d'ya hear?" I asked.

"Nothin'."

"Only heard 16s," I said.

"Yeah, didn't hear any return fire. Maybe someone got spooked."

As I talked to Bob, I saw Duke Snider and Chote, the first platoon's interpreter, running in our direction.

"What happened?" Bob asked.

"Greased nine of them cats layin' wire," Duke said as he used his sleeve to wipe the sweat from his face.

"Where were they comin' from?" I asked.

"East," Duke told us.

"Everyone okay?" I asked.

"Yeah, they didn't get off a round."

"What about Stik?" Bob asked. "He gonna follow the wires west?"

"Hell, they're already gone," Duke said. "We killed the VC after Stik moved out. I'd better get back to my people," he added as he and Chote headed down the line.

"Bac-si," Danh called in a hushed voice.

Whack-whack-whack. Whump-whump-whump. A stutter of M-16s and AK-47s fire broke the silence.

Bob grabbed the radio handset from Ly. I stood next to him and heard Stik calling the lieutenant with an urgency in his voice.

"We're in heavy contact," Stik yelled, followed by a rush of static.

Whump-whump-whump. Whack-whack-whack. Whoomph, whoomph. A cacophony of fire and explosions erupted on our opposite flank. The roar of automatic fire had reached the point where it was difficult to hear what was being said over the radio.

"Estimated company hitting the 2d Platoon," Ferguson yelled over the radio as a few rounds cut through the overhead foliage. "Get a FAC up. We're in deep shit."

"Roger, Two. FAC's on the way," Lieutenant Condon radioed. "Fox Four, are you there? Over."

"Roger, Control," Stik responded. He was out of breath.

"Four, this is Control. You gotta come to us. If we move to you, we're gonna get caught on low ground. Over."

"Roger, Control. We're on line and movin' in your direction," Stik responded. "We got wounded."

"Have I got everyone on the horn?" the lieutenant asked. "Fox One, are you there?"

"That's a roger," Duke responded.

"Fox Two?"

"Fox Two, here," Fergy answered.

"This is Fox Three," Bob added.

"Okay, I want a tight perimeter. No gaps," the lieutenant ordered. "One and Two: tie it in tight on the south side. Two and Three: one squad each on the north side until Recon breaks back in to fill the gap. Three: send out one squad to help recon reenter the perimeter. Any questions?" Condon paused. "Okay, stay off the horn unless it's important."

Bob turned to Thach. "Let's circle the wagons. Move the 1st Squad to the north side of the perimeter." Thach nodded. "Once Recon gets back, ya can move 'em back here," Bob added.

"Okay, *Trung si,*" Thach responded.

"Jim, you and I'll take the 2d Squad out to link up with Stik."

"I'll tell Rinh we've got wounded," I said.

I quickly moved down the line until I found Rinh.

"Recon's got wounded," I said. "Set up an aid station in that depression." I pointed to what appeared to be an old bomb crater.

"Okay, Donahue."

When I got back to Bob, he had the 2d Squad ready to move and was talking to Stik on the radio.

"Roger, Four. One squad movin' in your direction," he said. "We'll set up a skirmish line fifty meters out. Three, out."

The clatter of automatic fire punctuated by explosions continued on both flanks, and a few stray rounds thumped into the tree trunks.

"Let's move it," Bob ordered.

Thach led the squad out of the perimeter and headed northwest. Bob and I followed him, along with Ly and ten members of the second squad. While moving at a quick pace over the flat and relatively open terrain, Bob gave last-minute instructions to Thach.

"Three blasts on the whistle, and we fall back halfway to the perimeter," Bob said. "Keep 'em on line as we move."

"Okay, *Trung si.*" Thach nodded and used his scarf to wipe the sweat from his eyes.

"The second three blasts, and we fall back all the way to the perimeter," Bob added.

"Okay, *Trung si.*"

When we reached the fifty-meter mark, Thach stopped.

"Get 'em on line, five meters apart," Bob ordered.

Thach deployed the first five men to his right and the second five to his left. Bob and Ly took up a position in a small depression, and I hit the ground behind a tree to their right.

"Here they come," Bob yelled. "Hold your fire."

Looking up, I saw the Recon Platoon moving toward us through a thin layer of knee-high mist. The area between us and them was crowded with two- and three-story trees. It reminded me of a rubber plantation. The bottom halves of the trees were free of leaves, and almost no vegetation grew beneath them. It looked as if at least two men were being transported in a fireman's carry. Their white bandages stood out in the maze of greens and browns. As Bob talked on the radio, Thach took a prone position beside me.

"Fox Four, this is Fox Three. Over," Bob said.

"Three, this is Four," Stik rasped over the radio.

"Four, you're seventy-five meters out. Over."

"Roger, Three, I see ya."

As Recon drew closer, the volume of fire rose dramatically, and rounds began knocking chunks of bark from the trees. On the far side of Recon's wounded, the rest of the platoon was leapfrogging to their rear. It looked like one squad was carrying the wounded while the other two took turns laying down a base of fire.

As they closed to thirty meters, I smelled the caustic fumes of CS gas and could hear Stik yelling at his Bodes to keep on line. Seventy-five meters on the other side of the Bodes were the khaki uniforms and erratic muzzle flashes of enemy troops. The hair on the back of my neck began to tingle as I took a deep breath and slowly exhaled.

Here we go, I said to myself, as my system electrified with the familiar rush of adrenaline. I was always scared on the threshold of a battle.

"Over here," I yelled to Stik as the first of the Bodes carrying the wounded reached our position and flopped to their knees in exhaustion.

"Tell 'em they've got another fifty meters to go!" I yelled to Thach as I jumped to my feet and ran to the wounded.

The men were too spent to carry the wounded any farther, so I grabbed the nearest Bodes and helped them get the wounded on their backs. From what I could see, only one man was seriously wounded. He had been hit in the upper leg, and it looked as though the round shattered his femur and severed his femoral artery. Someone had improvised a tourniquet from a green platoon scarf and a small piece of bamboo, tied just above the wound. His trouser leg was soaked black with blood, but the leg appeared to have stopped bleeding.

Once the wounded moved through, I returned to my position behind the tree, where I found Stik taking well-aimed shots at the advancing enemy.

"You all right?" I asked.

"Yeah, give me some ammunition," he said, out of breath and drenched with sweat.

I reached down and pulled five magazines out of my BAR belt and handed them to him.

"Caught 'em eatin' lunch." He inserted a fresh magazine into his M-16. "One of 'em spotted us, and then a couple of platoons came right at us. Lucky we were on line when they hit." He pulled his bolt to the rear and released it, slamming a round into the chamber.

"How many were there?" I asked.

"At least a company," he said. "I burned up five hundred rounds. The Bodes kicked ass. But there were just too many."

"Keep movin'," Stik barked to his men. "Keep movin'."

The remainder of the Recon Platoon passed through our skirmish line. There was a short pause in the firing, then our 2d Squad opened up on the pursuing enemy. Stik and I squeezed off a few well-aimed shots, but the enemy was still too far out to hit.

Glancing to the rear, I saw that Recon was about half-way back to our perimeter. When Bob gave three long blasts on his whistle I fired three quick bursts and every-one jumped to his feet. Running with my back to the enemy was an uncomfortable sensation. I had the feeling that a round was about to crash into my back. Reaching the halfway point, we again hit the ground and resumed firing. Here and there brilliant white shafts of sunlight penetrated to the jungle floor, and the khaki-clad enemy soldiers ap-peared to flash on and off as they ran in and out of the shafts.

I again looked to the rear to check Recon's progress. When I turned to resume firing, I saw that the enemy had disappeared from view. I could still hear the reports of their AK-47s but couldn't see anyone. I thought their lead elements might have outrun their main body and were waiting for them to catch up. Whatever the reason, it gave us an opportunity to move again.

With another quick glance to the rear, I saw that Recon was almost back to the perimeter. Bob gave a second three blasts on his whistle, and we all again jumped to our feet and ran to the rear. Reaching the perimeter, we caught up with the last of Stik's men.

The Recon Platoon sergeant didn't give his men a chance to rest. He immediately deployed them along the northern side of the perimeter. Once they were in position, Bob and Thach moved our 2d Squad back to the 3d Pla-toon's sector of the perimeter.

The firing on our side of the perimeter had subsided to the point where there were only isolated shots or bursts of automatic fire, but there was still a constant roar of fire and explosions coming from Ferguson's and Hagey's sector.

"Hey Jim, over here."

To my right, Duke and Stik had set up behind a large fallen tree.

"What brings you up here?" I asked Duke as I took up a position between them.

"Wanted to see if old Stik was still kickin'." He laughed.

"He's too ugly to get killed," I said.

"That's true. Musta temporarily lost my mind."

"Any word on Fergy and Frank?" I asked.

"They've got their hands full," Duke said.

"Here they come!" Stik yelled.

I peered over the moss-covered tree trunk to see an estimated company of khaki uniforms moving through the emerald forest and knee-high mist. They were seventy-five meters out.

Whack-whack-whack. Poing . . . whumph. Ta-tow-tow. The Bodes opened up with M-16s, M-79 grenade launchers, and the M-60 machine gun.

To my left, Thach was moving down the line trying to slow everyone's rate of fire. When the advancing enemy line was fifty meters out, Stik, Duke, and I commenced firing. I was using tracer ammunition and carefully aimed and squeezed off each round. When the top of my front sight blade was chest high on an enemy soldier I squeezed the trigger and sent a crimson streak down range. Firing with both eyes open, my right eye sighted the weapon, and my left followed the luminescent line of the tracer's flight. Using tracer rounds gave me the advantage of tracking the exact trajectory of each bullet. If a round was to the left or right of the target, I made a slight adjustment and squeezed off another round.

Following each round, I noticed that most of them were being deflected skyward or into the ground. The M-16s lightweight 5.56mm ammunition didn't have much brush-cutting capability. Having a high velocity but small caliber, the bullets were easily deflected by branches and vines.

When the enemy soldiers were forty meters out, they suddenly changed tactics. Rather than trying to overrun us with a frontal assault, they began to fire and maneuver. Each man ran forward for a few meters, hit the ground, fired a couple of rounds, jumped to his feet, and then ran forward again.

I began firing three-round bursts and saw that with each burst at least one of my rounds was hitting home. When the crimson streak hit an enemy soldier, he fell and disappeared beneath the pearl mist.

Judging from the way they continued to fire and maneuver, I concluded that they were well trained, probably some of the best troops we'd ever encountered. As they closed the distance between us, Danh crawled up next to me.

"I stay you, *Bac-si,*" he said with a big smile.

I hoped he wasn't waiting for my heart. Moving a few meters ahead of the advancing enemy, I spotted what looked like an officer carrying an M-16. It appeared as though their assault was beginning to sputter, and he was screaming frantically at his men to keep moving. I raised to one knee to get a clear shot at him, but before I could get off a burst, I felt a warm breath hit the left side of my head, knocking me to my butt in a sitting position. I was dazed and uncertain as to what had happened.

I felt something warm flowing down the left side of my face and neck. Stik turned and looked at me with a shocked expression. I'd been hit! I glanced to the left and, out of the corner of my eye, saw bright red blood squirting out from the side of my head; was I dead?

I hesitated to touch my temple. I was afraid I'd find part

of my head gone, but I forced myself to slowly raise my hand and touch the wound. With warm blood pulsating on my palm, I cautiously pushed my index finger into a small hole just over my temple. I felt a great sense of relief flood over me when I realized that part of my head hadn't been blown away.

"Gimme a battle dressing!" I yelled to Stik.

"God damn, Jim, I thought you were dead," he said. "I was waitin for ya to fall over."

"Thanks; I need more friends like you," I said with a stunned smile as he removed a dressing from its wrapper.

Stik placed the dressing over the wound, and I held it in place as he tied it to my head. Warm blood was flowing down my neck and chest. Looking out over the top of the tree, I saw that we had broken the assault. Although there was still a lot of shooting, most of the enemy troops had taken up positions behind trees; a few were running to the rear.

"Get it tight!" I yelled as Stik tied it in place. "Gotta stop it." I was bleeding profusely but remained alert. In the corner of my mouth, I detected the metallic taste of blood.

"Don't wanna hurt ya," Stick responded.

"Don't worry. I've only got so much blood. If ya can't stop it, I'll be dead by dinner."

"It's as tight as I can get it, but you're still bleedin'," he said with an anxious look on his face. My collar, neck, and the side of my face were covered with blood.

"Need help with that?" Duke yelled.

"No," Stik said. "Keep an eye on Charlie."

"Get an Ace and two clamps outta the right pocket of my ruck," I told Danh.

My rucksack was only a few meters away, and Danh crawled over to it and returned with what I wanted.

"Take the dressing off and see if ya can spot a bleeder," I

told Stik. "Musta cut an artery. Danh, tell Rinh to bring the M-5 kit."

Whoomph! Something exploded on the far side of the fallen tree and showered us with dirt.

"You wanna clamp the bleeder?" Stik asked.

"Yeah, if ya can clamp it, Rinh can tie it off with surgical thread."

"I'll give it a shot," he said as he untied the dressing and looked closely at the wound.

"What d'ya see?" I asked.

"A bullet hole. Don't see a bleeder. Just a round hole with a lot of blood gushin' out of it. There's no exit wound. Bullet's gotta be lodged in your head."

"Okay, let's try pressure again," I said. "If that doesn't work, you're gonna have to open it up."

"You wanna open it out *here*?" Stik said as he tore open another battle dressing with his bloody hands.

"Are there any other options?" I asked as he placed the dressing over the wound. "Get it as tight as ya can. Don't worry about hurting me."

He tied the dressing as tightly as possible without ripping it. I could feel the additional pressure, but blood was still oozing from under the bottom half of the dressing.

"Put the Ace on top of the dressing," I said.

Rinh and Danh returned to where Stik was working on me. Rinh turned pale when he saw that I had been shot in the head.

"Rinh, give Stik a hand with the Ace," I said. "Danh, get back up on the line."

Danh picked up his Sten and moved back to the fallen tree, throwing a glance at me over his shoulder while Stik and Rinh applied the Ace bandage.

"As tight as ya can make it," I said as they rolled the Ace around my head.

"Should I start an IV?" Rinh asked.

"No, not yet. If ya can stop the bleeding, I won't need one."

When they finished wrapping my head with the Ace, Rinh covered it with three-inch surgical tape. The bleeding finally stopped, and I felt a great sense of relief.

"Chey-yo!" I yelled the Cambodian battle cry.

Danh turned and gave me a thumbs-up.

"Very good, Donahue!" Rinh smiled before moving back down the line in the direction of the aid station.

"You look like some damned Arab," Stik said with a relieved laugh. "If that bullet had been a hair to the right, it woulda blown your ugly head off."

"Up yours," I said with a weary smile.

"You dizzy?" Duke asked.

"I'm okay."

"Better get back to my people." He stood up and headed down the line in a low crouch.

"All you Marines have hard heads with nothing in between," Stik remarked to me before leaving.

News Clippings

Prime Minister Air Vice Marshal Nguyen Cao Ky this morning said that during the past two years, he has never had any thoughts or committed any actions which are contrary to the best interests of the people and the nation.   *Vietnam Press* (Saigon), July 18, 1967

Dr. Benjamin Spock, noted pediatrician and one of the nation's most vocal spokesmen for peace in Vietnam, indicated Monday that he might be available as a third party presidential candidate next year.
          Buffalo Evening News, July 18, 1967

The sharp dispute between General Westmoreland and Defense Secretary McNamara's Pentagon analysts revolves around the rate of enemy infiltration from North Vietnam.   *Newsweek,* July 24, 1967

June tourists: 99,410, a record high.
          Honolulu Star Bulletin, July 18, 1967

The public and private comments on the Vietnam War have seldom been further apart in Washington than they are today. The official comments remain moderately optimistic; the private comments are much more solemn and even gloomy.
          Courier Express (Buffalo), July 18, 1967

Doctor Zhivago starring Geraldine Chaplin—Julie Christie—Tom Courtenay—Alec Guiness—Ralph Richardson—Omar Sharif—Rod Steiger.   *Los Angeles Times,* July 18, 1967

Mr. FINDLEY: Mr. Speaker, the strike at Colt Industries, which has halted all production of M-16 rifles so badly needed by allied forces in Vietnam, is a major scandal which actually has an adverse impact on our troops more immediate and more direct than the short-lived rail strike which brought such prompt action by Congress.
          Congressional Record—House, July 18, 1967

With Mayor Daley of Chicago making a belated drive to take the 1968 political convention away from Miami Beach, which seemed to have a stranglehold on them, this is probably a good time to examine this quaint American folkway.   *Los Angeles Times,* July 18, 1967

Dear Abby: My wife and I are newlyweds. She wants to have a dinner party and invite all of her old boyfriends. All these fellows are still single. I told her I didn't think much of the idea.

Los Angeles Times, July 18, 1967

4

The smell of spent gunpowder hung heavy in air so hot and humid it seemed at times almost suffocating to breathe. An unyielding sun tortured the jungle with its heat; I was grateful that we were mostly shaded from its rays.

The exchange of fire had tapered off to sporadic shots and explosions, and only Danh remained at our firing position behind the fallen cypress. He was lying at the right end, squeezing off well-aimed shots from an M-16. He must have run out of ammunition for his British Sten.

My hands were sticky with blood that had caked with dirt, so I poured some water from my canteen and rubbed them clean. After drying off with my scarf, I pulled myself up to the fallen tree. No sooner had I eased my head over the top of the moss-covered trunk than two rounds slammed into its rotting bulk, splattering splinters of wood in all directions

"VC close," Danh said as I ducked. He crawled up next to me.

He brushed aside some rotting leaves and twigs from the ground between us and smoothed the damp soil with his hand. Using a twig to draw a map he explained that enemy troops were spread out along our entire front. Some

97

were as close as ten meters, while others were as far away as a hundred.

"Many VC," he said.

"How many?"

"Maybe one hundred, *Bac-si.*"

"Okay, partner," I said. "Get back to your position."

I removed an old MK-2 fragmentation hand grenade from my harness, pulled the safety pin, let the safety lever fly with a *ping*, counted "One-one thousand, two-one thousand," then tossed it toward whoever had shot at me.

Whoomph! The grenade exploded, and shrapnel sliced through the overhead foliage. I had no way of knowing if it had hit its intended target, and I wasn't about to check it out.

"*Bac-si, Trung si* Cole come," Danh called.

Bob, Thach, and Ly crawled up next to me, and Ly rested his radio against the tree.

"You all right, old buddy?" Bob asked with concern. "Got back as quick as I could."

"Yeah, I'm okay," I said. "Keep your heads down. Charlie's only a few meters out."

"Everyone's pinned down," Bob said as he used his scarf to wipe the glistening beads of sweat from his face.

"We tied in with Duke?" I asked.

"Yeah, we're tied in tight." Bob removed a canteen from his belt and drank as we talked. "What d'ya got here?"

"Maybe a company," I said. "In this terrain, they don't have the men to overrun us."

"A Mexican standoff." Bob paused. "We're gonna need air to knock 'em out of there. We're almost outta ammo."

"Thach, get an M-79," I told him. "Can't touch 'em with 16s."

The M-79 grenade launcher served as our artillery. Its high-explosive rounds could be fired accurately up to 375 meters.

"Okay, *Bac-si,*" he responded. "*Bac-si,* I give you," he said as he removed a small white Buddha and gold chain from around his neck. I was very moved by the gesture; I knew it had deep meaning to him.

"My friend, I think you should keep it," I said, trying to convey my gratitude.

"No, *Bac-si,*" he insisted as he struggled to slip it over my head but couldn't quite fit it over the bandage. With grungy, dirt-covered fingers, he managed to unclasp the chain and refasten it around my neck.

"Thank you, my friend. I'll take good care of it."

"I get M-79," he said before scurrying off through the brush.

Cautiously peering out over the tree again, I saw what appeared to be a squad running from right to left about 125 meters out.

"Look at that," I said to Bob.

"Blue uniforms."

"They carryin' rucks?" I asked.

"Think so. Yeah, they're all carryin' rucks. Wonder where they're headed?"

"Got me."

"Aw, shit!" Bob said as he pointed at what looked like a number of platoon-size units moving through the same area. They were all carrying rucksacks.

"I could be seein' things," I said as I tried to focus my good eye. "Are some of 'em carryin mortar tubes?"

"Yeah, a weapons platoon," Bob said. "Could be part of a battalion."

"Looks like we're in for a knock-down-drag-out," I said. "Wish I had a pair of binoculars."

"Thach come," Danh told us.

Looking back over my left shoulder, I saw Thach and Kien crawling toward us. Kien was carrying his M-79 and wearing an ammo vest full of high-explosive rounds. He was also toting a couple of Russian RPG-7 rocket-propelled grenades.

"Where'd ya get the RPGs?" I asked.

"He take from VC." Thach smiled defiantly.

"How's your foot doin'?" I asked.

"Foot good," Kien said as he chewed on an unlit cigar, rolling it with his tongue as he maneuvered it in the corner of his mouth.

"Tell 'im I better not find out he's been stealin' gold fillings," Bob said as he pointed to his teeth.

"No, *Trung si,*" Thach responded with intense brown eyes. "He not do." Obviously he didn't catch the jest in Bob's words.

Thach positioned Kien at the left end of the tree while I removed my map and spread it on the ground. As Bob and I discussed our situation, a confused roar of AK-47s, M-16s, and explosions resounded through the jungle announcing an end to the lull.

"Don't think they'll hit us here again," I told Bob as I looked at my map.

"Yeah, it's too open," he agreed.

"Gonna hit us down at the other end."

"Good bet," Bob said. "If they come through the thick stuff, we won't see 'em 'til they're on top of us."

"You said it."

"Tell ya what," Bob said. "I'll leave Ly and the radio with you. I'm gonna move the M-60 and a few extra men down to the other end. Why don't ya see if ya can find out what's holdin' up the air support."

"Okay."

"Meet ya back here," Bob said before crawling off to the left.

"Gonna check with the lieutenant," I told Thach. "Back in a few minutes."

I crawled ten meters in the direction of the center of the perimeter and, once out of the line of fire, walked in a low crouch. With automatic fire and explosions to the south and east, I suddenly heard Lieutenant Condon. Nearing the sound of his voice, I saw that he, S.Sgt. Roger "Ranger" Smith, and a couple of Bodes from the headquarters section had set up in a small depression. Handset pressed to his ear, the lieutenant was kneeling next to his PRC-25 radio. Roger was sitting at his side, acetate-covered map spread across his outstretched legs.

"Sidewinder, Sidewinder, this is Fox Control. Over," Condon said into the handset.

"Tryin' to get the FAC up," Roger said. "You okay, Jim?"

"Yeah, I'm okay."

"Fox Control, this is Sidewinder. Over," the FAC responded.

"We're in business." Condon gave us a thumbs-up.

"You look like you had a fight with an ugly stick, and lost," Roger said.

"Ssshh, listen!" I hissed, pointing to the west.

In the distance, I heard the faint groan of an approaching O-1E spotter plane. Roger placed his map on the ground in front of the lieutenant and stood up.

"Sidewinder, this is Fox Control," Condon radioed. "If you follow niner-zero degrees you'll come in right over us. Over."

"Roger, Control. I'm on niner zero."

"Jim, as soon as I can get a slick in here, I'll get you and the rest of the wounded out," the lieutenant said with genuine concern in his voice.

"Don't worry about me, sir. I'm okay."

"It gave ya a good whack," he responded. "The side of your face is black-and-blue."

"Let me check your pupils," Roger said as he looked into my eyes.

"They equally dilated?" I asked.

"Yeah, so far, so good. That round musta hit somethin' before it hit ya."

"How's it look in your area?" Condon asked.

"Got a company pinned down in single canopy," I said. "They can't move, and neither can we."

The map and grease pencil were lying on the ground, so I squatted and, using the grease pencil as a pointer, showed him where Bob and I had seen a weapons platoon with mortars and a possible battalion of infantry moving across our front.

"We figure they're gonna rush us through the thick stuff down at the southern end of the platoon."

"That's what I'd do," Roger said.

"Sir, it's gonna take 'em a while to set those mortars up," I said. "If we can get some air within the next few minutes, I'd like to put the first strikes in on the company that's out in front of us."

"You got it," Condon said as he studied his map. "If ya can knock 'em outta there, shift some of your troops down to the other end."

"Yes, sir." I nodded.

"If ya can't hold 'em, I'll reinforce ya with the head-quarters section," he added. "We gotta keep 'em outside the perimeter. If they break through, we got big problems."

"Okay, sir. I'll relay that to Bob."

"If they've got mortars, they're gonna need a clearing," Roger said.

"Yeah. I'll have the FAC keep an eye on the open areas."

"He's gonna have to watch that east-west trail," Roger

added as he squatted and pointed to the trail that was located just a short distance south of our perimeter.

"Yeah," Condon agreed. "They'll use it to bring in reinforcements."

The drone of the FAC's engine grew louder as he approached.

"Sidewinder, this is Fox Control. Over," Condon radioed.

"Control, this is Sidewinder. Over."

"Sidewinder, this is Control. I'll give ya a 'now' when you're directly overhead. Over."

"Roger, Control."

"Here he comes." Roger smiled as we looked up. "Just a little more."

"Now!" Condon yelled into the handset.

"Okay, Control," the FAC radioed. "I got ya."

Looking up, we heard him circling overhead but couldn't see anything through the blanket of green foliage.

"You low on ammo?" Roger asked.

"Yeah."

"What d'ya need?"

"Ah . . . everything." I shrugged. "See if ya can get us some canister rounds for the 79s. HE ain't worth a shit in the thick stuff."

"What kind of quantities we talkin' about?" Roger asked.

"Hell, we'll take anythin' we can get," I said. "Ain't worried about havin' too much."

"Okay, Jim, get on back to your platoon," Condon said. "I'll see what I can do."

"Yes, sir," I said before heading back to the perimeter.

Poing . . . whumph! As I neared my position, I heard Kien firing his M-79.

When I reached the fallen tree, I crouched next to Ly, and he handed me the radio handset.

"Sidewinder, this is Fox Three. Over," I radioed the FAC.

"Fox Three, this is Sidewinder. Over."

"Sidewinder, I've got a company pinned down northwest of my position. Over."

"Roger, Three. Gimme a smoke. I've got fast-movers five minutes out. Over."

"Smoke," I said to Ly. From his harness, he removed an olive drab canister and handed it to me. It was yellow smoke.

I pulled the safety pin and tossed it five meters out in front of our position. A few seconds later, a caustic plume of thick yellow smoke enveloped the area and billowed sluggishly skyward.

Whoomph! Something exploded above me, and a split second later, a hot blast knocked me flat on my face. I looked up and saw hundreds of leaves floating slowly to earth through a pall of gray smoke. I wasn't hurt, but my ears were ringing.

"RPG," Danh yelled. "It hit tree."

"Smoke attracted the fire," I said. "Everyone all right?"

Ly had been hit by a falling branch, but other than that, no one was hurt.

"Fox Three, this is Sidewinder. Are you there? Over."

"Sidewinder, this is Three. Over."

"Three, we have a problem," the FAC said. "Got yellow smoke in two locations. Over."

"Damn," I said to myself. Had someone accidentally pulled the safety pin on another yellow smoke canister? Maybe the enemy had intercepted our radio transmission and popped another yellow smoke to confuse the FAC.

"Another smoke," I said to Ly. He removed another canister from his harness and handed it to me. This time it had a red top.

"Sidewinder, this is Three. I'm popping another smoke," I said. "It's the same color as the socks of Boston's baseball team. I say again, the same color as the socks of Boston's baseball team. Over." I hoped he was a baseball fan.

"Roger, Three. I read you five by five."

I lobbed the canister a good ten meters off to my right front and waited. Seconds later a coil of bright red smoke drifted across the ground before coiling upwards through the foliage.

"Three, I got ya," the FAC radioed. "The air force is up top. Where do you want it? Over."

"Numba one, *Bac-si!*" Ly flashed me a big smile. "*Soc mau* VC."

"Sidewinder, this is Three. Gimme heavy ordnance one hundred meters northwest of the smoke. I say again, heavy ordnance one hundred meters northwest of the smoke, over."

"Roger, Three."

"Sidewinder, this is Three. If you bring 'em in on two-two-five degrees, they'll be flyin' parallel to our lines. Over."

"Roger, Three," the FAC responded. "Two-two-five degrees."

I had a lot of confidence in the FAC but didn't want the jets flying directly over our perimeter. If one accidentally dropped his ordnance a second early, his payload could land right on top of us. It wouldn't be the first time it had happened.

The FAC swooped down low, dipping his nose toward the target.

Whooosh . . . pop! His white phosphorous marking-round blossomed into a graceful umbrella of molten white streamers. In his radio communications with the jets, he would use it as a reference point.

"*Bac-si, Trung si* Cole come," Ly said. I looked over my left shoulder and saw Bob crawling toward us.

"How's it look?" Bob asked.

"Got fast movers stacked up," I said. "Condon's working on the ammo resupply."

"Good."

To the northeast, I heard the roar of the first jet knifing in just above the canopy. My pulse rate picked up. You never could tell for sure where that first bomb would land.

"Get down!" I yelled.

The whine of the jet's engine rose to a banshee-like scream.

Karoumph! Karoumph! Karoumph! A hundred meters out, a daisy chain of orange-black fireballs flashed across our front; a second later, the earth-rending concussion of 750-pound bombs pounded my eardrums.

"Sidewinder, this is Three. Over," I radioed.

"Three, this is Sidewinder. Over."

"Sidewinder, you're lookin' good. Over."

"Roger, Three."

Moments later, a second jet streaked in, and the jungle shook with violent seizures of fire and steel.

"Gonna start walkin' 'em in," I told Bob.

"Charlie's between a rock and a hard place," Bob said. "Gonna be forced to move on us."

"Move or die." I smiled.

Another load of heavy ordnance exploded across our front, sending slivers of red-hot shrapnel slicing through broad leaves, tree branches, and flesh. With each blast, the fluting wail of shrapnel punctuated the air overhead.

"Pass the word we're bringin' it in close," Bob told Thach.

Thach raised the HT-1 radio to his mouth and briefed the squad leaders.

Karoumph! Karoumph! Karoumph! Another string of bombs exploded across our front, and a steaming piece of razor-sharp shrapnel whistled through the air and plowed into the base of a tree just a couple of feet away. It weighed a good five pounds.

"Look at the size of that sucker," Bob said.

"Sidewinder, this is Three. Over," I radioed.

"Three, this is Sidewinder. Over."

"Sidewinder, can ya give us napalm at five-zero meters. I say again, napalm at five-zero meters. Over."

"Roger, Three. We aim to please."

Less than a minute later another jet began its approach to the target.

"Napalm," I yelled.

Using napalm always scared the hell out of me, so I could easily imagine what it did to someone on the receiving end. If it didn't cremate the enemy, its insatiable fireball killed him by sucking the air out of his lungs.

The jet roared over the canopy, and its napalm pods tumbled lazily end over end. There was a dull *thud* and a sickening *kawhooosh* as orange-yellow balls of liquid hell splashed through the jungle, consuming everything in their path. Even fifty meters away, an invisible wall of heat hit my face with surprising force. The pungent petroleum smell of burning gas quickly permeated the area, and I heard the screams of people in their death throes, agonizing human sounds that turned my stomach.

"Sidewinder, this is Three. You're on target. Over."

"Fox Three . . ."

"Here they come!" Bob yelled.

The volume of fire up and down the line reached a

deafening crescendo as dazed enemy soldiers began running and stumbling out of the firestorm.

Bob, Kien, Ly, and Danh were firing as fast as they could line their sights on targets while I crouched low and kept contact with the FAC.

"Three, this is Sidewinder. Over."

The frenzied gunfire was so loud I could barely hear the FAC.

"Sidewinder, this is Three," I yelled into the handset.

"Three, this is Sidewinder. How we doin'? Over."

I started to yell again, but caught myself. Why am I yelling? I'm the one who can barely hear.

"Sidewinder, this is Three," I replied in a normal voice. "You've got 'em movin' forward. Can you give me twenty millimeter or CBUs? Over."

"That's a roger, Three. Where do you want it? Over."

"This is Three. As close as possible. We need it now. Over."

"Roger, Three. It's on its way."

"Grenade!" Danh yelled, and I hugged the ground.

Whoomph! An explosion to our rear left my ears ringing.

I dropped the handset, picked up my M-16, and looked out over the top of the tree. Just a few meters away a half dozen crouched enemy soldiers were running at us with their weapons blazing. One was on fire and screaming. His khaki uniform was burned and most of his skin was charred a reddish black. I didn't have time to aim my weapon so I just swung it in his general direction, but before I could squeeze the trigger, he fired a burst that lashed the air over my head. A split second later, my burst caught him in midstride, blowing off his right arm and shoulder. The impact of the bullets spun him around, and a stream of blood sprayed from his amputated arm like water from a hose. Then he just stood there in shock, a strange apparition staring at me. I pulled the trigger again, but nothing happened. Someone else got off a burst that lifted and twisted him upward before dropping him into sitting position with his back against a tree. He just sat there with his mouth and eyes wide open.

Off to the north I heard another jet on its final approach.

"Get down," I yelled.

As the jet roared over our position, its 20mm cannons screeched like the rusty hinges on an enormous door. Peering out over the tree, I saw a storm of rounds cutting across the ground, ripping through the foliage and enemy troops remaining in the open. I picked up the handset.

"Sidewinder, this is Fox Three. Over."

"Three, this is Sidewinder. How we lookin'? Over."

"This is Fox Three. Like a cow pissin' on a flat rock. Over."

"Roger, Three."

I removed the magazine from my M-16 and pulled the bolt to the rear. A shell casing was stuck in the chamber.

"Cheap ammunition," I muttered to myself.

I gave Bob the handset and removed a pocket knife from my hip pocket. I tried to pry out the shell, but it was stuck tight. I freed the cleaning rod attached to my rifle with green tape and screwed its sections together. By ramming it down the rifle's bore, I was able to dislodge the shell. I then reached into the center pocket of my rucksack and removed a bottle of Hoppes #9 cleaning solvent and the rest of my cleaning equipment.

Another jet screeched across our front, its twenty-millimeter cannons blasting away.

I opened the bottle of Hoppes, dipped a bore brush in it, and pushed it through the rifle bore a half dozen times. The firing slackened to a few sporadic shots, and Bob continued to talk to the FAC. Using my chamber brush and solvent, I then scrubbed out the chamber. The strong smell of the Hoppes was pleasant; it reminded me of simpler times, hunting back home. As I scrubbed, black dissolved carbon dripped on my hands, and I wondered where the reinforcements from the 1st Division were. Over the radio, I heard Fergy and Duke requesting air support. After running a few patches through the bore and chamber, I wiped the entire weapon down with silicone cloth and reassembled it.

"Sidewinder, this is Three," Bob said into the handset. "If ya ever get up to Trang Sup, the 3d Herd owes ya a cold one."

"Roger, Three. I copy that."

Seconds later, the circling jets broke off and the sound of their engines faded to the east.

Except for tormented groans and cries coming from the killing zone, an uneasy silence descended over the 3d Platoon's sector. The jungle in front of us had been ripped apart. The foliage hung in blackened shreds from the charred trunks of trees. Many had been stripped bare of leaves and splintered. Blankets of bluish gray smoke thickened and thinned in wispy, ghostlike patterns as they drifted across our front, giving an eerie, almost haunting feel to the battlescape. Here and there, fires continued to burn. And over everything, there hung the acrid scent of burnt cordite, charred flesh, and jellied gas.

News Clippings

Secretary of State Dean Rusk said yesterday that one condition of terminating American raids against North Vietnam was a guarantee that the Marines holding key positions would not be attacked by North Vietnamese regulars.

St. Louis Post-Dispatch, July 18, 1967

Joe Frazier and George Chuvalo finished their training grind yesterday at their upstate resort camps for their 12 round heavyweight bout in Madison Square Garden tomorrow night.

The New York Times, July 18, 1967

A year ago, Ronald Reagan was a political unknown. Today, he is a governor of the nation's biggest state—and rising fast in public-opinion polls for the presidency.

U.S. News & World Report, July 24, 1967

"Steve McQueen at his best!" *The Sand Pebbles*

Los Angeles Times, July 18, 1967

The ambassadors of the seven allied nations in the Republic of Vietnam will meet Tuesday "to strengthen consultation and cooperation among these nations," the Foreign Ministry said Monday.

The Korea Herald, July 18, 1967

Colt Ind. $+3\frac{3}{4}$

The Wall Street Journal, July 18, 1967

Out of Robert McNamara's trip to the fighting front came a decision to slow the U.S. buildup, resist Vietnam's becoming entirely an "American War." Washington's problem: how to get the South Vietnamese to carry more of the burden.

U.S. News & World Report, July 21, 1967

Barefoot in the Park—A successful adaptation, by Neil Simon, of his Broadway comedy, well acted by Robert Redford, Jane Fonda, Mildred Natwick, and Charles Boyer. (Music Hall, 6th Ave. at 50th, PL7-3100)

The New Yorker, July 22, 1967

If the United States followed the Constitution and Congress declared war, then, the U.S. would be in a position to win the war in Vietnam, Brig. Gen. (Ret.) Richard B. Maoan said Monday night.
Courier Express (Buffalo), July 18, 1967

5

A blazing afternoon sun caused the burned-over expanse at our front to shimmer in the wavering heat. Even in the imperfect sanctuary beneath the jungle canopy, the relentless heat bore down on us. A hush had fallen over the battle, bringing a curious blend of relief and worried silence.

A short distance down the line and to our rear, Rinh had set up a makeshift aid station in an old crater, a meter deep and ten meters across. With some of the overhead vegetation blown away, a brilliant shaft of sunlight reached all the way to its moist, brown bottom, illuminating the small depression with an unearthly glow.

Nearing the rim of the crater, I saw that Rinh and the Recon Platoon medic were busy tending to a couple of the wounded. The ground around them was littered with blood-stained battle dressings, pieces of white gauze, empty syringes, and discarded penicillin and streptomycin bottles. The Bode from Stik's platoon who had been hit in the leg was lying on a poncho at the center of the crater. Rinh was hovering over him, tying a can of serum albumin to a four-foot section of bamboo that had been pounded into the soft dirt. The blood-volume expander flowed into a vein in the back of the Bode's hand through a thin, plastic tube.

On the left side of the crater, a Bode from the 2d Platoon was lying on his back with his head propped against a rucksack. The Recon Platoon medic was kneeling next to him, carefully covering his face with layers of white gauze. Stepping down into the depression, I rested my M-16 against a rucksack and knelt next to the Bode from the Recon Platoon. His lips were blue, and I could only see white slits through his half-open eyes.

"I gave him 600,000 units of procaine penicillin and a half gram of streptomycin," Rinh said as he knelt next to me. "The platoon medic gave him morphine when he was hit."

"Good." I checked the medical tag that was attached to his fatigue jacket and saw that his name was Luc. The green tourniquet on his left leg was tied tight a couple of inches below his crotch. His camouflage pant leg was caked with dried blood and dirt. Some fresh blood was still seeping through the coagulated crust.

"How's the other guy doing?" I asked Rinh.

"Shrapnel wound. It looks bad, but it's not serious."

"Okay, I'll take a look at 'im as soon as we finish here."

"Donahue, how is your head?" Rinh asked with concern.

"Got the world's worst headache."

"Do you want something for pain?"

"No, don't wanna dull my senses," I said as I checked the flow of the serum albumin.

It looked good. White surgical tape held the tube and needle firmly against the back of the wounded man's hand, and there was no swelling.

"He drifts in and out," Rinh said. "When he's conscious, he asks for water."

"Got a scissors?" I asked as I felt his pulse and watched the second hand on my Seiko. His wrist was cold and clammy, and his pulse was running about 120 beats a minutes.

Rinh removed scissors from his M-5 medical kit and handed them to me. Observing the movement of the Bode's chest, I saw that his breathing was rapid and shallow. He was mumbling incoherently.

"Check his blood pressure," I said as I used the scissors to cut through the bottom of his pant leg.

"His systolic was ninety-two."

"Check it again," I said. "He's in shock."

Rinh removed a blood pressure cuff and stethoscope from the M-5 kit, rolled up the Bode's left sleeve, and wrapped the cuff around his arm. I finished cutting his pant leg all the way up to the tourniquet and felt his now-exposed leg. It was cold and slippery with sweat. His light brown skin had turned a pale, sallow color as if he were already dead.

On the inside of his thigh a small, dark hole outlined with black oozed bright red blood. It was a few inches below the tourniquet and halfway between his hip and knee. Below the wound, his leg was cocked at an odd angle, a sure sign that the bullet had fractured his femur. I lowered my head close to the ground and at the back of his leg found the exit wound, a silver-dollar-size hole with small splinters of bone fragments imbedded in the flesh.

It didn't look all that bad, but that type of wound could be deceptive. When a fast-moving bullet tore through muscle, the shock often destroyed large amounts of the surrounding tissue, and considerable amounts of blood could seep through the walls of small blood vessels and pool in the damaged areas. Death from shock was always a possibility.

"His systolic is down to seventy-four." Rinh's voice mirrored his concern as he removed the stethoscope from his ears.

"Did ya give 'im epinephrine?" I asked.

"No."

"Gotta stabilize his blood pressure," I said. "Give him 0.2 milligrams of epinephrine, and get a normal saline IV going."

As Rinh prepared the injection, I placed four-inch squares of sterile gauze over the wounds, then covered them with surgical tape. Every time I touched his leg, he let out a hoarse groan from deep within his chest. Rinh didn't have any trouble giving him the injection but wasn't able to get the IV's needle into his nearly collapsed vessel.

"Do a cutdown if ya can't get it in," I said.

"One more try," he responded.

Using a thumb to hold a vein on Luc's left wrist in place, he finally worked the needle into it. "Got it!"

I smiled.

With the wounded Bode's blood pressure dropping dangerously, we had to move quickly. If we were unable to get it under control, he would likely fall into irreversible shock and die of kidney or liver failure in minutes. Judging by his condition, he had probably lost about a quart of blood before the tourniquet was applied. When he began to lose blood, his vessels had automatically constricted to compensate for the loss. But we'd reached the point where that defense mechanism was beginning to fail. I hoped the epinephrine would constrict his vessels again and increase his blood pressure.

Whoomph! An explosion just a short distance south of the crater startled me. While working on the wounded, I often became oblivious to the fighting around me, but something that close had a way of snapping me back to reality.

"Open it all the way," I told Rinh as he adjusted the drip

rate of the normal saline IV. With the regulator wide open, the clear salt water flowed into the wounded man's veins.

"I will splint his leg," Rinh said.

"Okay," I said. "No tellin' when we'll get outta here. Get someone to improvise a stretcher."

"Okay." Rinh nodded.

Normally we carried our dead and wounded in hammocks tied to bamboo, but in this case it was important to keep him as flat and stable as possible. His loss of blood contributed to the shock, but I was convinced that the primary cause was the excruciating pain. When recon had carried him all that distance without a splint, the sharp ends of his broken femur must have acted like a meat grinder on the surrounding tissue. I shuddered at the thought of the pain he must have endured.

"Should I loosen the tourniquet every thirty minutes?" Rinh asked.

"No, don't touch it," I said. "He's already lost too much blood. Any more, and we'll lose 'im."

If we were able to medevac him to an American hospital within the next few hours, they'd probably be able to save his leg. But, with his artery severed and his femur broken, the chances of saving the leg grew slimmer with each hour. What concerned me most was the possibility that the enemy would overrun our perimeter. If that happened, I knew the Bodes wouldn't leave him for the enemy. I also knew that if we got into a running gunfight with the Cong, there would be no way the Bodes could carry him on a stretcher. Those considerations foretold painful decisions to come.

"You been sendin' the wounded back to their platoons?" I asked as Rinh used safety pins to reassemble the wounded Bode's pant leg.

"Yes, Donahue. If they can walk, I send them back."

"Why don't ya keep the next two or three here for security?" I said as I moved to the other wounded Bode. "If Charlie gets inside the perimeter, he's gonna blow your ass away."

He nodded that he would.

"Okay, let's take a look at that face," I said as I knelt next to the second Bode.

I reached for the M-5 kit and placed it on the ground next to the Bode's head while Rinh instructed the Recon Platoon medic to take Luc's blood pressure every fifteen minutes and keep an eye on his IV. Kneeling at his side, I took his pulse and then removed the gauze from the side of his forehead, revealing a deep oozing gash that went all the way to the bone, starting a half inch below his hairline. When I removed more of the blood-soaked gauze, I saw that he had a second gash over his eye. The two cuts came together between his eyes forming a perfect V. When Rinh finished with Luc, he squatted next to me.

"His name is Ty," Rinh told me. "He was with Sergeant Hagey."

He looked at me through worried brown eyes as I peeled back the blood soaked gauze.

"Knhum slarb reu te?" he mumbled.

"He thinks he will die," Rinh said.

"Moen ei te, kom barom oy sos." I told him that he wasn't going to die.

"Tell 'im it's not as bad as it feels," I said. "We'll sew 'im up, and in a month there'll be nothin' left but a thin red line."

Rinh explained what we were going to do, and that seemed to relieve some of Ty's anxiety. He was a good-looking Bode, and the thought of being permanently disfigured no doubt terrified him. Normally, I didn't suture wounds in the field because in most cases you had to surgically remove the damaged tissue surrounding the wound. Failure to do so would result in death from gangrene. Facial wounds were an exception; it was generally advisable to sew them up as soon as possible. My decision to close him up immediately was also influenced by the possibility of the enemy's overrunning us at any time. I figured that if we had to fight our way out, he'd have a much better chance of surviving if his wound was closed. If he got stranded in the jungle with his face torn apart, he'd probably die of infection.

Removing the last layers of gauze from Ty's face, I saw that the jagged rip continued down the side of his nose until it ended near the corner of his mouth. It formed a perfect Y. The once light-brown skin of his face had swollen a deep purplish black.

"Tell 'im we're gonna cover his eyes to keep the soap out."

Rinh comforted Ty while I covered his eyes with gauze. Looking at his hands, I saw his fingers digging into the dirt. It reminded me a lot of my experiences in the dentist's chair. Once the morphine took effect, he'd relax.

"You give 'im antibiotics?" I asked.

"Yes." Rinh showed me where he had recorded it on Ty's medical tag.

I asked Rinh to ask Ty if Frank Hagey was all right, and Ty told us that he and Frank had killed many Viet Cong. He said that the last time he saw Frank, he was outside of the perimeter at the southern end of the 2d Platoon. He said that he hadn't seen Bill Ferguson, but thought that he was up at the other end of the platoon.

"Okay, let's clean 'im up," I said.

Rinh removed a plastic squirt bottle from the M-5 kit. It contained a mixture of pHisoHex and hydrogen peroxide. After shaking it up, he squirted some into the palm of my hand. The pHisoHex had a fresh antiseptic smell that reminded me of our medical training at Fort Sam Houston, Texas. As I rubbed my hands together, the white soapy liquid quickly turned brown with dissolved dirt and blood. Rinh then poured water from a canteen to rinse them clean.

"Tell 'im not to worry," I said. "In a couple weeks, he'll be back in Tay Ninh raisin' hell. I'll buy 'im a buffalo steak at the Bamboo Club."

Ty forced a smile as I dried my hands with a surgical towel. Rinh then removed a sterile suture set that was wrapped in a green surgical towel. After removing the tape that held it shut, he placed it on the ground next to me and peeled it open. I checked its contents: two straight and two curved five-inch forceps, a straight razor, a surgical knife with extra blades, gut and black silk suture thread, general surgical scissors, an assortment of curved surgical needles, four eighteen-inch surgical towels, an emesis basin, and a pair of tweezers. Everything we would need to sew him up.

It was a hell of a place to try to maintain sterile technique, but we would have to do our best. When I thought about it, I was amazed how few wounds became infected. The last one I could remember was a montagnard from a village near Duc Phong. After sewing up a flesh wound a few inches above his ankle, I told Doctor Yen to tell him that he would have to stay at the dispensary until I removed the stitches. That night the montagnard snuck out of camp and returned to his village. Three weeks later, four montagnards carried him back to the dispensary in a hammock. His wound was inflamed with infection, and half of the stitches had been ripped out by the swelling.

"Gimme a pair of 7s," I told Rinh.

He reached into the kit, opened a pair of paper-wrapped surgical gloves and laid them on the sterile field.

While I slipped into the rubber gloves, Rinh dropped a

few pieces of gauze into our sterile emesis basis and then hung a bottle of normal saline from a piece of bamboo he had pushed into the ground next to Ty's head.

I was ready to flush out the wound, when the level of fire picked up along the 3d Platoon's side of the perimeter. From the south, the whine of a jet engine rose to a scream as it streaked in low.

Karoumph! Karoumph! Karoumph! A string of bombs exploded, and the earth convulsed.

"Flush it out," I told Rinh as thousands of leaves drifted to the ground around us.

With the end of the bottle's plastic tube an inch from Ty's face, Rinh opened the regulator and flushed specks of dirt and a few blood clots from the wound. There was some oozing but no serious bleeding.

"Okay, let's scrub it," I said.

Rinh picked up the plastic squirt bottle and carefully filled the length of the wound with the mixture of hydrogen peroxide and pHisoHex. The hydrogen peroxide immediately began to bubble when it came in contact with the raw flesh.

After filling the wound with the soapy disinfectant, Rinh squirted some on top of the gauze, and I used a few squares to gently scrub the length of the wound. The morphine must have done the job because Ty wasn't clutching the dirt any longer and didn't appear to be experiencing any discomfort.

"Chheu reu te? " I asked if he was in pain.

"No, *Bac-si*."

When I finished with the wound, I worked my way farther and farther away from it until I had finally scrubbed his entire face.

That done, Rinh rinsed away the soap with normal saline. The white mixture flowed down Ty's neck and the side of his rucksack. When Rinh was through, he used a towel to dry the sides of Ty's head and neck and wipe the remaining soap from his ears.

When he finished, I draped the wound with the four eighteen-inch green towels that had been packed inside the sterile suture set. With his face wrapped, he looked like a nun wearing a green habit.

Rinh opened packages containing a plastic syringe and a twenty-three-gauge needle and dropped them both on the sterile field. I attached the needle to the syringe as he removed a bottle of lidocaine hydrochloride from the M-5 kit and wiped its rubber cap with a piece of alcohol-soaked gauze. He then held the bottle steady while I pushed the syringe's needle through the rubber cap and into the anesthetic. I then drew back on the syringe and filled it with the clear, pain-killing liquid.

After Rinh explained to Ty what we were doing, I carefully inserted the needle into the upper right corner of his Y-shaped wound. The injection of lidocaine caused the area around the needle to swell. Working my way down the right side of the Y, I injected the lidocaine every quarter inch. When I finished the right side, I did the left.

Karoumph! Karoumph! Karoumph! A string of bombs exploded, and more leaves fell to the ground. That was normally the easiest part of sewing up a wound, but it was made difficult by the fact that the earth was shaking beneath me. Finished, I pricked the wound with the needle. Ty didn't move. He had an impassive look on his face.

"He's numb," Rinh said.

"Yeah." I smiled. Between the morphine and the lidocaine, Ty wouldn't feel it if he got hit by a tank.

I placed the syringe next to the emesis basin and picked up a curved forceps and a three-eighths inch curved surgical needle. After clamping the center of the needle with the forceps, I threaded it with a piece of black silk surgical thread. To insure that all the edges of the wound would line up properly, I decided to put the first stitch in at the base of the V.

Gripping the flap of the V with the tweezers, I pushed the needle through the skin and into the underlying tissue. When it came out, I pushed it into the flesh on the other side of the gash and out through the skin. Using the forceps, I then tied a tight surgical knot and cut away the excess thread with the scissors. It looked good; everything lined up perfectly. I was pleased with myself.

"Bac-si," a voice called. I looked up and saw Thach and Kien carrying another wounded Bode into the crater. Thach had a leg under each arm, and Kien gripped him under his arms and around his chest.

"Bring 'im here," I said as another jet streaked in just above the treetops. "Behind me." It was Lieu. "Damn." I knew he'd never make it. We should have left him at Trang Sup.

Kawhoosh! A load of napalm splashed through the canopy somewhere south of the aid station.

"He stand behind little tree and shoot at VC," Thach said, shaking his head.

Lieu writhed on the ground as Rinh unbuttoned his fatigue jacket. An inch to the right of his navel there was a dark, dime-size hole ringed by a small circle of fresh blood. There was no sign of external bleeding, but he was in a lot of pain. I wanted to help him but couldn't contaminate my surgical gloves.

"I give him morphine," Thach said as Rinh and Kien rolled him onto his right side. Lieu grimaced.

"Got an exit wound?"

"No, Donahue," Rinh said as he searched Lieu's sides and back for a second wound.

I was surprised. Bullets to the stomach usually passed through the soft tissues and exited somewhere in the back.

Lieu continued to squirm and kicked a shower of dirt on Ty's legs.

"Watch it! He's gonna contaminate everything," I yelled as Thach and Kien tried to calm him down. I felt sorry for him. He was only a kid and was probably scared to death. This one mistake could cost him his life.

Rinh slowly rolled him on his back, covered his wound with a battle dressing, and buttoned his fatigue jacket.

The wound itself didn't look serious, but there was no telling what kind of damage had been done inside his abdominal cavity. If the bullet hit one of the main vessels, he would die quickly. If it ruptured his intestines, he could die of infection. If we didn't get him to an American hospital, his survival was a crapshoot. There were a lot of ifs.

"All we can do is control the pain and start an IV," I told Rinh. "If he's alive in thirty minutes, he might make it."

"I go," Thach said.

"Tell Bob I'll be back as soon as I'm done."

"Okay, *Bac-si*," Thach said as he and Kien headed back to the platoon.

While Rinh endeavored to comfort Lieu, I continued suturing Ty's face.

Starting at the top right of the Y, I repeated the suturing procedure every quarter inch until finally putting in the last stitch at the base of the Y.

"How's it look?" I asked Rinh as I removed the patches from Ty's eyes.

Rinh leaned over. "Very good."

Rinh removed an air force White Dot signal mirror from the M-5 kit and handed it to Ty. He tilted the mirror a few times to examine the wound. He seemed pleased with our work.

"Tell 'im that once the stitches are out, he'll look great,"
I said, as I covered the stitches with gauze and surgical tape.

When I finished, I removed the surgical gloves and took
a long drink of water from my canteen. Rinh picked up a
tube of ophthalmic ointment and squeezed a little into
each of Ty's red eyes.

"Hey, Rinh, you wouldn't have a cold Pepsi, would ya?"

"I wish I did," he said as he looked over at Lieu. "Donahue,"—his expression turned serious—"Thach feels very
bad about Lieu."

"So do I."

"No, Donahue, you do not understand. Lieu was afraid,
and Thach had to kick him and call him many bad names.
Now maybe he will die."

"He was doin' his job," I said. "I'll talk to 'im."

After checking Luc's IV, I squatted next to Lieu, and
using Rinh to interpret, I told him that within a few hours,
we'd get him to an American hospital. We even managed
to get a smile out of him when we told him that before he
knew it he'd be eating hot American food and chasing
beautiful nurses. Rinh laughed when he told Lieu about
the time he was medevacked to the 196th Light Infantry
Brigade's Mobile Army Surgical Hospital in Tay Ninh.

Whump, whump, whump. All along the 3d Platoon's side
of the perimeter, hundreds of small cluster bomb units exploded like a string of firecrackers.

Before leaving, I talked to Rinh about the possibility of
hiding Luc and Lieu in thick underbrush if it appeared we
were going to be overrun. It would be risky, but there were
no easy solutions. Rinh agreed and told me that he would
draw a map of their location so that we could return after
the battle to pick them up.

I was about ready to head back to the 3d Platoon when
a Bode from Duke's platoon slid into the crater and said

something to Rinh. Rinh told me that his name was Son and that a member of his squad had been shot in the head. After telling Son that I would go with him, I picked up our M-5 kit and followed him south through a maze of thorn-covered vines and tangled brush.

After twenty meters of slow going, we entered a sunny bamboo thicket with dense green bramble to our right. As we wove our way through the thicket, pieces of dead and decaying stalks crunched beneath our feet. It was a strange war. Except for the melodic chirping of small, pale green birds overhead, we were walking in solitude while only a few meters away men were desperately fighting for their lives.

Whump, whump, whump. An AK-47 opened up from behind a curtain of green to our right. I could see the bullets splintering stalks of green bamboo just a few feet in front of me, and I had the strange, trancelike sensation that they were traveling in slow motion.

It only took me a fraction of a second to flick the selector switch to automatic as Son and I hit the ground behind a small hill. We hugged the ground as the AK continued firing with the brittle cracking sound of rounds chopping through the bamboo stalks around us. I considered throwing a grenade in the direction of the firing, but the bamboo was just too thick. The grenade would probably have bounced back on us.

Son screamed something in Vietnamese, and the firing stopped. I cautiously peered over the top of the mound, but all I could see was a mosaic of greens. Except for a smattering of gunfire coming from Duke's area, everything was still.

Suddenly, I spotted movement—it looked like a face. I filled the air with tracers, firing a full magazine. There was a horrible scream, and the face disappeared. After I quickly changed magazines, we jumped to our feet and rushed forward. I felt dangerously exposed, crashing through the bamboo thicket. If the enemy soldier wasn't dead, he had the clear advantage. What if it was a trick? What if there was more than one of them? With each step, my heart beat faster.

A few meters into the thicket, we found a blue-uniformed Vietnamese soldier lying on the ground in twisted agony; his face and the front half of his neck had been blown away, and loud guttural groans, blood, and scarlet foam poured from what once was his neck.

Whack-whack. Son fired two quick shots into his chest, and it was silent again.

"What the hell did ya yell?" I asked as he gathered up the dead man's weapon and web gear.

"I Nguyen," he smiled, pointing to his chest. "I Vietnam, do not shoot."

We left the dead soldier where he fell and continued in the direction of Duke's platoon. As we walked, I heard the muffled *wap, wap, wap* of choppers far to the south. I hoped they were bringing in reinforcements. At the top of the hill, the terrain thinned, and I spotted Chote, Duke's interpreter, hunched over some bodies. Son and I ran forward and, with a great sense of relief, saw that the bodies were of enemy soldiers wearing blue uniforms and pith helmets. There were about a dozen corpses scattered around the clearing, and Chote was checking them for anything of intelligence value. From what I could see, most of them had been shot up pretty bad.

"Where's Duke?" I asked.

"Come, *Bac-si.*" He motioned me to follow him.

At the southern side of our perimeter, I found Duke kneeling behind a large fallen tree firing a captured AK-47.

I squatted next to him and could see the backs of the retreating enemy seventy-five meters away.

"Returnin' this ammo to its rightful owners," he said as he continued to fire. Looking south, I saw that, for at least a hundred meters, most of the foliage had been blown apart or burnt away. A few hot spots were still smoldering, and the entire area was blanketed by a mantle of gray smoke and haze.

"How's it goin', Jim?" he asked when he stopped firing.

"Could be the calm before the storm," I said. "What they hit ya with?"

"A company, maybe more. Made two good runs at us," he said as he used his scarf to wipe the sweat from his face. "We held our fire 'til they were twenty meters out, then let 'em have it with grazing fire and claymores. Greased a lot of 'em."

"Lucky they didn't roll up your flank."

"You're tellin' me. It was the weirdest thing I ever saw," he said as he took a long swig from his canteen. "Once they broke through, they just stood there like they didn't know what to do next."

"That is strange. I figured 'em to be some pretty good troops."

"They ran up the hill a ways and stopped," he said. "Caught 'em in a cross fire, but a few got away."

"We ran into one of 'em," I said.

"I'll tell ya, those sky-jockeys did one hell of a job. They're my landscapers." He laughed, nudging his AK-47 toward the blackened area in front of his platoon.

"Yeah, they won't come through there again."

"I'm gonna leave one squad here and move everyone else to the creek bed."

"Hey, would ya make contact with Fergy and tell 'im that

Hagey's outside the perimeter down at the southern end of his platoon?"

"Sure," he said as he picked up his radio handset.

"Bac-si." Son motioned for me to follow him.

"See ya later," I said as I stood up to leave.

As Son and I moved down the line, I could hear the FAC drifting a couple thousand feet above the canopy. By then, the choppers that I had heard a few minutes earlier were a short distance southwest of our position.

As we followed the southern edge of the perimeter, the Bodes were spaced five to ten paces apart and were busy taking advantage of the lull in the fighting. Some were digging holes while others were piling up pieces of trees in front of their positions. A few were feverishly cleaning their weapons.

Twenty-five meters down the line, we were met by one of Duke's squad leaders. He led us to a large gray-trunked cypress tree that was just a few meters to the rear of his position. Near its gnarled base, I found a wounded Bode lying in a fetal position on a blood-covered poncho. I didn't know his name but recognized him as one of the Bodes who had been with us since Ho Ngọc Tao. He was a good friend of Danh's. I assumed that his airway was partially blocked because every time he took in a breath, it sounded like he was snoring. I put our M-5 kit on the ground next to him, and Son told me that he and the squad leader would be on the perimeter if I needed anything.

When I squatted next to the wounded Bode, I saw that he was seriously wounded. Bloody saliva drooled from the corner of his half-open mouth and pooled on the poncho. The salty, sweet smell of fresh blood coating the rubber poncho was repulsive. It had the smell of a body bag.

"Chheu reu te?" I asked if he was in pain, but he didn't answer.

His jet black hair was matted with blood, and behind his left ear was a nickel-size bullet hole. In the shadowy tangle, smothered under layers of dark green vegetation, I found it difficult to see what I was doing. I had to get him into a sitting position, so I grabbed him under both arms and dragged him off the poncho and propped him up against the cypress trunk. The large ground roots formed a perfect chair to cradle him in.

With him sitting against the tree semiconscious, I saw that the bullet had shattered the right side of his jaw, passed through his mouth, then exited behind his left ear. I couldn't tell if the bullet had fractured or penetrated his skull. For his sake, I hoped that it hadn't. Jaw wounds were very painful, and this one was no exception. The platoon medic had attached an empty morphine syrette to his collar. Although morphine was our most potent painkiller, it wasn't supposed to be used in the case of head wounds because it increased pressure within the skull. It could also complicate the wounded man's breathing problems by further constricting his airway.

Using my pen flashlight, I checked his ears to see if there was any clear cerebrospinal fluid draining from them. I was relieved to see that there wasn't. When I checked his pupils, I found both dilated and glazed with the fish-eye look of shock.

When I tried to check his pulse, he started to gag and spit up blood. I stuck my finger into his mouth to make sure that it was clear and found it filled with pieces of bone and teeth. Putting my other hand under his chin, I pulled out pieces of a half-dozen or so teeth and the coughing stopped. If he was going to live, I'd have to figure out a way to stop the bleeding.

I was having trouble keeping him in a sitting position, so I straddled his legs and sat back on his knees. I tried to look inside his mouth, but found it too dark to see anything. In an attempt to get a better look at the damage, I pushed my pen flashlight partway into his mouth and saw a mass of torn flesh, bone, and blood. It looked like the bullet had fractured his jaw, knocked out some teeth, ripped open his tongue, and went up through the roof of his mouth before exiting behind his left ear. Most of the bleeding appeared to be coming from the hole in the roof of his mouth.

He was still having some difficulty breathing, but nothing life threatening. However, I was concerned that his torn tongue would swell, constricting his airway. If that happened, I'd have to cut an emergency airway. The biggest problem just then was stopping the bleeding between the roof of his mouth and the exit wound. A pressure dressing wouldn't do any good, and I couldn't get inside the wound to tie off the bleeding vessels.

In an effort to get a better look at the roof of his mouth, I pushed the light a little bit deeper inside. He started to retch, his body jerked, and he heaved a bellyful of warm blood and vomit into my face. The salty taste of blood and the nauseating smell of vomit turned my stomach. The heat and humidity only intensified the experience. I should have known it would make him gag.

Shifting off his legs, I removed one of my canteens, poured some water into my cupped hands, and splashed it on my face. My scarf was covered with blood and vomit, so I untied it and tossed it away. Using a half canteen of water, I then rinsed the front of my fatigue jacket. When I finished, I removed a green triangular bandage from the M-5 kit, dried my face with it, then tied it around my neck. After taking a couple of deep breaths and a drink of water, I was ready to go back to work.

When I looked at the wounded Bode, I concluded that

the only way I was going to be able to stop or slow the bleeding was to pack the space between the exit wound and the roof of his mouth with as much gauze as possible. With the hole packed tight, it might put enough pressure on the torn vessels to stop the bleeding.

I tore open a package of two-inch squares of gauze and dropped them into a stainless steel emesis basin. With a five-inch forceps in my hand I straddled his legs between my own to minimize movement. Then, holding his head against the tree with my left hand, I used my other hand to pick up a few pieces of gauze with the forceps. I knew it was going to be painful for him, but if it worked, it just might save his life.

Whirrrrr! The firing of helicopter gunships interrupted my thoughts.

With his head firmly against the tree, I slowly pushed the gauze into the hole behind his ear and carefully worked it deep into the wound; the deeper it went, the more he groaned. When I thought that the packing might be getting close to the roof of his mouth, I stopped and, using my flashlight, took a look inside. There wasn't any sign of the gauze. After pushing it another quarter of an inch, I took another look and could see blood-soaked gauze and the silver tip of the forceps protruding through the hole in the roof of his mouth. With the first piece of gauze in place, I unclamped the forceps and removed it from his wound. So far so good, I thought to myself.

I picked up a few more pieces of gauze and delicately worked them into the wound. Suddenly, I sensed movement to my right front. I froze. Was I seeing things, or was it another one of the enemy soldiers who had broken through the perimeter? I debated whether or not I should make a dive for my M-16 a few feet away. I decided not to move. With one hand over the Bode's mouth and the other holding the forceps, my eyes scanned the dimly lit foliage for movement. I could kick myself for not keeping Son for security. After a long minute, I was convinced that no one was there, and resumed packing the wound.

Whirrrrr! Helicopter gunships continued to work the eastern side of our perimeter.

When the hole was packed as tight as I could make it, I covered the wound with a couple of dry pieces of gauze and wrapped his head with an Ace bandage. I looked back inside his mouth and was relieved to see that there was no evidence of heavy bleeding.

When I finished, I turned his poncho over and, grabbing him under his arms, dragged him back onto it. I put him on his side with his face toward the ground so that if there was any more bleeding, it would drain from his mouth. With that completed, I started a slow-dripping normal saline IV and gave him some penicillin and streptomycin. That was about all I could do for him. There were obvious limits to what any medic could do in the field. If he didn't lose any more blood, and if there wasn't any brain involvement, he'd probably pull through.

I moved the short distance back to the perimeter and, finding Son, asked him and another member of the 1st Platoon to carry the wounded Bode back to where Rinh could keep an eye on his airway.

While they cut a ten-foot section of green bamboo and tied a hammock to it, I filled out a medical card and attached it to the wounded Bode's jacket. After carefully moving him into the hammock, they picked him up and carried him away.

Alone again, I began repacking the M-5 kit as I listened to the *wap, wap, wap* of helicopter rotor blades fading to the south. My ears were filled with a high-pitched ring, and my head felt like it was going to explode. I didn't want to take anything that would slow my reaction time or put me to sleep, so I removed a couple of Darvon capsules from my kit and downed them with a drink of water. I then removed my signal mirror to take a close look at my dressing. There was no sign of any fresh bleeding, but everything to the left of my nose was stretched tight from the swelling and had turned black and blue. When I pressed my fingers against my face, it felt like soft, spongy rubber.

News Clippings

In Saigon, American psychological warfare experts have drawn up a proposal to drop small transistor radios into communist North Vietnam in order to get allied views across to the North Vietnamese People.   *Eastern Sun* (Malaysian Edition), July 18, 1967

A Band-Aid on a cancer. In the rare moments when he allows himself the luxury of despair, that is how Vice President Hubert H. Humphrey describes the Administration's urban development program.
                    St. Louis Post-Dispatch, July 18, 1967

The Vietnamese Army, in reality, is deteriorating. Americans more and more are doing the fighting, of necessity. The trouble? Very incompetent leadership, an officer corps riddled by politics and a lack of ability.   *U.S. News & World Report,* July 24, 1967

Frank Robinson Fears He May Be Through For Season
                    Los Angeles Times, July 18, 1967

Vietnam Assembly approves ticket of Thieu and Ky.
                    Buffalo Evening News, July 18, 1967

COMBAT, 7:30 P.M. (7)   *Los Angeles Times,* July 18, 1967

The Americans inflicted heavy casualties on the North Vietnamese in two operations south of the demilitarized zone, U.S. High Command figures showed today.
                    The Guardian (Rangoon), July 18, 1967

Formation of a committee for Draft Resistance, a group of 70 including folk singer Joan Baez, was announced in San Francisco.
                    Los Angeles Times, July 18, 1967

Sen. George McGovern (D-SD) will receive the third annual Estes Kefauver Award Saturday night from Californians for Liberal Representation at the Beverly Wilshire banquet. The award, to be presented by actor Robert Vaughn, is given to a legislator who speaks with "a courageous and independent voice in the vigilant pursuit of peace and justice."   *Los Angeles Times,* July 18, 1967

6

1535 Hours

The battle had seesawed around the perimeter for several hours. The only constants were the oppressive heat and humidity of an ever-watchful sun. The time I'd spent working on the wounded had removed me from the heart of the action, and I wanted an update on what was going on.

I skirted the perimeter, and when the scarves changed from blue to red, I knew that I had reached the 3d Platoon's sector. The Bodes were still dug in along the east bank of the creek bed, firing and shouting catcalls and obscenities at the enemy who, in turn, was sniping at them from the far bank. As I passed behind their positions, the Bodes waved and joked about my head. But I could tell from the broad grins on their faces, they were glad to see me alive.

Thirty meters into the 3d Platoon's sector, I found Bob, Thach, and Ly set up in a shallow trench located just a few meters east of the creek. It measured about ten feet long, two feet wide, and four feet deep. Bob was kneeling in the center of the trench with the radio handset pressed to his ear. Thach and Ly were to his right and were squeezing off well-aimed shots.

"Get down," Bob said as I jumped into the trench to his left.

"Any word on the resupply?" I asked.

"Be here in a few minutes," he said as he monitored radio transmissions. "We're low on everything."

Running out of ammunition while being surrounded by the enemy had to be one of the worst feelings a person could experience. I wasn't worried about being killed, but the thought of being captured scared the hell out of me. A few weeks earlier, I had a nightmare about getting overrun. In the dream, I not only found myself out of ammunition, but as the enemy closed in around me, I could only move in slow motion as if struggling underwater. I was fighting desperately to escape when I bolted awake, soaked in a cold sweat.

"*Bac-si,* how Lieu?" Thach asked. An anxious look was etched into the lines of his face.

"If we get 'im out today, he should make it."

We were all concerned about Lieu, but Thach's concern went much deeper. I could tell by the worry in his voice. I couldn't understand why he was so concerned about him. Maybe there was more to their relationship than I knew.

I glanced up and down the trench and noticed that it extended farther to my left but was congested with a tangle of leaves and vines.

"Let's make some room here," I said, as I laid my rifle on the M-5 kit, removed my K-bar, and began cutting away the tightly packed vegetation. After slashing through four or five feet of growth, I hit the end of the trench and began tossing bundles of cut foliage to the rear. I was scooping up one of the last armfuls of dead fall, when I spotted something smooth and chalk-white partially submerged in the dirt and humus. I bent down to take a closer look when it hit me. It was a perfectly preserved human skull.

"Hey, look here," I said.

"What d'ya got?" Bob asked as he leaned over to look.

I picked it up and brushed off the dirt.

"A skull."

"Think it's American?" he wanted to know.

"No, don't think so," I said, as I used my finger to pry dirt out of the eye sockets. "Too much gold in his teeth."

"Any other bones down there?" he asked.

I scraped the floor of the trench with my knife.

"No, nothin'," I said. "You'd think there'd be part of a uniform or something. Pigs probably got to 'im."

"Uh-huh, they can do a job on ya," Bob said. "You sure this ain't a grave?"

"Naw," I said, rotating the skull in my hand and examining it. The possibility had never crossed my mind, but the thought of setting up in someone's grave was a bit unnerving.

"Hey, take a look at this," I said, handing him the skull. There was a perfectly round nickel-size hole over his left eye and a large three-inch hole at the back of his skull.

"Took a round in the forehead," Bob said, and handed the skull back to me. "Probably turned his brain to mush."

"Didn't feel a thing," I said, and stuck my finger in the hole.

"Lotta people coulda died here," he said as he adjusted the squelch on the radio.

Looking at the skull, I found myself wondering who he might have been. There was no way of knowing how long it had been there, but my guess was that it had been many years. What a story that skull could have told of past battles and forgotten dreams. Looking into his dirt-encrusted sockets, I had no way of knowing whether the dead man had been friend or foe. I guess it didn't really matter. For all I knew, he could have died fighting the Viet Minh, the French, or the Japanese. Maybe he was Japanese. Maybe his remains would be the last returned home from World War II. When I thought about it, I realized that with our uniforms and flesh stripped away we all looked pretty much the same. We all return to dust. We all share the same last home.

Thinking back to when we first entered the area earlier that morning, I remembered wondering if we were the first human beings ever to set foot on that ground; clearly we weren't. There really wasn't anything new under the sun, not even here. Ours was at least the third battle to have taken place. The first was fought by whoever called in the air strikes that had created the old craters pockmarking the area, and the second was fought by those who had dug the trench. And there could have been more battles, for all I knew.

It was hard to tell; the jungle had reclaimed many a hidden scar. Men could have been killing each other on that hill since the dawn of time. I thought to myself how intriguing it would be to return someday as an archeologist when the war had ended. The thought of excavating the area also got me wondering if anyone would ever know of the men who fought and died there. I knew it wasn't a Gettysburg or a Normandy or an Arlington, but it was a solemn resting place. No monuments would ever be erected in the solitude of that jungle, but somehow I felt that it was only fitting that they be remembered somehow, by someone.

"Jim." Bob's voice brought me back from my reflections. "You remember those skeletons we found in that chopper over in Phuoc Long Province?"

"Yeah, on Blackjack-33, south of Dong Xoai," I said. "Captain Johnson said he served with one of 'em at Fort Campbell. Wonder if they ever got a positive ID."

"I'm sure they did," Bob said. "They keep dental records on everyone. No two people have the same teeth."

That was a bizarre one. We had been busting brush

through thick jungle when, right in the middle of nowhere, we found a chopper in mint condition, just resting on the jungle floor as if it was on display. Examining the find, we saw two perfectly preserved skeletons through the Plexiglas. Still in their flight suits, strapped in at the controls, they looked as if they were still taking their job seriously. Everything was in such good condition that I half expected one of them to lift up his sun visor and say something like, "What took ya so long?"

My thoughts were interrupted by the faint *wap, wap, wap* of a chopper approaching from the southwest.

"Fox Control, this is Swamp Fox. Over." A familiar Oklahoma twang crackled over the radio.

"It's Major Gritz," Bob said with excitement in his voice.

"Bring it in," I said as a surge of adrenaline recharged my body.

"Swamp Fox, this is Control," Lieutenant Condon responded. "If you follow three-zero degrees you'll come in right over us. Over."

"Major Gri bring ammunition?" Thach asked.

"None too soon, old buddy." Bob beamed as he patted Thach on the back.

"Roger, Control. Gimme some smoke. Over," Gritz said.

"Swamp Fox, this is Control. You got it. Over," Condon responded.

"Put this in your ruck, will ya?" I asked Ly as I handed him the skull.

"Ohhh, *Bac-si,*" he responded with a wide-eyed look, shaking his head, then retreating to the far end of the trench. He was visibly shaken. For some reason it spooked him. Maybe it was some sort of superstition. Bob raised his eyebrows and gave a don't-ask-me look.

"Here, gimme," Bob said as he extended his hand.

I handed it to him, and he reached to the rear of the trench and stuffed it into his rucksack.

The Bodes were a strange group. Things that would terrify the average American didn't faze them a bit, while things like the skull could scare the hell out of them. I remembered an earlier mission when one of the Americans killed a large python. That limp snake shook them up so badly they could barely function.

I wanted to change the subject as quickly as possible because I knew that fear could be contagious. If it got hold of Ly, it could spread like a wildfire around the perimeter.

"How's the radio battery holding up?" I asked Ly.

"Good, *Bac-si.*" He nodded.

"Got any extras?"

"Two."

"Good."

The resonant slap-thumping sound of the chopper grew louder as it neared our position.

"Heads up," I yelled as it passed by overhead, half expecting a cascade of ammunition boxes to come crashing through the canopy.

Whump-whump-whump. The measured staccato of an NVA .51-caliber machine gun somewhere west of our position rang out.

Hoping to get an azimuth on it, I grabbed the compass that hung around my neck and raised it to eye level, but when I glanced down to take a reading, I found that the glass was coated with dried blood, and I couldn't read the numbers.

"We're takin' fire," Gritz radioed as the chopper banked sharply and veered to the northeast.

I used my fingernail to scrape off the dried blood, then took a quick azimuth on the machine gun.

"Swamp Fox, this is Control," Condon radioed. "Did ya make the drop? Over."

"Negative, Control," Gritz responded. "Too much smoke to get a fix on ya. Give me a flare on my next pass. Over."

"Roger, Swamp Fox."

"He's gonna shoot up a flare," Bob told us as he continued to monitor transmissions. "If that doesn't work I'll send up a few tracers."

"I read 280 degrees on that machine gun," I told him.

"Good," Bob responded. "As soon as the FAC gets back, we'll try to take it out."

"Here he comes again," I said as the chopper homed in from the northeast. "He'd better watch out for that fifty-one."

As the sound of the chopper grew louder, I crossed my fingers. If he stayed at treetop level, he might make it. Any higher, and he'd be blown out of the sky.

"Control, this is Swamp Fox," Gritz radioed. "Got your flare. Over."

"Roger, Swamp Fox."

Whump-whump-whump. The fifty-one opened up on the chopper.

"Comin' in low and fast," I said.

"Heads up," Bob yelled as everyone looked skyward.

I caught a glimpse of the chopper, and seconds later, boxes of ammunition tumbled through the canopy. Up and down the line, the Bodes jumped to their feet and cheered. A few of the boxes slammed into the ground to the rear of the 3d Platoon, but the others overshot our position and landed in enemy territory on the far side of the creek.

Moments after they hit the ground, the volume of fire coming from both sides of the creek picked up again. A few enemy troops could be seen leap-frogging in the direction of the boxes.

"If we don't get those boxes, it's gonna be all she wrote. You and Ly cover us," Bob said as he and Thach crawled out of the trench and then sprinted across the creek bed in a zigzag pattern.

As they dodged in and out from behind trees, Ly and I laid down a base of suppressing fire on the few enemy troops we could see. Although my tracers appeared to be right on target, I wasn't sure that I had hit any of them. I could tell by the way Charlie was going after the boxes that he must have sensed their importance to us.

Bob only had a few meters to go before he reached a box when a bright orange flash exploded at the base of a tree just behind him. By the time the sound of the concussion reached me, he had been picked up and blown forward like a rag doll.

"RPG!" Ly yelled as we jumped to our feet.

The thought of Bob being torn apart by shrapnel must have paralyzed me for a split second, but by the time his chest hit the ground, I found myself rushing toward him. When I reached the creek bed, he was on his side and through a cloud of blue gray smoke was waving that he was okay. The blast had bowled him over, but miraculously, the shrapnel must have missed him.

When I saw that Bob was all right, I hit the ground behind a large tree and continued to fire. After squeezing off a few rounds, Ly sprinted past me. When he reached Bob and Thach, the three of them began searching the underbrush for more ammunition boxes. I saw Bob pointing at something, and then the three of them disappeared into the vegetation. A long minute passed before they ran through the curtain of greenery. Bob had a box hefted onto his shoulder and was firing short bursts behind him as he scrambled back. Ly and Thach each had a box under their arms.

From my vantage point, I could see that they were headed in the wrong direction. I jumped to my feet and yelled to them, but they couldn't hear me over the noise of the battle. I feared that if they continued any farther to my right the Bodes down the line would spot their movement and open fire. We'd lost a lieutenant in a similar incident, and I didn't want a repeat of that tragedy.

As a last resort, I rested my M-16 against the trunk of the tree and fired a waist-high stream of fluorescent red tracers a couple of meters in front of them. It caught their attention and they began running in my direction.

As they ran, I watched for enemy movement but couldn't see any. When they were almost back to my position, I spotted two blue uniforms coming out of the thick vegetation near where they found the boxes. I let them take a few steps into the clearing, then emptied a magazine. By the time the last casing flew free, they had disappeared. I wasn't sure if I'd killed them or if they just dove for cover.

Once Bob, Thach, and Ly were safely across the creek, I fired two more shots into the area where the enemy soldiers went down, then ran to the rear. By the time I caught up with them, they were back in the trench, soaked with sweat and gasping for air.

"Whew, that was close," Bob said, still trying to catch his breath.

"You okay?" I asked.

"Yeah, just a little sore. There was a *pop* and the next thing I remember was flying."

"Don't see how that shrapnel missed ya," I said, shaking my head in amazement. "You sure you ain't pullin' a Frank Hagey on me?"

"Yeah, Jim, I'm sure. Must be my lucky day."

Thach put his arm around Bob and smiled a big-toothed smile.

The use of high-explosive fragmentation hand-grenade booby traps was limited only by Viet Cong ingenuity. This drawing shows a booby trap designed to toss a grenade five to six feet into the air, where an airburst would inflict maximum damage.

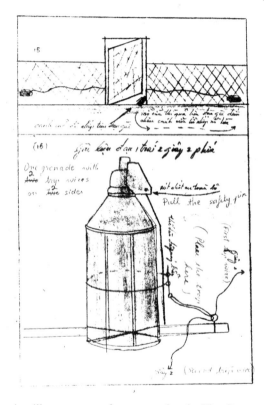

This drawing illustrates one of two ways that the Viet Cong used to booby-trap gates. They attached one end of the trip wire of a hidden high-explosive fragmentation hand grenade to its safety pin and the other end to the gate. They would also place a grenade with its safety pin removed under a gate so that the gate held the safety lever in place. In either case, any movement of the gate would detonate the grenade.

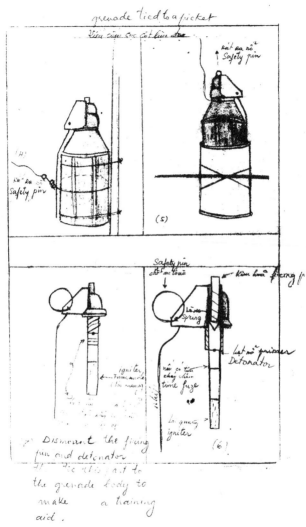

grenade tied to a picket

Although high-explosive hand grenades were designed to be thrown, this Viet Cong drawing demonstrates how the VC often removed the time-delay elements from the fuses to use grenades as booby traps that would detonate instantaneously when tripped. Grenades with the time-delay element removed were sometimes placed in cans where one end of the trip wire was attached to the grenade.

Our first night in Nha Trang

Special Forces Camp
at Duc Phong

"Dr. Yen" and a
montagnard village
chief

Cambodian company on
patrol near Duc Phong

A-1E fighter parachute
dropping napalm containers
full of supplies. The drops
were made every four days.

Children of the Luc Luong
Dac Biet (Vietnamese
Special Forces) at Song Be

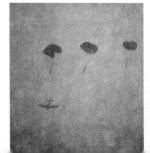

A patrol from Duc Phong takes a lunch break in a montagnard village.

Sgt. Jim Donahue and montagnard friends

Point man

Kim, a Cambodian medic, in the dispensary at Duc Phong

Viet Cong prisoners captured near Song Be

Lunch break with the yards

Montagnard soldier carrying
a PRC-25 radio

SFC Mike Holland (left) and
montagnard troops from Duc
Phong stop to shoot the bull
with a villager.

Morning formation
at Ho Ngoc Tao

Beachfront restaurant
in Nha Trang

Viet Cong captured during
the Black Box mission

Capt. Jim "Bo" Gritz throws Capt.
Steve Yedinak during hand-to-hand
combat training at Ho Ngoc Tao.

Bodes from the Recon Platoon dressed as Viet Cong

Capt. Steve Yedinak with the recovered top-secret electronic countermeasure (ECM) system 13A Black Box from the downed U-2 spy aircraft

Christmas Day, 1966. Top row, left to right: Sgt. Jim Donahue, Capt. Jim "Bo" Gritz, SFC George Ovsak, SFC Bill "Buck" Kindoll. Bottom row, left to right: S.Sgt. Dale England, SFC Pat Wagner, S.Sgt. Dennis "Monty" Montgomery, M.Sgt. Jim Howard.

SFC George Ovsak and snake. George was killed at Trang Sup.

M.Sgt. Jim Howard uses an international orange ground panel to signal a chopper during Blackjack-31. Jim was seriously wounded in '68 and was discharged as a sergeant major.

Seriously wounded Viet Cong POW just prior to his being medevacked

Trang Sup Special Forces Camp with Nui Ba Den, Black Virgin Mountain, in the background

Detachment A-303 in Bien Hoa after Blackjack-31. Top row, left to right: SFC Bill "Buck" Kindoll, SFC George Ovsak, SFC Al Doyle, S.Sgt. Dennis "Monty" Montgomery, SFC Pat Wagner, S.Sgt. Dale England, S.Sgt. Dick Jarvis, Sgt. Jim Donahue. Bottom row, left to right: M.Sgt. Jim Howard, Capt. Steve Yedinak, Capt. Jim "Bo" Gritz, Lt. Joe Cawley.

SFC Bob Cole (left) and SFC Ernest "Duke" Snider

Thirteen-year-old Winh with captured enemy ordnance. He was wounded near Chi Linh during Liberty Blackjack.

Members of Detachment A-304: S.Sgt. L. Brooks "Stik" Rader (top left), SFC Bill "Fergy" Ferguson (top, second from right), SFC Ernest "Duke" Snider (top right)

S.Sgt. L. Brooks "Stik" Rader (right) running the Bodes over the Tay Ninh obstacle course

SFC Ernest "Duke" Snider being presented the Silver Star by General Hay. To the general's left is SFC Bob Cole. The awards ceremony took place at Phuoc Vinh.

Taking a break

S.Sgt. Roger "Ranger" Smith enjoying breakfast while sitting in his hammock

SFC Bob Cole, July 1967

Lt. Jim Condon at a beer party in Trang Sup

S.Sgt. Donahue making a last-minute equipment check before departing Trang Sup for Quan Loi

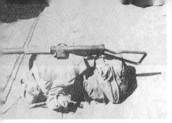

9mm MK-II British Sten
with silencer

FAC pilot in the cockpit of his
single-engine O-1E aircraft

SFC Bob Cole
near Quan Loi

Lt. Jim Condon
in the jungle north
of Quan Loi

SFC Bill "Fergy"
Ferguson (left)
and SFC Ernest
"Duke" Snider

S.Sgt. L. Brooks
"Stik" Rader

S.Sgt. Roger "Ranger" Smith and his troops moving through wet terrain

S.Sgt. L. Brooks "Stik" Rader

Moving cross-country

S.Sgt. Jim Donahue and Bodes from the Third Platoon

S.Sgt. Roger "Ranger" Smith and SFC Bob Cole moving through the jungle during Operation Blackjack-34

S.Sgt. Roger "Ranger" Smith with members of the Headquarters section

SFC Bob Cole taking a break

Viet Cong awards ceremony

Dead Viet Cong

Third Platoon moving
over open terrain

A member of the
Third Platoon waits
for the enemy.

Third Platoon
crossing a small
stream

Viet Cong soldier killed during Blackjack-34

Lt. Jim Condon and SFC Bob Cole decorating members of the Third Platoon at Trang Sup following the Quan Loi operation

M.Sgt. Bernie Newman (left) and SFC Ernest "Duke" Snider at a cookout on the beach at Long Hai

VC prisoners

VC prisoners

VC prisoner

Luc was the Third Herd's platoon sergeant until he was shot in the stomach near Phuoc Vinh. The author caught up with him at the 24th Evac Hospital in Long Binh.

Bob Cole at the Special Forces Association Convention in Fayetteville, North Carolina

Larry "Stik" Rader as the first sergeant of the Honor Guard Company of the United Nations Command in Yongsan, Korea, 1981

Bo Gritz (right) and Jim Donahue in Bangkok, Thailand, October 1982

First Sergeant Francis "Frank" Hagey back at Fort Bragg with the 18th Airborne Corps, 1973

Command Sergeant Major Ernest "Duke" Snider while assigned to the 10th Special Forces Group at Fort Devens, Massachusetts, 1983

Jim Condon in the Badlands of South Dakota, 1995

Tan Thach, Son Thai Hien, Rinh Kien, and Kim Lai in Cherry Hill, New Jersey, 1997

Roger "Ranger" Smith in front of his home in Las Vegas, Nevada, 1999

Duke Snider "gone fishing," 1986

Roger "Ranger" Smith (left) and L. Brooks "Stik" Rader outside of the Recon Team Hawaii hooch, 1971

CW2 Roger "Ranger" Smith with the 1st Special Forces Group at Fort Lewis, Washington, 1985

Left to right: author, Capt. Scott Whitting, LTC Ernst "Tom" Esser (German Army Reserve), Capt. Hank Humphreys, and Capt. Don Kieffer in Geilenkirchen, Germany, to compete for the German Sports Ribbon, 1994

Sandi and Jim Donahue chuted up to begin the 1984 Death Valley Marathon

Sgt. Maj. L. Brooks "Stik" Rader with the 1st Special Forces Group at Fort Lewis, Washington, 1986

Jim Donahue (right) meeting with President Ford in the White House Rose Garden, May 1976

"*Trung si* Cole numba one," he said.

"Numba one," Ly added as he raised his index finger.

"Hey, you guys did a great job," I said.

"Sure did," Bob added. "I appreciate it," he said as he bent over and kissed Thach's ear.

"Numba ten," Thach quipped as he rolled his eyes then wiped his ear with his sleeve in embarrassment.

Bob, Ly, and myself couldn't control ourselves and were laughing so hard that we could barely stand up.

"I open boxes," Thach grunted as he climbed out of the trench and began moving the boxes to the rear, trying to ignore us.

"Let's get serious," Bob said. "There's more out there. We gotta go out again."

As I listened to Bob, it suddenly registered that something was wrong; his eyes had a glazed look. The concussion from the explosion must have hurt him more than he was admitting.

"You're not lookin' too good," I said. "Better stay here this time. Ly and I'll get what's left."

"Look who's talkin' about lookin' good," he said. "Look, there's a box where we went the last time. I'll pick it up. You check off to the left."

"Okay, let's do it."

As soon as we reached the far side of the creek, I broke off to my left front and clambered up a gradual incline, searching the jungle for signs of the enemy and ammunition boxes. Shots were being fired to my left and right, but as far as I could tell, no one was shooting at me. When I was thirty meters out, I saw three blue-uniformed soldiers running from right to left about twenty-five meters ahead of me. A split second later, they spotted me. I fired a long burst at them then dove to the ground before they could return fire.

Whump-whump-whump. A burst of automatic fire stitched the ground a few inches to my right. As each round impacted, it kicked up chunks of moist soil then settled back upon itself. I couldn't see where the firing was coming from, but it sounded like it was from somewhere in the trees.

I was on relatively open ground so I quickly rolled a few meters to my left and took up a position behind a tree. As I searched the branches for a sniper, I felt dizzy, and my heart was pounding like a bass drum.

Whump-whump-whump. A second burst thumped into the trunk just above my head, pelting me with bark and pulp. This time, I spotted muzzle flashes and the partial silhouette of the sniper half-hidden in the branches of a large tree about twenty meters in front of me. I quickly lined up my front sight blade on the shadow and fired what was left in my magazine. There was a scream, a figure tumbled out of the tree, and a body hit the jungle floor with a hollow thud.

After slipping in a fresh magazine and chambering a round, I rose to my feet and strained to see movement in the bushes around the base of the tree, but it was too thick. I was about to move forward again when another shot was fired from higher up in the same tree. Without aiming, I sprayed the tree with tracers and then dove into some large ferns further to my left. Figuring that I was already too far into enemy territory, I decided to crawl a little farther to my left and then start working my way back to the platoon.

After crawling several meters through a wall of rotting leaves and congested vines, I realized I was forming a molelike tunnel as I plowed forward. The mottled leaves were of every size and shape. Some were long and narrow, some heart-shaped, while others were two to three feet long and over a foot in diameter. They were bunched together in various stages of decomposition, filling the stagnant air with the moist compost smell of decaying matter.

Using my hand and my M-16 to part the leaves, I had moved about fifteen meters when my hand touched someone. The unexpected contact sent jolts of adrenaline stabbing into my system and overwhelmed me with an icy fear.

Whack-whack-whack. I cut loose with my M-16, sending a flurry of leaves flying in all directions. As the rounds blew away the vegetation, I saw that it was a leg, but that was all. It had been severed just below the hip with a clean cut, its white bone protruding through the flesh like a shank of meat in a butcher shop.

By the time I inserted a fresh magazine, I'd regained my composure and detoured around the leg. I crawled a few meters more when I ran into loose dirt. I paused and listened. I could hear something that sounded like whimpering up ahead. Finally, it dawned on me that I was on the edge of a bomb crater. From where I was lying, I could tell that the crying was coming from inside the depression. I couldn't see inside, but on the far rim, I spotted a box of ammunition lying on the soft dirt. The opposite side of the crater came into view as I cautiously raised my head. A pith helmet was lying on the reverse slope, but there was no sign of whoever was crying. He must have been just below me.

With my finger on the trigger, I peeked over the edge of the berm and saw the jet black hair and shoulders of someone lying on his back. My first instinct was to fire a round into him, but the thought of taking him prisoner prevented me; besides, I had him cold.

With my rifle pointed at the top of his head, I slowly rose to my knees and called *"Dung lai!"* If I remembered my Vietnamese, that meant don't move! He didn't move, but continued moaning and crying. I wasn't sure, but by the plaintive tone in his voice, it sounded like he was calling for his mother. With my head extended over the crater's edge, my nostrils filled with the overpowering stench of death, and I had to fight back the urge to gag. The last time I'd smelled anything that bad was when a Viet Cong's body was blown apart by a booby trap during the black-box operation.

I kept my rifle trained on his head while I scooted a little to my right, then slid on my rear down the inside slope. When I got even with him, the sight of his wound took my breath away; everything from his waist down had been blown away. It looked as though someone had dumped a pile of Franco-American spaghetti down the slope beneath him. The blast had cut him in half, spilling his insides out on the ground. I'd seen a lot of bad wounds but nothing like that. I found it unbelievable that he was still alive.

"Ohhhh," he moaned.

He appeared to be only about seventeen years old. He had a boyish, clean-shaven face and a fresh haircut. His face had a taut, waxen look, but his brown eyes were alive and followed my every movement.

I considered applying a tourniquet but realized that it wouldn't do any good. He was still breathing and alert, but he was really dead. I looked at him with pity. He pleaded with me in Vietnamese. I think he was begging me to kill him. I nodded that I understood, moved closer, then raised my M-16 to his temple; a couple of ounces of pressure on the trigger, and he'd be out of his misery.

As he closed his eyes in anticipation, I couldn't help notice the tears running down his dust-covered cheeks. A couple of minutes earlier, I could have killed him in a heartbeat, but now I couldn't pull the trigger. He was just a boy lying there, his manhood shattered, crying for his mother.

He opened his eyes and looked at me.

"Xin loi." I told him that I was sorry. He was no longer the enemy, but a human being not so different from myself.

I removed a canteen from my belt and poured a little water on his lips; he didn't make any effort to swallow and let the water run down the side of his face into the dirt.

Although we had exchanged only a few words, I felt that something more had occurred, something deeper. I couldn't call it friendship, but it was intimate. Nothing like that had ever happened to me before. Whatever it was, I felt a strange mixture of joy and sorrow. Maybe we had touched something in common, had shared something.

Gotta get that box back to the platoon, I thought as I removed my scarf. After pouring some water on it, I used it to cover his eyes.

"Bac-si!" a voice called.

"Over here," I yelled as I clawed my way out of the soft dirt, picked up the box of ammunition, and headed in the direction of the voice. It was Thach.

"You go too long, *Bac-si,*" he said.

I followed him back toward the platoon, and at the creek's edge, we were met by Ly.

"I think VC *soc mau* you," he said as he ran his index finger across his throat. He grabbed the box from me.

"Almost, my friend," I said.

The three of us ran to an area a few meters behind the trench where we found Bob filling empty magazines.

"You get lost?" he asked as I knelt on the ground next to him.

"We'd better get some over to Stik," I said.

"Yeah," Bob said. "Get a count on the boxes."

Thach and Ly lined up the boxes in front of us while I made a quick inventory.

"Twelve boxes," I said.

"Go ahead and divide it up among the four platoons," Bob said.

"Okay."

"I'm gonna give the lieutenant an update," he said as he and Ly moved out.

I began breaking open the boxes, and Thach left to get a few men to carry the ammunition around to the other platoon sergeants.

"We give one box *Trung si Sau Lam*?" Thach joked when he returned with three men.

"Yeah," I laughed. "Give one to *Sau Lam*."

Trung si Sau Lam was a nickname that the Bodes had given to Stik Rader because he worked them so hard during training back at Trang Sup. It meant "Sergeant No-Good." They liked Stik, and it was their way of joking with him.

After we finished dividing up and distributing the ammunition, Son came by to pick up his share of the 7.62mm machine-gun ammunition. I always tried to avoid eyeball to eyeball contact with him because he was the most cross-eyed person I had ever seen. Just looking at him was enough to make me dizzy. I never could figure how he did it, but he could lay down a base of fire like no one I'd ever known. Somehow, being cross-eyed seemed to enhance his depth perception.

A few minutes later, Bob returned, and he, Thach, and I sat on the ground filling the last of our empty magazines. When Bob leaned forward to pick up some ammo, I noticed that his rear end was soaked with a large splotch of blood.

"Hey, you've been hit," I said as I leaned my M-16 against a tree, jumped to my feet, and squatted next to him.

"What?" he said in disbelief.

I grabbed him by the arm.

"You've been hit in the rear," I said.

He turned to look and appeared shocked to see the blood. When he touched the area, the palm of his hand turned bloodred.

"Take off your harness and drop your drawers," I said. "Thach, get the M-5 kit."

Thach returned with the medical kit and set it on the ground next to me, just as Bob finished unbuttoning his trousers.

"What d'ya see?" Bob asked as he dropped his trousers in a pile around his ankles. He looked pretty awkward standing half-naked in the jungle, while I examined his buttocks.

From what I could see, he'd caught a piece of shrapnel in the right cheek. It didn't look too serious.

"RPG," Thach said as he looked at the quarter-inch gash in Bob's skin.

"Yeah, looks like ya caught a piece of that RPG after all," I said. "Does it hurt?"

"My whole backside aches but nothin' that bad," he said. "What d'ya think?"

"Well, I'll tell ya one thing," I chuckled. "You won't be sittin' down on the job for a while."

"C'mon, Jim, this is serious! What d'ya think?"

"Ah, doesn't look bad," I said. "It depends on how deep it went." I gently pressed my finger against the wound but couldn't feel anything hard. "If it's lodged in the fat or muscle, you shouldn't have any trouble with it."

"Good. Cover it up," he said.

"When we get back to Trang Sup, you're gonna have to get it X-rayed," I said as I covered the wound with gauze and surgical tape. "They may have to surgically remove it."

"We'll worry about it later," he said.

After I gave him shots of penicillin and streptomycin, he returned to the trench while Thach and I finished reloading the last of our magazines.

"*Bac-si,* I must tell you," Thach said as he grabbed my arm. The intensity in his voice surprised me. His face was a study of conflicting emotions.

"Tell me what?" I asked as I pushed a round into a magazine.

"I not tell anyone."

"Tell anyone what?" I asked, looking into his blood-shot eyes.

"Lieu, *Bac-si.* He is son of my sister."

"I didn't know." No wonder he was so shook up about Lieu getting hurt.

"Her husband die at Dong Xoai. Now maybe Lieu die."

"I'm sorry," I said as I put my hand on his shoulder. "We'll get 'im to an American hospital, and he'll get the best treatment in the world."

"Thank you, *Bac-si.*"

"Look, my friend, it's not your fault," I said. "You're the best damn platoon sergeant in Vietnam. If it wasn't for you, we'd all be dead. Every man in the platoon owes you his life." I saw that his eyes were welling with tears.

"Okay, *Bac-si.*"

I snapped my ammo pouches shut, and we both headed back to the trench.

News Clippings

From left, the prisoners are Sgt. Isaac Comancho, Sgt. Kenneth Roraback, Sgt. Claude McClure and Sgt. George Smith. Comancho later escaped, Roraback was shot, McClure and Smith were freed.

Life, July 21, 1967

Sinatra—to any soldier with more than 18 months in service the name would have flashed to mind the great, golden voiced holdover from bobbysox days—Frankie. But to more than 100,000 troops who ogled while the latest Sinatra stomped her boots at 17 different Vietnam sites, the word now has another reaction—Nancy.

Army Digest, July 1967

Official statistics show that the burden of fighting in South Vietnam has recently passed decisively to American troops. A study of casualty lists since the first of the year showed that while more South Vietnamese troops were killed in the first weeks of January, the situation is now reversed, even though government forces outnumbered American troops by about 200,000.

Courier Express (Buffalo), July 18, 1967

Sides registering greatest proportionate upward progress this week:
1. "Windy" . . . The Association
2. "Can't Take My Eyes Off You" . . . Frankie Valli
3. "Light My Fire" . . . Doors

Billboard, July 22, 1967

President Marcos' trip to South Vietnam has reassured a continuing role for the Philippines to preserve freedom in the embattled nation, Manila newspapers said today.

Eastern Sun (Malaysian Edition), July 18, 1967

Sean Connery Is James Bond   "You Only Live Twice"

The New York Times, July 18, 1967

Gustav Crane Hertz is the highest-ranking American to be taken prisoner by the Vietcong. His kidnapping in February 1965 drew only brief attention. But now, 30 months later, he is still missing and a growing cause célèbre.

Life, July 21, 1967

Honeymooners—Kramden (Jackie Gleason) finds suitcase full of money and goes on a spree.   *Buffalo Evening News,* July 18, 1967

American C-130 transport planes carried 150 Congolese paratroopers to Kisangani in pursuit of an estimated 180 rebel mercenaries.
                                    Los Angeles Times, July 18, 1967

7

1620 Hours

Shadows were lengthening as the sun arched into Cambodia and the air grew cooler. Across the jungle, sunlight angled through holes in the canopy, creating a mesmerizing effect as dust and haze danced through the light.

Everything in the 3d Herd's sector appeared to be under control, so I told Bob that I was going to see if Fergy and Frank's platoon was experiencing any major medical problems. I had a gut-feeling that Mister Charles was getting ready for an all-out attack on our side of the perimeter, and I wanted to be able to get back before he hit.

The 2d Platoon was defending much of our eastern flank, so I just followed a ninety-degree azimuth across the interior of the perimeter until I spotted yellow scarves. When I reached their side of the perimeter, I immediately made contact with a couple of Bodes who were lying in a shallow foxhole. They told me that Fergy was set up just a short distance south.

Down the line, enemy bodies, discarded ammunition boxes, and medical supply containers littered the jungle floor. I had to step over small trees that had been toppled by high-velocity rounds. After moving a short distance, I spotted Fergy and his radio operator lying in a depression ten meters long, three meters across, and a half meter deep.

The area was heavily shaded by large three-story trees and thick vegetation close to the ground. Fergy was our intelligence specialist. With his tall lanky body, white skin, and sandy brown hair, he stood out like a sore thumb.

"Get down, J.C.," he yelled. "They'll get ya."

I hit the ground and began crawling the last few meters. I couldn't help smiling when I saw that he had a large nylon American flag tied to a tree branch just to the rear of the depression.

"I oughta kick your ass," I said jokingly as I crawled into the depression and took up a position next to him. "Are you the asshole who developed the intel on this operation?"

"Hey babe, don't blame me," he said. "When we were back at Quan Loi, some light colonel told Condon that it takes a long time to deploy a brigade."

"Think he was tryin' to tell us somethin'?"

"No shit."

"Did ya get the ammo?" I asked.

"Yeah, but at this rate—"

Whump-whump-whump. We hugged the ground as rounds lashed the air overhead, bullwhipping through the foliage.

"Damn Cong!" Fergy snarled as we lay face-to-face in the dirt.

"Ya know, that flag's probably attractin' fire like flies to a hog," I said.

"I'm sick of this clandestine bullshit," Fergy said as he raised his head and fired a burst in retaliation. "I want those bastards to know who they're up against." He smiled. "If the shit hits the fan, I got my beret in my rucksack."

"Got mine too!" I laughed with a feigned bravado.

"D'ya really?" Fergy replied, taken aback that I'd done the same thing.

"Yeah. In my ruck."

The automatic weapon stopped firing, and we slowly raised our heads. Fergy pointed out that it was coming from a position thirty meters east of us. The gun was firing from behind a tree stump that was located on the far side of a clearing. With its bark stripped away, the stump looked almost white in the sunlight.

"Enough is enough," Fergy snarled. "I'm gonna take the son of a bitch out."

"Hold on," I said as I grabbed him by his ammunition harness. "Let's not go off half-cocked."

"Brush is too thick to hit 'im with an M-79," he responded.

"What about air?"

"I've already called in strikes."

"We got a couple RPGs," I suggested.

"Nah, there's only one way to do it," he said. "I'm gonna get a couple Bodes to go with me."

"Okay, okay, but pop a smoke when ya get in position," I said. "We don't wanna grease your ass."

He nodded and crawled off to our right. As he crawled out of the depression another Bode from the 2d Platoon dropped in, wincing in pain. He had been shot in the ankle, and the bone was shattered. While I checked his wound, Fergy's radio operator began firing well-aimed rounds from a captured AK-47 at the area around the stump.

The bullet had passed all the way through both sides of the wounded Bode's ankle. The nylon webbing of his jungle boot had turned black with caked blood and dirt, but most of the bleeding appeared to have stopped. I thought about removing his boot, but figured I'd never get it back on again.

Whump, whump, whump. Another burst lashed the foliage, but as long as we kept flat, the gunner couldn't hit us.

When the firing stopped, I removed a large battle dressing and an Ace bandage from my M-5 kit. After giving him a syrette of morphine and loading him up with penicillin and streptomycin, I covered the entrance and exit wounds with the dressing and wrapped his ankle with the Ace. It was a little awkward working prone but at least it kept us out of the line of fire. As soon as I got a chance, I'd improvise a bamboo splint that would extend a couple of inches below the heel of his boot. He'd probably be able to walk on it if he had to.

"Bac-si," the radio operator called. I looked up and saw a knotted plume of red smoke billowing up in front of the white stump. I grabbed my M-16 and took up a position next to the radio operator. Through the smoke, I suddenly saw the shadowy outline of figures moving behind the stump.

"Hold your fire," I said as I took up the slack on my trigger.

Whack-whack-whack. An M-16 opened up, and seconds later two Bodes and Fergy bolted through the smoke and into the clearing. Once out of the smoke, they hesitated for a second, then began running in our direction. Fergy was carrying someone slumped over his shoulders.

I jumped to my feet, ran forward ten meters, and took up a position behind a tree on our side of the clearing. If there was an enemy soldier anywhere along the edge of the clearing, he'd have a clear shot at them.

As they scrambled toward me, I had the helpless feeling that they were about to be blown away.

"C'mon on, Fergy!" I yelled. "Move it, move it!"

"I got one," he yelled as he approached.

"You crazy bastard, are you out of your gourd?" I yelled as we ran the last few yards together.

"Didn't have time to go the long way," he said. "They're gettin' ready to come at us again."

When we reached the depression, he flopped the black-clad soldier on the ground next to the wounded Bode and then dropped to his knees out of breath.

"Whew! Ain't as young as I used to be," he gasped.

"You're gettin' older, but ya sure as hell ain't gettin' any smarter," I added.

"Hey!" Fergy yelled as the wounded Bode began kicking the prisoner in the ribs with his good foot and screaming something I couldn't understand.

Fergy and I dragged them apart. I looked into the soldier's terror-filled face. Clearly, he was convinced that we were going to kill him. Fergy lit a cigarette and handed it to the prisoner, trying to calm him down, but the Viet Cong continued to follow the Bode's every move. His face and right shoulder were covered with blood, but other than that, he appeared to be in pretty good shape.

"What a break," I said to myself as I looked at his shoulder. He could provide us with valuable intelligence information.

"I got within five yards of 'im before he saw me," Fergy said. "Had to knock 'im down with a shoulder shot. He had a spider hole behind the stump. Every time we tried to take 'im out, he jumped in it."

"Who says someone ain't gonna use that same hole?" I asked.

"Buried two toe poppers in it," he said. "No one's gonna use it for a while."

"What happened to his face?" I asked. He looked a little worse for wear. His right cheek was red and puffy, his eye nearly swelled shut, and sticky blood caked in the clefts of his nostrils and upper lip.

"He wasn't all that enthused about comin' with me." Fergy gave a sardonic smile. "Had to butt stroke 'im."

I watched Fergy give the prisoner a drink of water and felt a great sense of accomplishment because, for us, it was a war of few prisoners. None of our men ever surrendered, and the few Viet Cong we captured were usually wounded.

"Trung si!" the radio operator shouted.

A sting of prickly heat rushed up my spine when I turned to see a line of black-pajama-clad Viet Cong coming at us from the far side of the clearing.

Whump-whump-whump. Adrenaline shot into my system, and my heart rate doubled as the ripple of muzzle flashes flickered through the scattered foliage. I threw myself to the ground, flipped the selector switch to automatic, and sighted in on the onrushing tide.

Out of the corner of my eye, I saw the wounded Bode raise his M-16 in the direction of the prisoner, but before I could yell "No!" he fired.

Whack! The round hit the Viet Cong in the back of the head, and in what appeared to be slow motion, his nose flew from his face in a crimson spray of blood, brain, and bone fragments. He was dead by the time he slumped to the ground even though his feet continued to twitch in nervous spasms.

I was furious and wanted to smash the Bode's head in, but the advancing enemy were only twenty meters out and closing fast.

I lined up my front sight blade on the closest target and began firing two- and three-round chest-high bursts. Out of the corner of my eye, I spotted what looked like a black baseball coming right at me. It quickly grew larger and, a split second later, passed a foot over my head leaving a trail of gray smoke.

Whoomph! The rocket-propelled grenade exploded somewhere behind us.

Above the roar of rifle fire and explosions, I could hear screaming and yelling. Fergy yelled something at me, but with all the noise, I couldn't understand a word. When the enemy was only a few steps away, I fired the last round in my magazine.

"Chey-yo!" I yelled as I sprang to my feet. Someone immediately ran into me with a tremendous force and knocked the breath out of me. I fell backward and somehow landed on my chest with someone on top of me. It was a Viet Cong. With all of my strength, I twisted and hit him in the jaw with my elbow. He let out a grunt that followed the crack of his jaw. I rolled to my back with him on top of me and was shocked to see how old he was. He had a cracked, weather-beaten face the consistency of parchment paper, yellow rotting teeth, and a few scraggly white whiskers hanging from his chin. He clutched at the shoulder of my fatigues, squeezing and twisting with his clenched fist, screaming at me in shrill Vietnamese as he desperately clawed at my throat with his other hand.

I couldn't reach his eyes, so I grabbed his Adam's apple with my right hand and tried to tear the windpipe out of his scrawny neck. He started to gag and cough a foul, fish-smelling breath into my face. I felt something cut the side of my neck.

A knife! I thought. He's cutting my throat! I let go of his neck, grabbed his right arm with both hands, and pushed it away from my throat.

My God! His right hand had been shot off just above his wrist and a piece of sharp white bone extended out of the bloody stump. He was trying to drive the bone into my throat!

Whack! A deafening shot exploded a couple feet from my ear, and the enemy soldier flew off my chest and out of my hands as if he'd been hit with a wrecking ball. I turned and saw that it was the wounded Bode who had fired the shot. Looking back to our front, I saw that the attack had been broken and that a couple of Bodes were already checking the enemy dead. I got to my feet and felt so dizzy I sidestepped and nearly fell back to the ground. I bent over to pick up my M-16, when I heard a raspy groan. The old soldier let out a tired sigh and died.

"You all right, J.C.?" Fergy asked, placing his hand on my shoulder.

"Yeah, a little dizzy," I said as I bent over with my head lowered to the ground for a couple of seconds.

"Bac-si," the wounded Bode called in a soft voice. I turned and saw that he had been hit again. This time it looked like a flesh wound halfway between his wrist and elbow. I removed another battle dressing from my M-5 kit, knelt next to him, and began tying it over the wound.

"VC numba ten," he spat contemptuously.

I just finished working on his arm when I felt something warm sliding down the left side of my neck.

"I'm leaking again," I said to Fergy as I reached up and found that my bandage had unraveled during the scuffle.

"Want me to put on a new Ace?" he asked.

"Yeah, will ya get one out of the kit?" I asked as I sat and removed the layers of old bandage. As I unraveled the Ace, it released the pressure on the wound and fresh rivulets of blood drained down my neck and chest. As soon as I got it off, Fergy knelt next to me and began applying the new one.

"As tight as ya can," I said.

I found myself looking at the old Viet Cong as Fergy wrapped my head. Staring into his lifeless eyes, I felt a sense of tragedy. Maybe it had something to do with his being an old soldier. He had probably been fighting all his life, and it had come down to this. I also found myself wondering if he was still aware of what was going on around him. I knew he was dead but wondered how long his brain would continue to function.

"That should hold ya, J.C.," Fergy said as he finished attaching the bandage.

"Can't see outta my left eye," I told him.

"Yeah, it's swollen shut," he said as he used his finger to gently press on the puffiness. When Fergy finished, I picked up my M-16 and M-5 kit.

"You see Frank?" I asked.

"Not since we first made contact," he said as he knelt next to his radio and picked up the handset. "Last I heard, he and the machine-gun section were down at the other end of the platoon."

"I'll see if I can find 'im," I said. "Will ya give Bob a call and tell 'im I'll be back in a bit?"

"Sure, J.C.," he said. "If you see Frank, tell 'im to get his ass up here."

"Okay. Catch ya later," I said as I headed down the line.

"Hey, J.C." Fergy smiled. "Stop in anytime."

"Forget it." I laughed. "I ain't ever visiting you again."

As I moved down the line, I saw that the Bodes were taking advantage of the lull in the fighting, busy cleaning weapons, fortifying positions, or scarfing rations. Others were just stretched out on the ground, taking a much needed break.

While looking for Frank, I thought about the loss of the prisoner. I had felt disappointment and anger, but my anger passed as I came to realize that if the Bode hadn't killed him, he just might have been able to change the outcome of the assault. If he had been able to tie up just one of the four of us for a couple of seconds, it would have reduced our firepower by twenty-five percent. As close as things turned out, the prisoner's death could have been the difference between life and death for everyone involved.

As I neared the end of the 2d Platoon's sector, my concern mounted when I couldn't find Frank. When the platoon scarves changed from yellow to blue, I really became worried. A couple of Duke's Bodes told me that they hadn't seen Frank, so I backtracked until I hit the yellow scarves again. After talking to a few Bodes, I found one who spoke some broken English. He pointed south and told me that Frank was down by the creek. I checked my map and couldn't figure out what he was doing that far outside the perimeter. Given the level of enemy activity in the area, he could easily be cut off and killed or captured. I sensed that his life was in grave danger.

Going outside the perimeter again wasn't something I relished doing, but since Frank was without a radio, there weren't any other options. After telling the Bode to pass the word that I was going out, I took a compass heading in the direction he gave me and started out. I took an azimuth because when I was ready to return I wanted to take a back azimuth and, I hoped, reenter the perimeter at the exact same spot. It was easy to get disoriented in the jungle, and reentering the perimeter in another location could be lethal.

A few meters outside, I entered a thicket of lime green bamboo, and I heard M-16 fire farther south. It had to be Frank. The more I thought about the situation, the more anxious I became. I had no idea who was where or who was firing in what direction. For all I knew, there could be a hundred Viet Cong between us. Zigzagging through the bamboo, I stopped and squatted every five or six meters and listened and watched for signs of the enemy or Frank. I didn't hear or see anything, but the firing increased to the north and west. It sounded as though they were probing Fergy's and Duke's sectors again.

The farther out I got, the more I thought the whole thing could be a trap. What if Frank was surrounded, and they were just waiting for someone to come out for him. The cold fear of the unknown began to grip me. I could envision a horseshoe-shaped ambush just waiting for me to walk into it.

"Don't let your imagination get outta control. It can distort reality," I told myself. I remembered a night ambush where I had convinced myself that a tree was an enemy soldier trying to sneak up on us. At times like that, the senses could play tricks, conjuring up images that only accentuate uncertainty.

Only a few moments had passed, but it seemed like an eternity by the time I hit the bank of the stream. Most of it had dried up, and the dark brown mud had cracked and curled in the hot air. The few still pools of water that remained were crusted with green algae over which hung a stagnant stench and swarms of blue-green flies.

I extended my head out over the creek bed. To my left, the ribbon of mud disappeared into a tunnel of tangled leaves and vines.

Whack-whack! Two rounds of M-16 fire startled me. I dropped to one knee and watched for movement. Thirty meters downstream, I spotted someone on the five-foot-high bank, kneeling behind what looked like a large fallen tree. It was Frank!

I wanted to yell to him but would risk giving away my position to any enemy troops who might be in the area.

The brush along both sides of the creek was a solid wall of thorn-covered vines, so I slid down the bank into the mud.

Slowly working my way in his direction, my boots cracked through the hard-shelled potsherds of the creek bed before sinking several inches into a creamy black muck that smelled of mold. Frank was busy watching whatever was going on the other side of the log and ducked when what appeared to be a grenade flew over his position and landed in a pool of water behind him.

Whoomph! The grenade exploded and showered him with mud and water. Frank raised his head over the top of the log and again hit the ground when a second grenade flew over his head.

Whoomph! The grenade again exploded in the water behind him. A split second later, he popped up and fired two quick shots over the top of the fallen tree.

Whoomph! The force of a third explosion on the opposite side of the tree caught him in a firing position and hurled him backward.

"God no," I said to myself as he flew spread-eagle through the air until landing on his back with a soupy splash.

I tried to run to him as fast as I could, but the creek's muddy suction slowed me to a walk. He had to be dead or seriously wounded.

"God," I muttered. "If he isn't dead, he'll drown."

Struggling forward, I had visions of Frank's wife and eight kids crying over his grave. What a tragedy to survive so much only to die in a pool of slime.

As I closed the gap between us, the waves quickly faded to a few ripples. In the middle of the stagnant pool, I saw his head. It was dead still and looked like a white pool ball sitting in the middle of a green felt table.

Suddenly, his shoulders rose above the green.

He's alive! I thought as he struggled to his feet in the waist-deep water and staggered toward the bank. My sense of relief was overpowering, and I let out a loud "Yaahoo!"

"You look like a drowned rat," I said, as I reached the water's edge and extended my hand to pull him out of the pool, dripping with green slime and mud, smelling like something that had crawled under the porch and died.

"He was a brave son of a bitch," he said, shaking his head. "He threw one grenade long and one short. The short one got me."

"You okay?" I asked as I put my arm around his waist and helped him to the bank.

"Jimmy," he said after sitting down on the trunk of a small tree. "Let me catch my breath."

I could tell that he was in a lot more pain than he would admit. His face was red from the blast. He was obviously disoriented, and his whole body was quivering in spasms.

"Here, take a couple of these," I said after removing two codeine tablets from my M-5 kit. "You'll feel better in a few minutes."

"What luck," he said as he swallowed the tablets. "If it wasn't for the water, I woulda broke my back."

Suddenly, I realized that there weren't any Bodes up on the bank.

"Where's the Bodes?" I asked.

"I had four," he answered.

"Where are they?"

"One got hit. It took two to carry 'im back to the perimeter."

"What about the other one?"

"Well," he said while rubbing the back of his neck. "When the machine gun broke down, I couldn't get it workin', so I had 'im take it to Stik. Don't know if he made it."

"You telling me we're out here all alone?"

"Looks that way," he said as he leaned forward to stretch his back muscles. "When we first made contact, Fergy was up on the north end and got hit hard from the east."

"Where were you?"

"On the south end," he said. "I got hit from the south, and the platoon got divided into two sections. After they broke contact, we got the platoon back together, and I tied us in with Duke's people."

"Yeah, but how did ya get out here?"

"I don't know if it was luck or what, but as soon as I got everyone tied in, they hit us again from the south. That time, we had our shit together. The Bodes were in position, and our claymores were out."

"So what happened?"

"When they broke contact and started to run, I took the machine gun and a few Bodes and counterattacked." He smiled. "We chased 'em all the way to the creek, and I've been here ever since."

"Hey, we'd better get up on the bank."

I extended my hand and pulled him to his feet. Grabbing a few roots, we pulled our way up the bank. Once on top, I looked out over the fallen tree and was surprised at the view. The entire area south of Duke's platoon could be seen, a clear shot at anything that moved within a hundred meters. All along the blackened front, wispy tendrils of smoke curled upward from smoldering hot spots. The charred bodies of enemy soldiers lay twisted and torn in the late afternoon sun.

"We put flankin' fire on 'em every time they moved on Duke's platoon," he said as he pointed over the top of the tree. "For a while it was a turkey shoot. Then they spotted us." He pointed to a blue-clad soldier lying on his side about twenty meters out. "That's the bugger that got me. I caught 'im in the chest just before that third grenade exploded."

Whump-whump-whump. An automatic weapon opened up to our left front. We ducked behind the rotting trunk as rounds slammed into the wood, splattering chunks of bark over us. After the initial burst, we both popped up to return fire but couldn't find a target. Frank then discovered that he was out of ammunition.

"You see 'em?" I asked as we knelt face-to-face against the tree.

"In a ravine about thirty meters out," he said. "Got a couple mags?"

I reached down and unsnapped one of my BAR belt pouches and pulled out five magazines.

"Here ya go," I said as I handed them to him.

"Thanks," he said, slipping four into his empty ammo pouch and one into his M-16. "Would ya believe I fired my last two rounds into that guy?"

Peeking out over the top of the fallen tree again, I spotted movement in the ravine and fired three quick bursts. Just as I ducked, they returned fire, and out of the corner of my eye, I saw Frank lob a grenade toward the ravine.

"On target," he said as he ducked. I slowly counted to "five one thousand" but nothing happened.

"A dud," I said as we both looked and saw a gray cloud slowly filling the ravine.

"Did you throw gas?" I asked.

"Who, me?" He laughed.

Both of us started laughing uncontrollably and sank to sitting positions with our backs against the tree.

"You need an R & R," I said.

"Hey, Jimmy, what d'ya say we go to Hong Kong?"

"Right now I'd settle for Trang Sup," I said.

Looking at the front of Frank's fatigue jacket, I stopped laughing when I saw that it was perforated with small holes.

"Oh, no," I mumbled. He must have multiple chest wounds. "Unbutton your jacket," I said as I knelt in front of him.

As he started opening the buttons, empty M-16 magazines fell out on the ground. His jacket was packed with them.

"Been sticking 'em in there so I wouldn't lose 'em," he said.

As they continued to spill out, I noticed that some were dented.

"They absorbed the shrapnel," I said.

"Yeah," he said as the last one clinked to the ground.

With his shirt unbuttoned, I took a look at his chest. Much to my relief, it was just red with scrapes and bruises.

"Looks okay," I said, feeling for broken ribs. "How does it feel?"

"Like I got kicked by a mule."

"Gonna send ya down to Saigon for tests," I said. "Could have internal injuries."

When he started to button his jacket, I noticed that the upper part of his left sleeve was covered with dried blood.

"Wait a minute," I said, grabbing his forearm. "What's wrong with your arm?"

"Ah, just a flesh wound."

"You wouldn't bullshit a friend, would ya?" I asked as I helped him unbutton his jacket.

With his jacket removed, I saw that his shoulder was covered with a couple of blood-soaked four-by-fours and a few pieces of surgical tape. I pulled away some of the tape, lifted the gauze, and took a look at the wound. From what I could see, it was a fairly deep flesh wound. Fortunately, there didn't appear to be any bone involvement.

"What d'ya think, Jimmy?" he asked.

"Gonna have to debride it and sew it up, but right now let's get ya back inside the perimeter."

Things seemed a little too quiet, so as soon as Frank got his jacket back on, I took a look over the trunk. Seventy-five meters southwest of us, I saw what looked like at least a squad running toward the creek.

"Better get outta here," I said. "They're gonna flank us."

"They'll come down the creek bed."

"Come on," I said as I picked up my M-5 kit.

I started to slide back down the bank but stopped when I saw that he couldn't get up.

"Hey, buddy, let me give ya a hand," I said as I grabbed him under each arm and lifted him to his feet.

"Just a little stiff," he said.

"I'm gonna recommend you for the Liar of the Year award," I said as I helped him down the bank. We retraced my footprints back to where I first dropped into the creek bed, then turned left into the jungle. As I took a quick back azimuth with my compass, we could hear the high-pitched sound of Vietnamese voices coming from the area of the downed tree.

"Don't stop," Frank whispered. "They're right behind us."

I nodded and picked up the pace as we slipped through the bamboo thicket. I kept us moving in the right direction and watched for the Bodes while Frank walked backward with his weapon at the ready.

When we reached the far side of the bamboo thicket, I knew we were nearing our perimeter. I didn't want to startle the Bodes so I stopped to watch and listen. I hoped they remembered that we were out here. Seeing Frank bent forward with a hand on one knee, I could tell that he was busted up more than he was letting on. He hadn't fully recovered from hitting that mine on the Saigon–Tay Ninh Highway, and now he was injured again.

"Wetsu!" Frank yelled when he spotted a Bode.

"Wetsu," the Bode responded.

"We're home, Jimmy." Frank smiled as three Bodes ran out to meet us.

"*Trung si* Hagey, *Trung si* Hagey." They beamed as they grabbed him around the waist and patted him on the back.

"They're glad to see ya." I smiled.

"Not as glad as I am to see them." He beamed.

Once we were again inside the perimeter, a few more of Frank's Bodes gathered around him to welcome him back. As he talked to them, I thought of his comment about us making it home. I guess everything's relative.

"Frank, I'd better get back to the platoon," I said.

"Okay, Jimmy. Thanks. I'm gonna check in with Fergy," he said as he shook my hand. "Haven't seen 'im since this mornin'."

"See ya later."

"God and country." Frank smiled as he turned and headed north.

News Clippings

According to U.S. officials, the Communists have lost a total of 207,500 men in the war.

Buffalo Evening News, July 18, 1967

In a commentary today, the Hanoi daily *Nham Dan* condemned the U.S. imperialists for using B-52's to bomb both southern and northern parts of the demilitarized zone and the Vinh Linh area in the DRV on July 13.

The Guardian (Rangoon), July 18, 1967

New York Police who ducked beer cans, eggs and milk bottles in their latest fight with the "hippies" must now see some merit to the slogan, "Make Love Not War."

Buffalo Evening News, July 18, 1967

The White House called on the National Liberation Front, the political arm of the Vietcong, and on North Vietnam today to permit the impartial inspection of American prisoners and to return the seriously sick and wounded among them.

The New York Times, July 18, 1967

Pretty Miss Lynda Bird Johnson, in London for the first time and trying to see everything she can see, went shopping on Carnaby St. But she did not—repeat not—buy a miniskirt as some papers reported.

The Miami Herald, July 18, 1967

Robert Komer, the U.S. Pacification Chief in South Vietnam, said that the pacification program has been "very slow" but it should make considerably more progress in the future.

Sabah Times (Malaysia), July 18, 1967

Howard Hawks Presents John Wayne & Robert Mitchum in *El Dorado*.

Los Angeles Times, July 18, 1967

In Miami Beach, Secretary of State Rusk said peace might be achieved in Vietnam "if we could sit down with Hanoi."

The Wall Street Journal, July 18, 1967

Johnny Bench, who drove in the Buffalo Bisons' first run in Monday night's baseball 2-1 victory over Columbus, raised his batting average to .249. The super rookie leads the Herd in runs batted in (44) and home runs (15).

Buffalo Evening News, July 18, 1967

8

The jungle was still steaming from the day's bake. The relentless glare of the sun had only lost a touch of its intensity.

When I reached Bob, Thach, and Ly, I found them huddled behind a fallen mossy tree trunk near the center of the 3d Platoon's sector. Bob had his map spread out on the ground and was pointing to locations on it as he gave directions.

"Hey, turkey, glad ya made it back," he said as I squatted next to him.

"Got tied up with Fergy and Frank," I said. "How's it goin'?"

He looked at his map and pointed to an area just west of our position.

"At least a battalion of 'em out there," he said. "Gettin' ready to hit us again."

"Beaucoup VC," Ly said as he pursed his lips and shook his head.

"Ammunition almost gone," Thach added grimly.

"Great! What about a resupply?" I asked.

"Chopper's inbound," Bob replied. "Don't think it's gonna make it on time."

"How much time we got?"

"None."

I jumped to my feet. "I'd better talk to Rinh about the wounded."

"Wait up, Jim," Bob said as he rose to his feet and tucked the map back into his hip pocket. "We're gonna have to split up."

"How d'ya want to do it?"

"You and Thach take the north end," he said. "Ly and I'll take the south."

"Okay."

"Look," he added, "I'll keep the machine gun with me."

"Sounds good. Where's the FAC?"

"Quan Loi," he said. "Had to refuel."

"Any scuttlebutt on reinforcements?"

"Condon's tryin' to get the Mike Force."

"We'd better get goin'."

"See ya later," Bob said.

"Take care."

"Mike Force come, *Bac-si?*" Thach asked as we moved down the line in a low crouch.

"Let's hope so."

Even if reinforcements were sent in, I wondered if they'd be able to land anywhere in the area. There were a number of large clearings that would make excellent landing zones, but the enemy surely had them covered with automatic weapons. It was the oldest trick in the book: surround a unit and then ambush and wipe out the reinforcements on the landing zone.

As we worked our way north, Thach encouraged the Bodes, and I tried to figure out why Bob had sent Thach and me to the northern end of the platoon. He knew that the enemy would have to be crazy to come at us again over open ground. They'd have a much better chance of breaking through our lines if they attacked through the thick brush at the southern end. Was Bob trying to keep Thach and me away from the worst of what was yet to come? I wouldn't put it past him.

When we reached the aid station, I told Thach to get the troops ready for the assault, and that I'd join him after talking to Rinh.

"I do, *Bac-si*," he said as he continued north and I headed a few meters east to the crater.

Approaching the depression, I saw Ty sitting on its rim with his M-16 pointed in my direction. In the shaded greens and browns, his bandage-covered face stood out like a flashlight in the dark. Someone had to start making green gauze, dressings, and surgical tape.

Behind Ty, Rinh and two of our platoon medics were working in a crater filled with wounded. The concave floor of the crater was carpeted with the camouflage uniforms of wounded Bodes sprawled around the circular slope with arms and legs splayed at awkward angles. A half-dozen glass bottles hung from bamboo poles with tubes running into the arms of those below. Scattered around the outside rim of the crater were pieces of cardboard, paper, discarded blood-stained dressings, and empty IV bottles.

"How's it goin', Ty?" I asked.

"*Trung si* Hagey okay?" he asked as I checked his bandages for fresh bleeding.

"Yeah, he's okay."

The areas around his mouth and eyes were the only parts of his face not covered by the mummy dressings. He still had a smile on his lips.

I was somewhat surprised by his concern for Frank and guessed that he must have been the Bode who Frank sent to get his machine gun fixed; probably got hit somewhere along the way.

"Are you Hagey's machine gunner?" I asked slowly.

"Machine gun." He nodded.

"Where's the machine gun?"

"*Trung si* Rader say no fix."

I nodded that I understood.

Standing on the rim of the crater, I watched Rinh kneeling at Luc's side taking his blood pressure. A bottle of normal saline hung on a section of bamboo and flowed into a vein in his arm. I was relieved to see that his leg wound hadn't killed him.

I started down the slope of the saucer-shaped crater and carefully stepped over Lieu. He was lying on his back with his eyes closed and his mouth gaped open. A shaft of sunlight danced on his face through a hole in the overhead foliage. I wasn't sure that he was alive until I saw the white dressing on his stomach slowly rise then fall as he drew a labored breath. That he was still alive was a good indication that the bullet hadn't severed any major vessels. Thach would be pleased with the news.

While looking at Lieu I heard the faint *wap, wap, wap* of a chopper. I strained to listen for a few seconds until I was sure it was the telltale beat of an approaching chopper. I hoped it was the ammunition resupply.

"Rinh," I called. He appeared startled by my voice.

Evidently he had been so involved in his work that he hadn't noticed my return.

"Donahue." He smiled as he stood up and removed a clean white handkerchief from his breast pocket.

"How do you feel?" he asked as he rechecked my dressing.

"Got some bad news, my friend; we're gonna have to hide everyone who can't walk."

"Why?" He looked at me with uncertainty in his voice.

"Ammunition's almost gone," I said. "They're gettin' ready to hit us again."

The expression on his face turned cold as he removed his glasses and looked at me through tired eyes.

"The VC will find them," he added as he used the handkerchief to wipe the greasy film from his lenses.

"Look, they're gonna cut through here like a hot knife through butter," I said. "If we have to break out with the wounded, they're gonna slow us down and no one's gonna make it—including the wounded."

"How long will they be left?"

"If we get the Mike Force in here and get resupplied, we'll be back by first light."

He looked at the ground and replaced his glasses.

"Okay, Donahue."

"Do it quick," I said. "Once they get inside the perimeter, it'll be too late."

He took a deep breath and nodded.

"I'll be up on the north end of the platoon," I said as I turned and carefully stepped over the wounded. Near the rim of the crater, I heard a loud grunt. When I looked, I saw that it was the Bode from Duke's platoon who had been hit in the mouth. He was still lying in a fetal position with an IV hooked up to his arm, but he mustered enough strength to flash me a feeble thumbs-up. I returned the gesture, then continued on my way.

I found myself agonizing about the wounded as I made my way back to the perimeter. The thing that worried me most was the thought that the Bodes might kill them rather than risk letting them fall into the hands of the enemy. I was also worried about what Thach's reaction would be to leaving Lieu.

"Damn." I stopped and headed back to the crater. This was one of those problems that didn't have an easy solution. No matter what you did, it would probably cost lives.

"Rinh," I called as I approached. He looked and ran in my direction.

"What is it, Donahue?" he asked tensely.

"You're right," I said. "Got too many to hide. Maybe two or three, but not this many. They'll find 'em for sure."

"What should we do?"

"Get the walkin' wounded back to their platoons and the rest in hammocks," I said.

"Okay." He smiled. "I was afraid to hide them."

"This way they'll have a chance. It may not be much, but at least it's a shot."

"I will get them ready," he said.

"Okay, my friend. Let's do it."

He nodded and began barking orders to the two medics who were working in the crater.

"Rinh," I called as I walked away. "As soon as ya get everyone outta here, come up to my position."

He waved, and I headed back to the perimeter. I felt a great sense of relief about the wounded and our decision not to cache them. Besides, I thought, if we could hang on until it got dark, we could break down into squad-size units and work our way south to Quan Loi or northwest to Loc Ninh. There was no way Charlie could seal the entire perimeter, especially at night.

When I reached the perimeter, I spotted Thach giving last-minute instructions to the troops. Most of them had attached bayonets to their M-16s. As I headed up the line toward him, an ominous foreboding settled over me. An oppressive silence had enveloped the line. The Bodes were too quiet. They were bunched in groups of two or three, some with looks of grim resignation, some with gaunt distant stares, others with tension etched on their faces, but no one said a word. All along the line, the biting stench of burnt flesh hung as a portent of imminent death and dying.

"Bac-si." Thach motioned for me to follow him.

We moved north until we found Danh and Kien set up at both ends of the same fallen tree where we had fought earlier in the day.

"Many VC come," Danh said as Thach and I took up positions near the center of the tree and used our hands to clear the ground of spent cartridges.

"Bac-si." Kien pointed out over the top of the tree. Looking west through a broken haze of white, gray, and black smoke I was shocked to see a long line of uniformed soldiers extended all across our front. Because of the distance and the blankets of haze, I couldn't tell if they were wearing blue or khaki uniforms.

Watching the enemy move into position, I was nauseated by the gaseous stench of putrefying bodies. Enemy troops who had been torn apart or burned by bombs earlier in the day had been lying in the tropical sun for several hours. Just a few meters in front of our position sat the same khaki-clad soldier I had shot hours earlier. His mouth was still locked open with a wide-eyed look of disbelief. The irritating hum of hungry flies buzzing about the dead only underscored the carnage.

As we waited for the enemy assault, I found myself recalling a book about Shaka, the great Zulu chief. I was in high school when I read it, and I remembered wondering how his enemies must have felt with his regiments closing in on them. Now I knew.

"They come," Thach said as he pulled his bolt to the rear and rested his M-16 on top of the fallen tree.

From a distance of 125 meters, I saw their officers running up and down the line. It looked as though they were trying to get their men on line and properly spaced as they advanced. When they closed to ninety meters, I could see that they were wearing blue uniforms, pith helmets, and web gear. Most were toting AKs. They must have been the same troops we spotted moving across our front earlier in the day.

As I watched, the blue line moved forward at a slow walk. I removed the few full magazines I had left and placed them on the ground near my right knee. When I looked up again, I saw that they had changed from a slow stride to a quick walk. As their pace picked up, my heartbeat began to accelerate. Suddenly, a volley of heavy firing erupted at the other end of the platoon. At seventy-five meters, they broke into a dead run and began firing and screaming. All along their line, their muzzle flashes blinked on and off like a hundred strobes.

Here we go, I said to myself. I wiped the sweat from my palms for the last time, braced myself, and took up a firm firing position. "Just a little bit closer, a little bit closer," I mumbled.

Thooomp! Thooomp! Thooomp! The hollow cough of enemy mortars sounded from somewhere west of our position. Shivers raced down my spine. I glanced over at Thach, and he flashed a panicked "Oh no" look. Something about mortars scared the hell out of me. It was probably the random, unpredictable pattern of impact. Our only hope was that they'd explode in the canopies of the larger trees and that most of the shrapnel would be absorbed by the foliage before it hit the ground. Based on what I knew of enemy tactics, I figured the assault was probably timed so that the mortars would start tearing us apart when the enemy troops were fifty meters away; these guys had their shit together. With the enemy drawing near, I crouched low as I heard their rounds cutting through vegetation and thumping into tree trunks.

At sixty meters, the Bodes opened fire. I lined up the top of my front sight blade on the chest of one of the leading attackers. He was running zigzag, so I aimed in front of his chest and squeezed. An instant later he fell to the ground and disappeared beneath the mist and smoke. With my left eye completely shut and my right partially closed, I found that my field of vision was becoming increasingly narrow. It was becoming more and more difficult to get a fix on a target, a lot like viewing the battlefield through a narrow pipe.

Whoomph, whoomph, whoomph. Just as I lined up my sights on a second attacker and was about to pull the trigger, he was vaporized in an explosion of fire and smoke. One second I could see him running at me, and a second later, there was nothing there.

"What the hell was that?" I yelled to Thach.

"Mortar, *Bac-si*," he shouted, as gray-black bursts mushroomed to our front, tearing through the enemy ranks with red-hot slivers of shrapnel.

I was almost paralyzed as I watched the rounds rip the assault to shreds. I couldn't believe it. As the mortar rounds walked among the enemy, they cut down the nearest troops like a razor-sharp scythe cutting through saw grass. Each explosion brought a bright orange flash followed by hot shock waves that rushed through the heavy air like ripples expanding on a pond.

After a long barrage of bursting mortar rounds, the ghostly figures of blue-clad troops stumbled and staggered out of the smoke. Most of them appeared dazed and wounded, and the Bodes easily cut them down before they reached our lines.

When the layers of smoke began to dissipate, I saw that those who hadn't been killed were walking or running to the rear. I couldn't help thinking that some mortar commander was going to get his ass chewed on this one.

I wiped the layers of sweat and grime from my face and slumped to the ground in nervous exhaustion. I was

replaying the turn of events, when Thach let out a loud
"Chey yo," which startled me. I turned to see him jump
on top of the fallen tree and start screaming and shaking
his fist defiantly at the retreating enemy. Suddenly Danh
joined him on the moss covered hunk, and they both began
dancing and singing:

> *"Puc a puc a* Ho Chi Minh
> *Puc a puc a* Ho Chi Minh"

Soon, gleeful Bodes all along the line jumped to their
feet and started singing:

> *"Puc a puc a* Ho Chi Minh
> *Puc a puc a* Ho Chi Minh"

"We sing 'fuck Ho Chi Minh.' " Danh grinned and continued dancing what looked like an oriental jig.

"Hey, Jim." I turned to see that it was Bob lugging a box of
M-16 ammunition and two bandoliers of M-79 ammunition.

"Did ya see what happened? Buddha must be lookin' out
for us." He grinned as he dumped some of the M-16 ammunition on the ground and handed Thach the two bandoliers.

"You got that right," I said.

Thach leaped down from the fallen tree, grabbed Bob
around the waist, and started dancing with him as he continued to sing.

"Hey, Thach," I said, "would ya write down the words
for me."

"Okay, *Bac-si*." He laughed.

"Could be a best seller." I chuckled as Danh and I knelt
to fill our empty magazines.

"Yeah, it's got a good beat." Bob laughed. "Definitely
Top 40 material. We'll get it on *American Bandstand*."

"You get an azimuth on those mortars?" I asked.

"Yeah," Bob answered as the dancing and singing died down.

"Hey, I'd better get back," Bob added as he scanned the battlefield. "They'll be back. You can count on it."

"Thanks for the ammo," I said as he headed back down the line in a low crouch.

"There's another load on the way," he yelled as he disappeared into the brush.

I was going to ask him if he wanted me to join him down at the other end of the platoon, but in all of the excitement, I forgot to bring it up.

While sitting on the ground filling the remainder of my empty magazines, I realized how really good I suddenly felt. The fear and exhaustion that I had experienced only a few minutes earlier were gone, and I found myself refreshed and ready to go. In some ways the day had been a lot like running a long-distance race. There were times when I felt I was not going to make it, and there were times when I felt as if I could go on forever. Just then I was soaring.

"Bac-si." I looked to my rear and saw that it was Kien. He was carrying one American and two large, round Chinese DH-10 claymore mines. The military-green devices measured a good foot in diameter and were supported by metal stands.

"Where'd ya get 'em?" I asked with excitement as he placed them on the ground next to me. He just smiled and continued to gum his soggy cigar butt.

"Hey, Thach. Tell Kien that cigars aren't good for his health." I winked as Kien spat tobacco juice at the ground.

Thach said something to him in Cambodian, and they both broke up.

"What he say?" I asked.

"Ah, he say if he worry, he not come Mobile Guerrilla Force." Thach laughed.

"No sweat," Kien said, nodding.

"Out to the left," I told Kien as I handed him one of the Chinese mines and pointed. "To the right," I told Danh as I handed him the other DH-10.

They indicated that they understood, so I took the American claymore and my M-16 and crawled over the top of the tree. After moving ten meters, I reached a dead enemy soldier. He was sitting in a rigor-mortis position against the tree where he had died. His skin had turned gray, and his still-open eyes were covered with small black bugs. As I crawled past him, I gave him a push, and he slumped to the ground in slow motion.

Crawling with my face close to the ground, I noticed that most of the grass, bushes, vines, and small trees had been cut by lead or shrapnel. The smell of shredded foliage reminded me of a freshly cut lawn on a hot summer day.

A few meters farther out, I reached the top of a small hill and stopped. There was still a lot of firing going on, but I didn't think that anyone was shooting at me. At least I didn't see or hear any rounds hitting near me. In the distance, I saw a long line of enemy troops forming for another assault. I didn't detect any movement in my immediate area but could hear voices and groaning coming from somewhere near. My best guess was that when we broke the assault, some of the enemy found sanctuary in the craters that pockmarked the bombed-over moonscape.

My claymore came in a green cloth pouch with holes cut in its bottom so that its retractable steel legs could be extended and quickly stuck in the ground. After extending them, I looked out over the top of the hill, aimed it in the general direction of the enemy, then pushed the legs into the soft mud. I tried to aim it so that its C-4 charge would propel its hundreds of steel ball bearings parallel to the ground. I didn't want it to fire harmlessly over the enemy or into the jungle floor. If it was aimed just right, it could do one nasty job on troops in the open.

"*Bac-si,* they come," Thach yelled.

When I was satisfied that the mine was angled properly, I opened the flap on the bag and removed the firing device and S-rolled wire that had been packed on top of the mine. I noticed a banana plant lying on the ground, so I snapped off a couple of its broad leaves and covered the mine. Holding the mine's firing device and the S-rolled wire in my left hand, I worked my way back to my firing position, uncoiling the wire as I went. As the thin strand of wire unraveled, I kept looking up and around for any sign of enemy troops. As I reached the tree, an automatic weapon opened up and rounds thumped into the trunk only a couple of feet from my head. The Bodes immediately returned fire while I scurried back over the top of the tree and placed the claymore's firing device next to me on the ground.

"Don't blow 'em until I blow mine," I yelled as I looked up and saw another long blue line moving at a slow gait across our entire front. I hoped they understood what I was saying because the Bodes tended to blow them too soon. If we waited until the last possible second before detonating them, we could do some real damage.

I remembered the time back at Duc Phong when the Viet Cong set up a Chicom DH-10 claymore just a couple hundred meters outside the front gate of the camp. Even though the Bodes were spread out in single file, it killed or wounded more than a dozen of them.

The enemy's advance through the mist and smoke, which lay low over the battlefield, reminded me of a locomotive slowly picking up speed. At seventy-five meters they broke into a full run and began firing and yelling. To our left, I could hear the distinctive *ta-tow-tow-tow* of our M-60 pouring out a steady stream of fire. Bob must have been in deep shit.

Although the ground in front of us looked relatively flat, it must have had a number of draws and shallow ravines because, as the enemy advanced, they slowly sank from view. A few seconds later, bobbing waves of pith helmets would reappear and then a line of bodies would gradually rise into view.

"Hold your fire," I yelled.

For some reason the words of my drill instructor at the rifle range at Parris Island started running through my mind: "All ready on the left; all ready on the right; all ready on the firing line; watch your targets; targets!"

Whack-whack-whack. Poing . . . whumph! At sixty meters, the Bodes opened up. I, too, began picking individual targets and squeezing off two- and three-round bursts. I couldn't figure out why they persisted in assaulting us over open ground. Since all of us were armed with automatic weapons, frontal assaults in the open were suicidal. Their commander must have been a real meathead. It was going to cost him a lot of good men.

When the long blue line reached forty meters, the firing and explosions reached a deafening roar. I could see the determined expressions on the faces of the enemy. Their mouths were wide open and screaming as they ran. It was probably intended to scare the hell out of us, but I imagined that it also helped them counter their own fears. Glancing to my left and right, I saw that Kien and Danh were getting anxious to blow their claymores. I picked up my firing device and, when the leading enemy troops reached thirty meters, squeezed it.

Whoomph! Whoomph! Whoomph! We fired the three

claymores, and enemy troops, leaves, and branches were blown back as though they had been hit by a tremendous gust of wind. Through the dust and smoke, I saw that we had blown gaping holes in their formation. For a few seconds the blasts staggered their advance, then the remaining soldiers surged toward us again.

I fired a whole magazine in a broad waist-level sweep across my front, spitting a brassy stream of casings all over the fallen tree. I ducked to reload and started to look up, when I saw a blue blur coming over the top of the tree. I fired a quick burst that must have hit him high because he did a complete reverse flip as his head was knocked to the rear and his lower body continued forward. As he went flying by me, I looked to the rear to make sure he was dead and saw that he had landed on top of a Bode who was lying flat on his back. I couldn't see either of their faces.

Jumping to my feet I fired another long burst across my front and then turned and pulled the dead enemy soldier off the Bode. That's when I saw that it was Thach. I turned back to fire the rest of what was left in my magazine but couldn't find a target. There was still heavy fighting off to our left, but the enemy to our immediate front had vanished.

Looking back at Thach I didn't see any blood, but the dirt around his head appeared wet. He wasn't moving, but his eyes were following my movements, and his chest was moving up and down as he breathed.

"Were ya hit?" I yelled as I searched for a wound. He didn't say a word, just looked at me through sad bloodshot eyes.

After searching his trunk for a wound, I worked my way up to his neck and head.

"Oh, no! It's his head," I said to Danh as he knelt on Thach's other side. "He's hit in the head."

I knelt at his side, carefully slipped my hand under his

neck, and slowly elevated his head. When I had enough room, I slipped my other hand under it. Oh, my God! I could feel his warm, dirt-covered brain resting in the palm of my hand. The back of his head had been blown away.

I looked at Danh. He didn't say a word, but tears were rolling down his cheeks. As I cradled Thach's shattered skull in my hand, Danh removed a canteen and rinsed the dirt from his brain. He then untied his red platoon scarf and spread it on the ground under Thach's head.

I felt a consoling hand on my shoulder. It was Rinh. He knelt at my side and removed a large battle dressing from his M-5 kit. As I held Thach's head, he gently applied the dressing over the wound.

Rinh finished with the dressing, and as we carefully lowered Thach's head onto the scarf, Thach grabbed my hand.

"Bac-si," he said in a soft voice. "I die."

I tried to say something, but was too choked up to utter a word. I took a couple of deep breaths and looked away, trying to fight back the tide of emotions.

"You'll be all right," I said as I felt my eyes pooling with warm tears.

"Bac-si, take me to my wife," he said.

I didn't know what to say to him.

"Rinh, get an IV goin'," I snapped.

He clutched my arm. "Let him die, Donahue," he whispered in my ear. I looked into Rinh's weary eyes and knew that he was right. Even if we were at Walter Reed Hospital, Thach wouldn't make it.

"Are you in any pain?" I asked as he squeezed my hand and gave a long, fluttering sigh. There was no response, only blank glassy eyes, which stared back with that faraway look that seemed as if they were looking right through me. I felt his neck for a pulse, but there was none.

"He's gone," I said.

No one said a word. For a long moment, everyone sat in silence while I removed the gold chain with the white Buddha he had given me earlier and carefully refastened it around his neck.

"Good-bye, my friend," I said as I closed his eyelids and ran my hand through his hair in a final farewell.

With the firing to our south reduced by then to an occasional shot, Danh and Rinh spread a camouflage poncho liner on the ground next to Thach, and then the three of us lifted him and placed him on it. Watching Thach's body lying on the liner, I found myself longing to talk to him; too many things had been left unsaid.

Before wrapping him in the nylon poncho liner, I removed the chrome-plated Browning automatic pistol from his holster and handed it to Rinh.

"Give it to his wife."

"I will, Donahue."

I unbuttoned Thach's breast pocket and removed the clear plastic bag that contained his wallet. Looking inside I found a folded piece of yellowed paper. When I opened it, I discovered that it was the write-up on a Bronze Star we had presented to him a few months earlier. Even though it was wrinkled and stained, I could still read the type:

> By the direction of the President of the United States of America and the Commanding Officer of Detachment A-303, 5th Special Forces Group (Airborne), the Bronze Star Medal for heroism in ground combat in the Republic of Vietnam is hereby presented to . . .

As my eyes followed the commendation, I remembered the day back at Trang Sup when we presented it to Thach. Of course, it hadn't been approved by the president, but it really didn't make any difference; it was his most prized possession. Whenever he went into Tay Ninh, he wore it on his chest and went walking down the street with a peacock-proud, kick-my-ass-if-you-can strut.

Looking further through his wallet, I found the actual medal pinned to one of its inside compartments. I thought it was the right thing to do, so I removed it and pinned it to his breast pocket. The red, white, and blue ribbon and the bronze medal looked clean and fresh against his dirt-covered camouflage jacket.

Looking at him lying on the poncho liner, I realized how lucky I was to have known old Thach. He was a special person. I knew that he would have given his life for me and that I would have done the same for him. He was my friend.

News Clippings

It is the American Soldier—not equipment or techniques—that is the heart and soul of the Army. . . .   *Army Digest,* July 1967

The loss of more than 2,100 planes over North Vietnam marked a big error and a heavy defeat of the U.S. imperialists in both the tactical and strategic fields.
                                        North Vietnam News Service, July 18, 1967

Miss USA, Sylvia Louise Hitchcock, who is a graceful blonde, was named Miss Universe of 1967 Saturday night.
                                        The Guardian (Rangoon), July 18, 1967

The President's decision, arrived at after several days of anxious contemplation, was a typical Johnsonian compromise. There will be more American troops in Viet Nam at the end of the year than originally scheduled, but not so many as General Westmoreland wanted.
                                        U.S. News & World Report, July 21, 1967

Carla Thomas, 25, daughter of a Memphis disc jockey, was recently voted the favorite singer of U.S. servicemen in Viet Nam, an honor won last year by the Supremes.   *Time,* July 21, 1967

What is clear is that Ho Chi Minh at least at one time regarded the Americans in his hands as "war criminals," covered by the 1945 Nuremberg Charter under which some Nazi leaders were tried and sentenced to death or imprisonment, and not as prisoners of a war protected by the Geneva Convention.   *Look,* July 25, 1967

The Dirty Dozen is a cautionary tale, warning us of what can happen to conventional morality in time of stress.   *Life,* July 21, 1967

U.S. artist Rockwell Kent defended Monday his donation of $10,000, part of a Lenin Peace Prize, to the Viet Cong women and children despite a U.S. prohibition of gifts to Vietnamese Communists.
                                        Courier Express (Buffalo), July 18, 1967

6:30   Walter Cronkite   *The Atlanta Journal,* July 18, 1967

9

1805 Hours

As the late-day sun receded slowly into Cambodia, the greens, browns, and yellows began to lose color.

"Jim, Condon wants to see us right away," Bob yelled as he and Ly ran up to where Rinh, Danh, Kien, and I were standing in somber silence around Thach's body.

"Thach's dead," I said. Rinh pointed to the poncho liner and the expression on Bob's face dropped.

"Gimme a minute," he said.

While he knelt next to Thach and whispered a few words, the five of us waited in respectful silence. After a few seconds, he rose to his feet and used his sleeve to wipe his eyes.

"Let's go," he said as he, Ly, and I headed in the direction of the *bo chi huy*.

"Hey, wait up," a voice called. It was Duke Snider coming up the line. "I'm gettin' too old for this shit," he said as he joined us.

"What's goin' on?" I asked as we walked together.

"It's time to shit or get off the pot," he said.

"If they hit us again, it'll be at last light," I said.

"There they are." Duke spotted Roger, Fergy, Frank, and Stik waiting for us. They were clustered around the lieutenant while he knelt on one knee with a radio handset pressed to his ear.

"You're holdin' up the show," Stik quipped as we walked into the depression and joined the circle around the lieutenant.

"Got everyone?" Condon asked as he stood up.

"Yes, sir," Roger responded.

"Okay, listen up. I wanna make this short," Condon said. "We just got word that reinforcements are on the way."

"Yeah, and the check's in the mail," Frank shot back.

"We've heard that bull before," Fergy added in agreement.

"No," the lieutenant reassured us. "The Mike Force is already airborne."

"All right! Let's get those Chinamen on the ground and get the hell outta here," Frank said. Everyone cheered and smiled.

"Okay," Condon said. "We've got a good-sized clearing a klick to the southeast. As soon as the Mike Force secures it, we'll link up with 'em."

"Gotta think Charlie's gonna have it covered," Stik said while looking at his map.

"FAC's gonna work it over with TAC air and gunships," Condon said. "When we move, we'll have gunships workin' our front, flanks, and rear."

"It's now or never," Bob said.

"You got that right," the lieutenant said. "Gotta get the dead and wounded out while we still have light."

"Don't have much time," Roger added.

"Sir, how d'ya wanna move outta here?" Frank asked.

"Hell," Duke chimed in, "let's move just as we are."

"Right," Condon agreed. "Two parallel columns with the *bo chi huy* in between. Second and first on the right," he said as he pointed to Fergy and Duke.

"Yes, sir." Duke blew his nose with his finger pressed against one nostril.

"Got enough demo to booby-trap the area?" Condon asked him.

"Yes, sir. I'll keep 'em off our ass."

"Okay," the lieutenant said. "Recon and Three on the left."

"Sounds good," Stik said. "I'll cover our rear."

"Okay," Condon said. "Jim, how d'ya wanna handle the wounded?"

"Let's keep 'em together behind the *bo chi huy*," I said. "We'll follow ya out."

"Okay," he agreed. "Get back to your platoons."

"Keep it slow," I added. "If we rough 'em up, some of these guys are gonna die."

"Gonna move 'em in hammocks?" Roger asked.

"Yeah, four men on each hammock," I said. "Two to carry and two to rest. We'll switch every hundred meters."

"Any questions?" Condon asked.

"Let's do it," Duke folded his map.

"Okay, get back to your platoons," Condon said. "We move in ten."

Everyone was pleased with the plan and headed back to relay the good news to their platoons.

"How d'ya wanna work it?" I asked Bob as we stepped over fallen branches and splintered stalks of bamboo.

"You take care of the wounded," he said. "I'll get the troops ready to move."

Nearing the fallen tree, I saw that Rinh, Danh, and Kien were crouched behind it trading well-aimed shots with the enemy.

"I'll catch ya on the LZ," Bob said as he and Ly broke off to our left and headed down the line.

"We go, *Bac-si*?" Danh asked as I knelt next to him.

"Yeah." I smiled. "Mike Force is gonna secure the LZ."

"What about the wounded?" Rinh asked.

"Medics are bringing 'em up to the *bo chi huy*," I said. "Get your gear. I'll meet ya there."

"Okay, Donahue."

"Danh, you and Kien get Thach ready," I said.

"Okay, *Bac-si*," Danh said.

When I finished giving directions, I moved down the line in a low crouch and found my rucksack lying where I had left it earlier in the day. Picking it up by one strap, I swung it over my right shoulder and headed for the *bo chi huy*. No longer packed with five hundred rounds of extra ammunition and half a dozen smoke, gas, and high-explosive grenades, it was a lot lighter than before the battle.

Crunching through splintered bamboo once again, I heard the muffled drone of the FAC overhead. Looking up through the trees, I caught a glimpse of the plane as it floated through one of the small holes in the overhead canopy. Outlined against a clear blue sky, the O-1E looked like a large black bird drifting on outstretched wings.

Approaching the *bo chi huy*, I saw that it was buzzing with activity. A mounting sense of urgency permeated the air. The lieutenant had his radio handset pressed to his ear while the Bodes were lifting their rucksacks to their backs and preparing to move out. From every direction, like metal filings attracted to a magnet, the wounded were being carried to the center of the perimeter.

On the west side of the *bo chi huy*, I found a small clear area and dropped my rucksack to the ground.

"Over here, over here," I yelled to the Bodes carrying the wounded. When they saw me, I raised my arm over my head and, by rotating it in tight circles, signaled them to come to me. As they neared, I saw that it wasn't going to be an easy trip to the landing zone. With heavy rucksacks on their backs, they were having difficulty carrying the extra weight of the wounded.

"Donahue." Rinh arrived and lowered his rucksack to the ground next to mine.

"Make sure they keep the IVs elevated," I said. "Four men on each hammock."

"I will keep them together," he yelled as a jet streaked just above the canopy. We looked at each other and smiled; it was a welcome sound.

"I'll bring up the rear," I said.

"Okay."

As the wounded began arriving, Rinh gave instructions to the porters.

Wap, wap, wap. A gunship was hovering directly overhead, and its pulsating downdraft filled the air with the smell of burnt aviation fuel and thousands of leaves.

Ta-tow-tow-tow. Whoomph, whoomph, whoomph. The gunship opened up with machine guns and rockets on suspected enemy positions.

"Bac-si!" I turned and saw Danh carrying Thach over his shoulders.

I grabbed Thach and helped Danh lower him to the ground.

"Jim," Roger yelled as he ran up to me. "Recon and Two are movin'. The wounded ready?"

"Kien come," Danh said as he pointed. Looking to my left, I saw Kien and a half dozen Bodes moving in my direction at a slow run.

"Two minutes," I told Roger. "Keep it slow."

When Kien arrived with the additional men, Rinh quickly assigned each of them to help carry specific hammocks. Keeping an eye on the *bo chi huy*, I saw that the first of them were moving east.

Whoomph, whoomph, whoomph. Ta-tow-tow-tow. Choppers laid down fire ahead of our columns. If they did their jobs, we'd be moving through a lead corridor.

"Get 'em ready," I told Rinh.

He yelled something, and the Bodes carrying the hammocks squatted and positioned the bamboo poles on their shoulders. When they rose to their feet, the hammocks lifted the wounded off the ground.

"I will go now," Rinh said.

"Okay, partner, you and Kien stay with the IVs," I said. "Danh and I'll bring up the rear."

"I stay you," Danh smiled.

"If you carry my ruck, I'll carry Thach," I said.

"Okay, *Bac-si*."

Danh already had his rucksack on his back, so I leaned my M-16 against a stump and picked up my rucksack. While I held it against his chest, he slipped its straps over his shoulders. Once it was in place, I let go, and he bounced a couple of times to settle the weight. With rucksacks mounted front and rear, he looked pretty well balanced.

"If ya have a problem, dump my ruck," I said. "Just make sure ya get my hammock and beret."

"No sweat." He smiled.

When I bent over to pick up Thach's nylon-wrapped body, I found that I couldn't get a grip on him.

"Nylon's slippery," I said as I looked around for help. Danh was the only one left, and he was carrying so much weight that he couldn't bend over. I unraveled Thach from his nylon cocoon and tried to get him on my back. Shit. I didn't have the strength to pick him up.

Grabbing Thach under his arms, I lifted him to his feet and then propped him up against a small tree.

"Hold 'im against the tree," I told Danh.

He moved to the rear of the tree, grabbed hold of Thach's collar, and held him in position.

With the side of my neck pressed against Thach's stomach, I was in a position to grab him behind his knees.

"Let 'im go," I said.

When Danh released his grip Thach slumped forward, his dead weight folding across my shoulders.

"Good, *Bac-si,*" Danh said, as I shifted Thach's weight to balance him on my shoulders. Once I had him positioned, I was able to grab his wrist with my hand. With my other hand free, I picked up my M-16.

"We go." Danh smiled.

Looking southeast, I saw that the last of the litter teams were already thirty meters ahead of us. From the sound of the gunships, I figured that their machine guns and rockets were pulverizing the terrain about three hundred meters to the southeast.

"Better catch up," I said as he led the way out.

Taking one last look around, I saw that most of the bamboo and small trees had been cut knee-high. The area was strewn with empty ammo boxes and cartons and the plastic and cardboard containers that our medical supplies had been packed in. Within a few weeks, the jungle would reclaim everything, and no one would know what had taken place on that small kidney-shaped hill. Looking out over the still perimeter, I detected movement seventy-five meters northwest of our location.

"Psst," I hissed. Danh stopped and looked to his rear. I pointed my weapon in the direction of the movement.

"VC," he whispered as two uniforms came into full view.

From what I could see, it looked like the point element of at least a squad. They might have been trackers.

Holding my M-16 with one hand and the butt gripped tightly in my armpit, I aimed in their general direction and squeezed off a long burst. Halfway through the magazine, they disappeared and didn't return fire. I probably didn't hit them, but at least I'd slowed them down.

"Let's get outta here!"

We moved out at a quick pace, hounded by an unseen enemy tailing close behind. When we entered the killing ground in front of what was the 2d Platoon's sector, I was awed by the extent of the carnage. The once-thick jungle had been ripped apart as though it had been hit by a tornado, and deep, moonlike craters pockmarked the earth. The area looked like the floor of a slaughterhouse. Bodies and severed limbs littered the ground, and pieces of intestines and an eyeball dangled from branches that had been stripped of their leaves.

When we reached the bottom of a gradual incline, we crossed a small finger-shaped hill where we ran into Duke and a few of his men. They had come across thirty to fifty enemy rucksacks that were lined up in three neat rows. They must have belonged to some of the troops who hit Fergy and Frank's platoon earlier in the day. Duke was using his knife to cut the shoulder straps off each of the rucksacks while the Bodes were dumping their contents on the ground.

"Don't have time to do a real job on these," he said as we approached.

From what I could see, they each contained a couple of blocks of dried fish, some uncooked rice, cooking utensils, a hammock and blanket, and a few personal odds and ends. I didn't see any maps or documents or anything else that would be of any intelligence value.

"Better get your butts outta here," I said. "Charlie's movin' in."

"I'll be right behind ya," he said as he sampled a piece of fish. "Whew, that shit's bad," he said spitting out a half-chewed chunk.

"Gonna booby-trap the area?" I asked.

"Yeah, don't touch anything," he said.

"Don't worry," I said as Danh and I continued on our way.

"Hey, Jim," Duke called. "Keep an eye out for Stik. He's settin up a stay-behind ambush."

"Will do," I said. "See ya on the LZ."

Danh and I entered a thick tangle of leaves and vines, and I soon realized that we had lost visual contact with the rear elements of the column, but I figured they couldn't be too far ahead. Fortunately, the ground was damp and spongy. It wasn't difficult to follow the footprints through the trampled undergrowth.

As we continued east, the jungle began to thin, and we soon found ourselves moving through a bamboo thicket. Our boots crunched through a carpet of dead and decaying bamboo as tall green stalks squeaked and clattered and a jet screamed in low from the south.

Karoumph, karoumph, karoumph. To our rear, Duke was calling in air strikes on what was once our perimeter.

Wap, wap, wap. What sounded like a score of helicopters was approaching from the south.

"Mike Force?" Danh asked as he stopped and pointed south.

"Must be." I stopped for a couple of seconds to adjust Thach's weight on my back. Laboring to catch my breath, I realized that trying to carry him might have been a mistake. I had thought that once I had him on my back, I wouldn't have any trouble, but I was feeling completely drained of energy. Every step was more difficult than the one before.

Moving out again, we soon passed through the last of the bamboo and entered an area of waist-high grass and scrub brush. Out in the open, without the shade of the canopy, it felt like the temperature shot up a good twenty

degrees. The glare of a low-slung sun hit my eyes and
forced me to squint. The searing heat was doing a number
on my aching head. And, as the sun beat down, my good
eye kept closing because salty sweat ran into it. I felt myself growing weaker, and I struggled to maintain visual
contact with Danh. I was nauseated and dizzy. Suddenly, I
found myself alone, disoriented, and pushing through a
wall of eight-foot elephant grass. The air was so close with
heat, it was like breathing inside a plastic bag. I began to
feel a panicky sense of claustrophobia. I had to get out.
Using all the strength I could muster, I parted the knifelike
blades of grass. I felt like I had stumbled into a sauna. My
pores opened like a faucet.

The putrid taste of hot vomit rose in my throat; the surrounding greens and browns began to spin. Then everything went black.

When I awoke, I was flat on my back. Thach was sitting
next to me, his back resting against the wall of elephant
grass. For a second, I thought he was alive, but then my
eyes cleared, and I realized that I was dreaming.

"Sorry old buddy." I slowly rose to my knees and then to
my feet. I didn't know how long I had been out. I removed a
couple of salt tablets from my pocket and swallowed them
with a long drink of water, realizing that I had probably lost
more blood than I originally thought. If I had been smart, I
would have hooked myself to a normal saline IV.

After the water, I felt much better and thought that if I
could work my way back to the main trail, I would either
run into Danh coming back for me or Duke or Stik moving
toward the landing zone.

"Bac-si," a voice called. It was Danh.

"Over here."

Seconds later, Danh and Kien came crashing through
the elephant grass.

"Boy am I glad to see you guys," I said as Danh grabbed me around the waist.

"I look to see you, *Bac-si,* but you go."

"Yeah, let's get moving," I said. "Lemme get a couple things outta my ruck so you can leave it."

He pulled the straps off his shoulders and dropped my rucksack to the ground. After opening it, I removed my beret, my hammock, and my Olympus camera, and stuffed them into empty pockets.

"Give your ruck to Danh," I told Kien. "You'll have to carry Thach." I could see that he didn't understand.

"I take Thach?"

Danh interrupted and said something in Cambodian.

"No sweat, *Bac-si,*" Kien said as he removed his rucksack and helped Danh mount it on his chest. As soon as Danh had both rucksacks settled, he took a few steps back toward the trail. Kien couldn't resist removing the few cans of C rations I had packed near the top of my rucksack.

"Let's go," I said as he stuffed them into his pockets and then picked up Thach in a fireman's carry. With everyone ready, we backtracked until we hit the trail, then headed east again. Within a few minutes, we moved out of the elephant grass into a flat, swampy area covered with soft mud and clumps of stunted sun-bleached grass. The clearing extended far into the distance, at least four hundred meters, and was surrounded by the tall gray trunks of cypress trees. A few meters into the open, we crossed a shallow north-south stream.

Ta-tow-tow-tow. As we splashed through ankle-deep water, the red tongues of tracer fire from at least a half dozen choppers probed the tree lines on both sides of the clearing. Darting in and out, the gunships looked like angry dragonflies as they raked the jungle fringe.

Whack-whack-whack. As I watched the aerial display,

several bursts of M-16 fire broke the silence to our rear. Stik's tail gunners must have made contact with enemy trackers.

"Hey, Jim!" a voice called.

I stopped and looked to my rear. It was Duke and his radio operator.

"Wait up," he yelled as I stopped and let Kien move past me.

"What d'ya hear?" I asked as he caught up and we walked together.

"Mike Force is on the ground." He smiled.

"They got the LZ secured?"

"Yup."

"China Boy, this is Fox Control. Over," Lieutenant Condon's voice crackled over the radio.

"Fox Control, this is China Boy." It was the Mike Force. "Come to the yellow smoke. Over."

"There it is," I said as I pointed ahead to a yellow plume drifting against the pale blue sky. To our left and right, I saw the camouflage uniforms of Mike Force troops standing in the wood lines on both flanks. Above them, with machine guns firing, choppers hovered protectively at treetop level. Higher in the sky, the ever watchful FAC was drifting in a lazy circle.

After moving another two hundred meters, I saw that, in the middle of the clearing, we were setting up a circular inner perimeter that measured about a hundred meters across. Near its center, it looked as if most of the Americans from the Mobile Guerrilla Force were meeting with members of the Mike Force.

When we reached the inner perimeter, Duke and his radio operator broke off and headed for the 1st Platoon while Danh, Kien, and I headed toward the center. We found Lieutenant Condon, Roger, Fergy, Frank, and Bob talking to a couple of Americans from the Mike Force. To their right, Rinh had the wounded lined up and ready to go.

"Got everyone?" the lieutenant asked Roger.

"Everyone but Stik and one Recon section," Roger answered.

"Okay, listen up," Condon yelled. "If Charlie catches us out here, he'll kick our ass, so let's do what we have to do and get outta here."

"Sir, how many choppers?" I asked.

"Seven," he said. "One at a time."

"Got a final count on the wounded?" Roger asked.

"Thirty that have ta be medevacked," I said.

"Okay," Condon said. "Get 'em ready."

Bob and I ran to where Rinh was waiting with the wounded.

"They ready to go?" I asked.

"All ready, Donahue."

"Okay," I said. "Let's get the most serious ones on the first chopper."

"*Trung si* Donahue," a voice called from behind me. I turned to see that it was a tall, well-built Chinese Nung I had met when the Mike Force was helping us build our camp at Duc Phong.

"*Chao ong,*" I said as I shook his hand. "Good to see ya again. How's everything goin'?"

"Too much operation," he said with a smile.

"Helicopter," Rinh told me as the lieutenant popped a red smoke.

Wap, wap, wap. Looking south, I saw the bulbous green hull of a Huey gliding in over the tree line. Seconds later, its underbelly flared up and its skids swayed as it kicked up a cloud of dust before settling twenty meters from the wounded. As the rotors popped and thwacked, Rinh had the porters carry five hammocks to the side door. After directing the loading of the wounded, I talked to a member of the crew.

"You know where Trang Sup is?" I yelled over the noise of the engine and rotors.

"Tay Ninh Province," he shouted. "Near the base of the mountain."

"Good," I hollered. "The dead go to Trang Sup, and the wounded to either the 3d Field Hospital in Saigon, the 24th Evac in Long Binh, or the MASH Hospital in Tay Ninh."

"The Viets go to Cong Hoa hospital in Saigon," he barked back.

"Bullshit," I yelled. "These are Cambodians. They're goin' to an American hospital."

Bob must have overheard what was being said, and joined the conversation.

"I'll tell ya what," he yelled as he pointed his finger threateningly in the guy's face. "If I find out they didn't go to an American hospital, I'll personally look you up. You got that?"

"Okay, okay," he said as Bob walked away. "That guy crazy?"

"That's right," I said. "Everyone on this team's crazy."

Rinh tugged on my sleeve. "All loaded, Donahue."

I gave the pilot the thumbs-up, and everyone around the chopper ran in a crouch back to where the rest of the wounded were lying. The pilot pulled back on his collective, and the chopper shook as it lifted to a few feet off the ground. With a final surge of power, it tilted forward, then climbed across the clearing, thrashing the tops of the canopy with its departing downdraft.

"I'll see ya back at Trang Sup," Bob said as he shook my hand and put his arm around my waist.

"Take care of yourself," I said. "Get your butt X-rayed."

"Right."

"I don't know where I'll end up," I said. "If they send me outta country, would ya get my gear to me?"

"Don't worry. I'll take care of it," he said as another chopper touched down amid a flurry of wind that whipped the hammocks of the wounded and caused us to shield our eyes. As Rinh supervised the loading, I heard Fergy yelling at Frank to get on the chopper and Frank yelling back that he wasn't leaving.

"Frank"—the lieutenant grabbed his arm—"I want ya to make sure the Bodes get taken care of. I want ya to go."

"All right, sir, I understand."

"Damned Frank's a bullhead." Fergy laughed, shaking his head.

As Bob and I listened to the conversation, someone grabbed me from behind and kissed my ear. It was Stik.

"Damn it, Stik!" I wiped my ear. "One of these days, I'm gonna kick your skinny ass."

"That'll be the day." He laughed. "Hey, you take care of yourself. I'll catch ya back at camp."

"Chopper comin' in," Roger yelled, as another Huey glided in just above the trees.

"Get Thach on this one," I yelled to Rinh above the noise.

As the chopper touched down in blowing grass, Rinh, Danh, Bob, and I picked Thach up. Once we had the wounded on board, we carefully slid his body across the Huey's metal floor.

"Hey," a member of the crew protested. "What's that slope doing with a Bronze Star?"

"Listen, you fat fucker." I shoved the muzzle of my M-16 into his belly. "That man's the best soldier you'll ever see."

"Take it easy," he said as he squirmed in his seat.

"Come on, Jim," Bob said as he grabbed my arm. "Don't let that sorry ass get to ya," he added as we ran back to where Rinh, Danh, and Kien were waiting with the next load of wounded.

"Keep 'em movin'," the lieutenant yelled.

"Yes, sir," I hollered as the fourth chopper landed.

As soon as the chopper was loaded, Rinh ran back to where I was standing. While Frank and Roger helped load the fifth and sixth Hueys, I went over the company's medical needs with Rinh. Although no American medics would be left on the ground, I had complete confidence in his abilities.

"Jim," the lieutenant called as he walked over and shook my hand. "Last chopper's comin' in. You and Frank make sure they take good care of the Bodes."

"Will do, sir."

"Good-bye, Donahue," Rinh said as he and Danh grabbed my arm and shook my hand.

"Good-bye, my friends." I could feel myself being overcome by emotion. "You guys take care of Bob."

"No sweat," Kien nodded.

"Come on, Jimmy," Frank said as he grabbed my arm.

"Hey, J.C.," Fergy yelled, "you guys stay outta trouble, ya hear?"

I gave him a thumbs-up, and Frank and I ran around to the right door of the chopper and climbed aboard. All of the seats and most of the floor space were already occupied, so we sat in the doorway.

With our feet dangling out over the skid and the main rotors slapping the late-day air at over three hundred RPMs, the pilot pulled back on the collective, and we lifted to a few feet off the ground. I flashed everyone below a V, and they waved back.

"We made it," Frank yelled as we transitioned to forward speed and began picking up speed and altitude.

As we rose high above the trees, the cool air felt clean and fresh as it blew through the open cabin, tugging at my fatigues. To the west, a copper-colored sun slowly sank into a pastel haze, burnishing the matted jungle greens with an iridescent orange. It was good to be out, but somehow, I felt bad about leaving.

As we flew south over the broccoli-topped jungle, I couldn't stop thinking about the guy who referred to Thach as a slope. The remark had angered me, but when I thought about it, I realized that he was probably the victim of his own experiences in Vietnam. Tragically, most Americans only came in contact with those Vietnamese who were trying to kill them, and the pimps, prostitutes, and Saigon cowboys who were trying to take their money. Few had the opportunity to get to know the people.

It was a short, low-level flight back to Quan Loi. When we landed next to the airstrip, the last light of day had turned the sky a fiery crimson. Shortly after touching down, Frank and I were picked up by a dirt-covered jeep and driven to a nearby general-purpose tent divided into two sections. While Frank waited in one end, I was taken to the other and told to have a seat on a stack of C-ration boxes. A few minutes later, an Oriental wearing what looked like French Army camouflage fatigues walked in and told me that he wanted to debrief me on the operation.

My first impression was that he was Vietnamese, but after talking to him for a couple of minutes, I realized that he was probably a Filipino. His black hair, worn over the ears, was too long for someone in the military, so I assumed he must have been a civilian associated with one of the intelligence agencies.

In my discussion with him, I was able to provide a detailed description of enemy uniforms, weapons, and tactics but wasn't able to give him any precise information regarding the identification of enemy units involved in the battle. I suggested that Lieutenant Condon or Fergy might be able to provide him with that information.

A medic entered as we talked and took my pulse and blood pressure. When he left, a sergeant carried in a half dozen enemy weapons that we had brought out with us. My interrogator didn't say much about them, but I could tell that he was impressed by the fact that they were all factory new and excellently maintained. When he finished with the debriefing, he scribbled down a few comments in a small notebook and asked me to send Frank in.

I returned to the other end of the tent where I found Frank sitting on a stool with his pants rumpled in a heap around his ankles. To my surprise, I saw that he had also been hit in the leg. It was only a flesh wound, and a doctor was covering it with a dressing.

"Your turn on the hot seat," I said as he stood and pulled up his trousers.

"Who is that guy?"

"Some spook," I shrugged as he left.

"Sergeant Donahue?" the doctor asked.

"Yes, sir."

"Take a seat over here," he said, pointing to a stool next to the table. As soon as I sat down, I heard the whine of a jeep transmission as it downshifted and pulled up outside the tent. A few seconds later, Major Gritz strode in.

"Damn, Jim," he said as I rose to shake his hand. "Sit down, sit down." He laid his Swedish-K submachine gun on the table. "I just got word that you and Frank had been hit. How serious is it?"

"Frank's got a couple of flesh wounds and possible internal injuries," I said as the doctor used a light to check my pupils and ears and then began to unwind the Ace from my head.

"If I'd known, I would have gotten you guys out earlier," he said as he watched the doctor. He winced as the doctor tugged at the blood-caked bandage.

"Probably best you didn't, sir," I said. "We only had eight Americans on this one."

"How's the rest of the team?"

"Well, sir, old Bob's got some shrapnel in his butt. Other than that, they're in good shape."

"Good."

"You had us worried." I smiled.

"Why's that?" he replied, not quite sure of what I meant.

"When you flew in with that resupply, we thought that fifty-one got ya."

"No." He grinned. "We came in so low he couldn't get a clear shot."

"This might hurt a little," the doctor said as he placed my bloody dressing on the table and picked up a stainless-steel probe. As he slowly worked it into the hole over my left temple, I gritted my teeth and gripped the edge of the table until my knuckles turned white. I hoped the expression on Gritz's face wasn't any indication of the seriousness of the wound.

"What d'ya think?" Gritz asked the doctor.

"Well, Major," he paused, placing the probe on the table, then began applying a new dressing. "All I can tell you is that the projectile lacerated a couple of his temporal vessels, and it's still in there."

"So, where do we go from here?" Gritz wanted to know.

"Down to Saigon for further examination and surgery," he said as Frank returned to the room.

"Good to see ya, sir," Frank smiled as they shook hands heartily.

"Frank, I hope to hell you don't feel as bad as you look."

"I feel pretty good, sir," he said. "It could be worse."

"When you get back to Trang Sup, I'm gonna restrict you to camp," Gritz said with a laugh. "Every time you go out the front gate you get hurt."

"Seems that way," Frank mused.

"Look." Gritz picked up his Swedish-K. "As soon as I get the company back to Trang Sup, I'll be down to see you guys."

"How much longer they gonna be in the field?" I asked.

"One day, two at the most."

A medic walked into the tent.

"Sir, the aircraft's ready to leave for Saigon," he told the doctor.

"See ya in a couple days, sir." Frank and I shook Gritz's hand then followed the medic from the brightly lit tent to a jeep parked outside. I climbed into the back of the jeep and found that the tent's lights had ruined my night vision. I couldn't see a thing until the medic started the engine and turned on the headlights. Peeling away in a cloud of dust, we sped down the runway toward the waiting C-130. While I hung on for my life, our headlights cut through the evening mist, splattering juicy bugs against the windshield. As we neared the waiting transport, we saw that the prop blasts from its outboard engines were kicking up clouds of rust-colored dust, so the driver looped around to its rear before coming to a stop at the foot of the lowered ramp. With the smell of burning aviation fuel filling my nostrils, we climbed out of the jeep and onto the ramp. I looked up into the cabin and saw shadows moving in the red glow of its night lights.

"Hold it," a nurse yelled as she ran down the ramp. "Do you have any grenades, claymores, or explosives?" she yelled over the roar of the engines.

"We're clean," Frank hollered back, raising his hands over his head.

"Need any assistance?" she asked as the three of us walked up the ramp.

"How about a cold beer," Frank joked.

"I'll get you some orange juice." She led us to two empty nylon seats on the left side of the aircraft and buckled us in.

"I think I'm in love," Frank yelled in my ear.

Looking around the cabin, I saw that they already had the Bodes and a few other wounded Americans on board. Some were strapped into seats on the other side of the aircraft, while others were tied down on stretchers. A half dozen nurses and medics were busy preparing them for takeoff. I was happy to see that the Bodes were still with us.

Once the medical personnel had everyone secured, the hydraulic whine of the retracting ramp signaled our preparation for takeoff. The pilot taxied the lumbering C-130 to the end of the runway before swinging the nose around and coming to a complete stop. A moment later, the fuselage began to vibrate as the engines revved to a scream. Suddenly we lurched forward and raced down the runway before leaping into the night sky above Quan Loi.

We had only been airborne for a few minutes when the nurse brought us each a glass of orange juice. As we sipped it, the steady hum of the engine lulled most of the wounded to sleep. By the time we finished our juice, the cabin had cooled enough that we were shivering uncontrollably.

"Can I get you a blanket?" one of the medics asked.

"Yeah, we're freezing our asses off," Frank said.

A minute later, he returned with a blanket for each of us and a couple cups of steaming coffee.

"Now that's service." Frank smiled as the medic wrapped one of the blankets around him.

Sitting in the soft glow of the cabin lights, we sipped coffee and watched the nurses shuttle among the wounded, checking their IVs and dressings. As we watched, we talked about the Bodes. In the afterglow of battle, it dawned on me how attached I had become to them and to Vietnam. I remembered going home on leave a few months earlier. It was good to see friends and relatives again, but I also remembered how much I missed what I'd left behind. When my return flight touched down in Bien Hoa, I remember feeling that I was back where I belonged, with my brothers-in-arms. Something rare had quietly taken place: a deep camaraderie had been formed that seemed to transcend relationships half a world away.

As I sat reminiscing about other times and places, my thoughts were interrupted; Frank's head slumped to my shoulder. He was sound asleep. He was still holding a half-full cup of coffee, so I removed it from his hand and placed it on the floor under my seat.

A short time later, the plane banked to the left, giving me a clear glimpse of Saigon's lights sparkling against the blackness. As it banked again, the plane's landing gear groaned as they were lowered, and we started our final approach.

A minute later, its wheels touched down at Tan Son Nhut with a screech, and the smell of scorched rubber filled the aircraft. Halfway down the runway, the pilot reversed the pitch on the props, quickly slowing the plane to a crawl and forcing me to grab hold of my seat.

As we taxied down the runway, our cabin's white lights were turned on, and the plane came alive with the last-minute activity of nurses and medics hurrying to prepare everyone for departure. I gave Frank a nudge.

"Hey Frank, we made it."

"What?" he said rubbing his eyes and squinting.

"We're in Saigon."

"Musta been dozin'," he said as he yawned.

"Dozin' hell. You were snoring so loud, they had to issue ear plugs."

When we finally came to a complete stop, the ramp whined down, exposing a number of ambulances with flashing lights. Seconds later, one of them backed up to the ramp, and a medic holding a clipboard climbed up the ramp and began talking to one of the nurses. When they finished talking, he walked over to where Frank and I were sitting.

"Staff Sergeant Donahue?" he asked.

"Yeah."

"Sarge, we've got a chopper waiting to take ya up to the 24th Evac in Long Binh."

"What about the Bodes?"

"The who?" He responded with a confused look on his face.

"The Cambodians," I said, pointing to the Bodes. "Where they going?"

"Oh," he said. "It depends on the injury. Most of 'em 'll be goin' to the 3d Field Hospital in Saigon."

"Okay," I said. "That's all I wanted to know."

"You got an SFC Hagey on your list?" Frank inquired.

He ran his finger down the clipboard.

"Here we go, Sarge. The 3d Field."

We stood up, and I put my arm around Frank's neck.

"Take care of yourself," I said.

"I won't be here long," he said. "As soon as I escape, I'll be up to see ya. Want anything from the PX?"

"Two cheeseburgers with everything, a double order of fries, and a chocolate malt."

"You got it," he said.

The medic led us down the ramp. The sultry night air caressed my face with its warm breath along with the smells of diesel exhaust and pungent oriental cooking. Exiting from the well-lit cabin made the night seem especially calm and dark. A few airport lights, with their subdued halos glowing a misty white, stood out against the velvet backdrop. When we reached the bottom of the ramp, they loaded Frank into one of the waiting ambulances. I walked across the tarmac to a medical chopper with its rotors slumped at rest. Once I was strapped into my seat, the pilot started the engine, and within a couple of minutes, we were flying high above Saigon. When we reached the Saigon to Long Binh highway, we followed it northeast. A few miles up the highway, I saw the outline of Ho Ngoc Tao Special Forces Camp on the left side of the road, and that brought back memories of the days when we were training the Bodes there.

A few minutes past the camp, we banked and began our final approach to the 24th Evacuation Hospital. As we neared the ground, I suddenly remembered that I had been there about a year earlier. A helicopter door gunner had suffered a serious sucking chest wound near Song Be, and on the flight back to the 24th, I managed to keep him from drowning in his own blood by using a 50cc syringe to aspirate the blood from his lungs. Within a couple of minutes of landing, they had him in the operating room with IVs going and his chest opened wide. It was probably the most efficient emergency medical work I had ever seen, but the thought of them doing the same kind of thing to my head had me worried.

As our chopper hovered over the landing pad and slowly sat down, I saw four people waiting for me with a stretcher.

"Aw shit," I said to myself. "Here we go."

"Sergeant Donahue," one of them yelled as he grabbed me and tried to lift me onto the stretcher.

"Hey, I can walk," I hollered as I stepped out of the chopper and followed them into a nearby building. Once inside the emergency room, they took my M-16 and web gear and gave me an envelope for my camera, beret, compass, watch, and wallet. I told them that if they didn't mind I'd like to hang on to my montagnard bracelet. They didn't.

I'd been in the jungle a few days so everything in the emergency room seemed especially clean and sterile. From what I could see, a half dozen hospital personnel were busy treating three patients.

"Here, take everything off and put these on," a medic said as he handed me a set of pajamas and a pair of slippers, then escorted me to a chair located behind a curtain. After removing my boots and fatigues, I dropped them on the floor and slipped into the pajamas. They smelled as though they had just been laundered, and it didn't seem right to be putting them over the filth I had accumulated. When the medic returned, he picked up my gear with a sneer, clutching it at arm's length as if he was holding a dead rat.

"Hey, don't throw 'em out," I said.

He gave me a you-gotta-be-kidding look and kept on going.

A couple of minutes later, a specialist six came in and asked me a few personal questions concerning my age, height, weight, allergies, etc. When he left, a doctor and nurse entered. The doctor checked my eyes, ears, nose, and throat, and when he left, the nurse took my vital signs. I was a little bit surprised to see that my blood pressure was up to 146/74. Maybe it had something to do with my phobia of hospitals.

When she got everything she needed, she told me that a Doctor Beazley had ordered a hematocrit and a tetanus toxoid. She also let me know that when I was finished in the emergency room, I'd be going to X ray and then to a Doctor Lawrence in the operating room. She told me that he had been an enlisted man during the Korean War and that his nickname was Snake. A few minutes after she left, the same medic returned with a wheelchair and rolled me out of the emergency room and into X ray. It was 0200 hours.

The X-ray technician hadn't arrived yet, so the medic helped me onto the X-ray table and then left. Waiting on the cold, hard table, I felt out of place and began to shiver. For some reason, I didn't like the smell of the room; there was something unnatural about it.

When the X-ray technician finally arrived, he quickly took several films of my head and left. The medic returned a few minutes later and wheeled me into the operating room. Waiting alone in the dimly lit room, my palms began to perspire as I envisioned the worst. The antiseptic smell of surgical soap and rubber only accentuated my nervous sweat. After a long wait, I was startled when a major walked in carrying a large envelope.

"Staff Sergeant Donahue?" he asked as he turned on a couple of additional lights.

"Yes, sir."

"I'm Doctor Lawrence," he said as he opened the envelope and removed the X rays. He attached them to a viewing screen and turned on the light.

"How do they look, sir?"

"Take a look for yourself."

I wheeled over next to the screen, and he pointed to a dark spot on one of the X rays.

"You have something lodged in the area of your middle ear."

"Any evidence of a fracture or skull depression or anything like that?" I asked nervously.

"No, everything appears to be intact." He smiled.

"That's a relief! I was worried there might be some brain involvement."

"No, nothing that serious. The one thing we have to watch for in a wound like this is a blood clot between the skull and the brain, a subdural hematoma. We'll have to keep an eye on you for a few days."

"Sounds good to me. Is it gonna require general anesthesia?" I asked as he slipped the X rays back into the envelope.

"No, I think we can handle it with a local. Let's get you on the table."

After helping me lie down on the operating table, he turned on a bright overhead light, removed my dressing, and slipped on a pair of surgical gloves.

"I'm gonna give you a few small injections that might sting," he said while filling a syringe with 1 percent Xylocaine.

"The doc's okay," I said to myself as he anesthetized the wound. I had a skin feeling that he was one of the best doctors I had come across. He had that special bedside manner that immediately put me at ease and instilled confidence.

When he finished numbing the wound, he told me that he was going to open it up and remove the devitalized tissue so that it wouldn't become infected when he sewed it up.

"Do whatever ya have to do, sir."

As he worked on the wound, we struck up a conversation, and he told me that he was an avid hunter. I told him about my experiences at Duc Phong and with the Mobile Guerrilla Force. He remarked that as soon as I regained my strength, he would take me on a tour of the hospital and that he would get me any medical supplies or equipment I needed. I told him that the next time I got into Saigon, I would bring him an M-1 sniper rifle with a leather cheek pad, side-mounted scope, and flash suppressor.

In the middle of whatever he was doing, I saw him pick up a straight forceps and could feel him insert it into the wound. A few seconds later I felt something tugging in my middle ear. It wasn't a sharp pain, but I could feel a dull pulling sensation.

"Must have a barb on it," he said as he used the forceps to gently pull and twist. "There you go," he said as he pulled out a piece of blood-covered metal and showed it to me.

"The brass jacket of an AK-47 round," I said as he dropped it into my palm. "Musta gone through some bamboo before it hit me."

"Keep it as a souvenir."

"Thanks, Doc," I said as I closed my hand around it.

When he finished irrigating the wound, he closed it with silk surgical thread and applied a fresh white dressing.

"That should do it," he said as he sat me up and helped me back into the wheelchair.

"How do you feel?"

"Dizzy and nauseated."

"Get a few hours sleep, and you'll feel better."

"Won't argue with that."

"I'll see you at ENT in the morning," he said as he slipped out of his surgical gloves.

"Okay, sir, thanks for everything." He turned off the overhead light and left the room. A short time later, the medic returned and wheeled me out of the building and down a covered walkway.

"Ward Eight," he said as we turned and wheeled into another building.

When we entered the darkened ward, I saw rows of occupied bunks along both walls. Halfway down on the right, we passed a nurse who sat on the edge of a bed trying to comfort someone who was in pain. When we reached the last bed on the right, I was rolled alongside, and the medic pulled down the sheet for me.

"In ya go, Sarge," he said as he helped me out of the wheelchair and onto the edge of the bed. From where I was sitting, most of the wounded appeared to be in bad shape. The guy in the next bed had tubes running out of his mouth and nose, and his shaved head appeared at least double its normal size.

"He's a captain with the 11th Armored Cav. A rocket hit his APC," the medic whispered before leaving. Watching the captain lie there so near to death, I realized how fortunate I was.

"Bac-si," a voice whispered from the shadows.

I turned to see that it was Luc. Seeing him for the first time since Blackjack-33, I was shocked by his appearance; he was skin and bone and looked like one of the walking dead. The skin that covered his protruding cheekbones was stretched tight, and his eyes were sunk deep in their sockets.

"Luc, *sak sa bai,*" I said as he hugged me and then sat at the foot of my bed.

"Hospital numba one," he said. "Have movie at night."

"Glad ya like it."

"We same cowboy, VC same Indian." He smiled.

"How's the food?"

"Much food, *Bac-si;* not good." He pursed his lips in disdain and shook his head. "All food taste same potato."

"They don't put *nuoc mam* on the food?"

"No *nuoc mam*," he said with a serious expression on his face.

"Look like ya lost a little weight."

He lifted his shirt and showed me an eight-inch scar on his stomach.

"I have big operation," he said proudly.

"What's going on here?" a blonde nurse interrupted.

"Just sayin' hello to an old friend."

"You'll have plenty of time for that in the morning," she said, extending her hand and helping him off the bed.

"I come back, *Bac-si*."

"Okay, my friend, see ya in the morning," I said as he and the nurse left, the sound of their voices fading into the night.

Alone in the silent ward, I rested my head on the cool, soft pillow and wondered how Bob and the Bodes were doing. In less than a breath I was deep in sleep.

It had been a long day . . .

News Clipping

Both the U.S. and South Vietnamese commands reported scant ground activity yesterday in South Vietnam.

The Courier-Journal (Louisville), July 19, 1967

EPILOGUE

Tho' much is taken, much abides; and tho'
We are not now that strength which in old days
Moved earth and heaven, that which we are, we are;
One equal temper of heroic hearts,
Made weak by time and fate, but strong in will
To strive, to seek, to find, and not to yield.

ALFRED, LORD TENNYSON

On 1 August 1967, the Mobile Guerrilla Force was redesignated Project Rapid Fire (Provisional Detachment B-36) and under B-36, Detachments A-303 and A-304 became A-361 and A-362. B-36 was also augmented with twenty long-range reconnaissance patrol personnel from the American infantry divisions in the III Corps Tactical Zone of South Vietnam.

In September 1967, Detachment B-36 moved from Trang Sup to a site on the South China Sea at Long Hai. When Projects Omega and Sigma were transferred to MACV-SOG on 1 November 1967, Detachment B-36 assumed the added responsibilities of developing tactical and strategic reconnaissance for II Field Force Vietnam. Project Rapid Fire was redesignated the 3d Mobile Strike Force on 23 May 1968, and grew to a force of three light infantry battalions, a reconnaissance company, and a headquarters company.

In July 1969, the Khmer Serei leader, Dr. Son Ngoc Thanh, sent a representative to Phnom Penh, Cambodia, to meet secretly with Gen. Lon Nol, commander of Cambodia's military forces. Gen. Lon Nol and Dr. Son Ngoc Thanh were unhappy with Prince Norodom Sihanouk's policies toward the Communists and feared the estimated forty-five thousand North Vietnamese and Viet Cong troops in eastern and northeastern Cambodia. At the meeting, it was decided that Special Forces–trained Khmer Serei troops from Vietnam would assist the thirty-two thousand poorly trained troops of Gen. Lon Nol in the overthrow of Prince Sihanouk.

Khmer Serei leaders within the 3d Mobile Strike Force were informed of their role in the pending coup d'état in January 1970, and sent Thach Rinh to Phnom Penh for a final planning meeting with Gen. Lon Nol. In May 1970, the Cambodians of the 3d Mobile Strike Force were flown by U.S. Air Force C-130 aircraft from Long Hai to Phnom Penh's Pochentong Airport. Shortly after their arrival, they engaged Main Force North Vietnamese Army troops, and over the months that followed, were integrated into the Cambodian army.

THE AMERICANS AND CAMBODIANS

Jim Condon—Commander, Mobile Guerrilla Force

In October 1986, the Department of the Army informed me that they had located a James Condon who had served in Vietnam in 1967. They weren't sure that he was the same person that I had been looking for, but after many years of searching, it was my first substantial lead.

That same afternoon I called a Dover, New Hampshire, telephone number and a woman with a southern accent answered the phone. It was Jim's wife, Gail. When she put him on the phone, I immediately sensed that nothing of any real importance had changed; he was still the same person I had known twenty years earlier.

During our conversation, Jim told me that he left Vietnam in 1968 and was assigned to the U.S. Army Training Center at Fort Jackson, South Carolina. Later that year, he volunteered to return to Vietnam and served as a company commander with the 196th Light Infantry Brigade at Landing Zone Baldy.

In 1970, Jim received orders to report to the Infantry School at Fort Benning, Georgia where he became an assistant operations officer in the communications-electronics department. While stationed at Benning, he also graduated from the Advanced Infantry Officer's Course.

Following graduation, he joined the 1st Armored Division at Erlangen, Germany, where he served as the company commander of a mechanized infantry company. In 1975, he was transferred to Ansbach where he became the division's assistant civil-military affairs officer.

In 1977, Jim left Germany and reported to the 24th Infantry Division at Fort Stewart, Georgia. While there, he earned a bachelor's degree in human resources administration and a master's degree in management.

Jim retired from the army in March of 1980, and he and his wife, Gail, now live in Dover, New Hampshire. When I asked Gail how someone from Georgia ended up in New England, she told me that when Jim retired, he closed his eyes and pointed to a spot on the map. It turned out to be Dover.

Jim's military awards and decorations include the:

> Silver Star
> Bronze Star
> Army Commendation Medal (3d Award)

Good Conduct Medal
National Defense Service Medal
Vietnam Service Medal
Republic of Vietnam Campaign Medal
Vietnamese Cross of Gallantry (2d Award)
Armed Forces Reserve Medal
Combat Infantryman's Badge
Master Parachutist Badge
Vietnamese Parachutist Badge

Rinh Kien—Chief Cambodian Medic

Rinh remained with the Mobile Guerrilla Force, Project Rapid Fire, and the 3d Mobile Strike Force until 1970. With the American-sponsored overthrow of Cambodia's Prince Norodom Sihanouk in the spring of 1970, he was airlifted to Phnom Penh, Cambodia. Once the government of Gen. Lon Nol was in power, Rinh was selected to attend the Khmer National Military Academy in Phnom Penh. He graduated in 1973 and quickly rose to the rank of captain.

By 1975, the Khmer Rouge had taken over in Cambodia and were systematically tracking down and murdering everyone who had served with the Americans or the Lon Nol government. Rinh avoided capture and, in April, headed back to Vietnam on foot. Twenty-nine days later, he arrived at his former village in Vinh Binh Province. By then, the Communists had also taken over in Vietnam, but with the help of friends, Rinh managed to conceal his past from the Communist authorities.

Rinh's luck ran out in July 1982 when an informer told the police that he had worked with Special Forces. Rinh once again averted capture and headed back to Cambodia, where he hid and lived as a woodcutter near Kampong Speu. Vietnamese security forces were soon on his trail, but he evaded them and headed northwest to the city of Battambang.

When he arrived there, security forces from the Cambodian National Front arrested and jailed him. After four days of intense interrogation, Rinh convinced his captors that he had never worked for the Americans or the government of Lon Nol. He also convinced them that he was on his way to a job in Paris and that if they didn't execute him, he would send them money from France. They believed his story, and a few days later, Rinh made it to the Thai border and the Site #2 refugee camp. While at Site #2 he applied for permission to emigrate to the United States. In January 1987, he made it to Seattle, Washington, where he found part-time work as a medical interpreter.

In November 1997, I linked up with Rinh for the first time in over thirty years. When I asked him if he ever sent the money to the members of the Cambodian National Front he said, "No, Donahue. I lost their address."

Danh—Silent Weapon Specialist, 3d Platoon

Danh was killed in Cambodia.

Robert "Bob" Cole—Commander, 3d Platoon

In 1978 I decided that I was going to write a book about the Quan Loi operation, and during the years that followed, I located all of the surviving American members of the team.

I reestablished contact with Bob when I ran into him at the July 1979 Special Forces Association convention in Washington, D.C. More than ten years had passed since I had seen him, but it didn't surprise me that he was still as soft-spoken as ever. Over a spaghetti dinner that night, I tried to get him to talk about the war, but it proved difficult.

When I finally got him to open up, he told me that he left Vietnam in 1968 and was assigned to the 7th Special Forces Group (Airborne) at Fort Bragg, North Carolina, where he taught small-unit tactics. Later that year, he was transferred to the 46th Special Forces Company (Airborne) in Thailand, where he worked with the Thai Special Forces at Nampungdam.

Bob told me that he volunteered to return to Vietnam in 1969. When he arrived in country, he was assigned to MACV-SOG's Command and Control North at Da Nang. About halfway through his yearlong tour at Da Nang, he took a weekend R & R and caught a flight south to visit some old Vietnamese comrades who lived in Tay Ninh. On his first night back in town, he took a couple of friends to the Bamboo Club for grilled buffalo steaks and cold Beer 33.

Bob completed what was to be his last tour in Vietnam in 1970 and returned to the 6th Special Forces Group (Airborne) at Fort Bragg to retire as a master sergeant. As a retiree, he told me, he found himself faced with a dilemma. He was originally from Brooklyn and couldn't decide whether to return there or remain in North Carolina. He decided to flip a coin. If it turned up heads he'd go back to New York, and if it was tails, he'd stay in North Carolina. Well, New York lost, and Bob moved to Charlotte, North Carolina, where he went to work for the post office. He worked for the post office for twenty-one years and retired in September 1994.

Bob has five grown children and in his spare time enjoys surfing the net and fishing for trout and smallmouth bass.

Bob's military awards and decorations include the:

Silver Star
Bronze Star (2d Award)
Purple Heart

Army Commendation Medal
Good Conduct Medal (4th Award)
National Defense Service Medal
Vietnam Service Medal
Republic of Vietnam Campaign Medal
Vietnamese Cross of Gallantry
Combat Infantryman's Badge
Special Forces Tab
Senior Parachutist Badge
Thai Parachutist Badge
Thai Fourragere

Tan Dara Thach—Khmer Serei Representative

From Cao Lanh, Tan continued to provide recruits for the Mobile Guerrilla Force, Project Rapid Fire, and the 3d Mobile Strike Force.

In October, 1970, Tan was flown to Phnom Penh, Cambodia, where he became the chief of staff of the Cambodian Army's 48th Infantry Brigade. While assigned to the 48th, he attended training at the U.S. Army Intelligence School on Okinawa. In December 1972, he became the assistant director of the Khmer Republic's Foreign Aid Office in Phnom Penh. Tan graduated from the Khmer National Military Academy in September 1973 and was promoted to lieutenant colonel in early 1975. Shortly after his promotion, he received orders to attend the Command and General Staff College at Fort Leavenworth, Kansas, but his plans were interrupted when the Khmer Rouge took over in April 1975.

Following the Khmer Rouge takeover, Tan and his wife and daughter escaped from Phnom Penh and hid in the forest near the village of Bang Crum. In July 1975, he and his family again narrowly evaded capture by Khmer

Rouge security forces and walked back to the village of Ke Sach in Kien Toung Province, Vietnam. By then, the Communists had also taken over in Vietnam, and to avoid arrest, Tan and his family fled to Saigon where they adopted Chinese names and hid with friends in Cholon.

In September 1975, Tan, his family, and a few friends made it to Hue where they hoped to cross the borders into Laos and Thailand. Shortly after their arrival in Hue, they were arrested, jailed, and interrogated by Vietnamese security forces. Tan convinced his captors that he was a Cambodian-born businessman who didn't speak Vietnamese. He was released from jail in November 1975 and returned to Saigon.

While in Saigon, Tan again convinced the authorities that he was a Cambodian-born businessman and obtained visas for himself and his family. In October 1978, they flew to Paris where he found work as a dispatching agent with the Renault Automobile Company.

In August 1980, they immigrated to the United States, where Tan earned a bachelor's degree in mechanical engineering and a master's in engineering. Tan is the president of the Khmers-Kampuchea-Krom Federation and devotes much of his time to promoting the interests of Khmer Krom who live in Vietnam and abroad.

Men—Rifleman, 3d Platoon
  Men was killed in Cambodia.

Sarine—Grenadier, 3d Platoon
  Sarine was killed in Cambodia.

Set—Rifleman, 3d Platoon
  Set was killed in Cambodia.

Francis "Blackjack" Kelly—Commanding Officer,
5th Special Forces Group (Airborne)

Blackjack returned to Fort Bragg in July 1967 to assume command of the Institute of Strategic and Special Operations. In June 1970, he was transferred to Denver, where he served as the senior military adviser to the state of Colorado.

The colonel retired from the army in August 1972 to become a professor of economics and political science at Loretto Heights College in Denver. Blackjack authored nine books and wrote the foreword to my second book, *Mobile Guerrilla Force*.

Colonel Kelly died on 26 December 1997 and is buried at Fort Logan National Cemetery.

Blackjack's military awards and decorations include the:

> Silver Star
> Legion of Merit (4th Award)
> Bronze Star (2d Award)
> Purple Heart
> Air Medal (5th Award)
> Order of Military Merit
> National Defense Service Medal
> European-African-Middle Eastern Campaign Medal
> Army of Occupation Medal (Germany)
> Armed Forces Expeditionary Medal
> Vietnam Service Medal
> Republic of Vietnam Campaign Medal
> Combat Infantryman's Badge
> Special Forces Tab
> Master Parachutist Badge
> Vietnamese Cross of Gallantry
> Vietnamese Parachutist Badge

Son Thai Hien—Machine gunner, 2d Platoon

In November 1997, I linked up with Son for the first time since September 1967. When I arrived at the Philadelphia airport, I spotted him standing in the crowd. He didn't say a word and was waiting to see if I would recognize him. Of course I did, and after an emotional reunion, he took me to a Vietnamese restaurant for lunch. Over jasmine tea and bowls of steaming Vietnamese soup, we looked at faded photographs and talked about old friends.

Son told me that as a member of the 3d Mobile Strike Force, he attended jump school in Nha Trang and that his company was airlifted to Phnom Penh in the spring of 1970. After the overthrow of Prince Sihanouk, he was assigned to the Cambodian Army's 43d Infantry Brigade at Borey Keila. In October, 1971, he was selected to attend leadership training in Chi Lang. Following graduation, he rose to the rank of captain and became the commander of the 271st Battalion at Kampong Cham.

In a December 1973 battle with the Khmer Rouge at Chero, Son lost his right leg—above the knee—to a claymore mine. He was evacuated to the 701st Military Hospital in Phnom Penh and, in April 1974, was fitted with an artificial leg.

On 17 April 1975, the Khmer Rouge took over in Cambodia, and to avoid execution, Son decided that he, his wife, and two children would attempt to walk back to Vietnam. It took them seventeen days, and when they arrived in Tay Ninh, he was arrested by Communist authorities and sent to Tra Vinh prison. For five years, he was beaten and interrogated regularly but never admitted his involvement with Special Forces.

When Son was released from prison, he told his wife that he couldn't live under communism, and he started to plan his escape to Thailand on foot. In September 1981, he, his wife, and three children began their long march across Vietnam and Cambodia and, during their thirty-three-day ordeal, had many close encounters with Vietnamese and Khmer-Rouge security forces and bandits.

When they reached Thailand, they were sent to the *Khao-Y-Dang* Refugee Camp and remained there for almost two years. In September, 1984, he, his wife, two sons, and four daughters immigrated to the United States. Currently, they live in Philadelphia. Son is the president of the United Cambodian-American Association and devotes much of his time to helping his fellow Khmer Krom veterans.

Kien—Grenadier, 3d Platoon

Kien was killed in Cambodia.

Kim—Rifleman, 3d Platoon

Kim was killed in Cambodia.

James "Bo" Gritz

While attending the 1979 Special Forces Association convention in Washington, D.C., I linked up with Bo. At that time, he was staying at a friend's home in suburban Washington and invited me to stay with him while I was in town. The following morning, we were up before first light, doing push-ups on the front lawn. By the time dawn cracked, we were well into a long-distance run over the rolling suburban hills.

While working up a good sweat, Bo told me that he left Vietnam in 1968 to attend the army's Chinese Language School in Monterey, California. When he completed language training in 1970, he received orders to attend the Command and General Staff College at Fort

Leavenworth, Kansas. After graduating in 1972, he moved to Washington, D.C., to become an aide to Gen. William C. Westmoreland, who, at that time, was chief of staff of the army. Later that year, Gen. Creighton W. Abrams replaced Westmoreland as chief of staff, and Bo received orders to enroll in a full-time graduate program at the American University in Washington.

Upon completion of his graduate studies in 1974, he became the commander of the 3d Battalion, 7th Special Forces Group (Airborne), in Panama. In 1976, he returned to Washington and the Pentagon to become the chief of congressional relations for the office of the secretary of defense.

That night over dinner, Bo told me that he had been asked by Lt. Gen. Harold Aaron, deputy director of the Defense Intelligence Agency, to retire from the military to organize and command a civilian prisoner-of-war rescue operation. He explained that General Aaron and others within the military and intelligence establishments knew that American prisoners of war were being held in Southeast Asia.

Bo retired from the army in 1979 and was given a cover position as a program manager with the Hughes Aircraft Company in El Segundo, California. Gen. Eugene Tighe, Aaron's superior at the Defense Intelligence Agency, also made the necessary arrangements for Texas billionaire H. Ross Perot to front the "private-sector" operation.

Since his retirement, Bo has organized four major prisoner-of-war rescue missions: Velvet Hammer, in early 1981; Grand Eagle, in late 1981; Lazarus, in late 1982; and Lazarus Omega, in early 1983.

Bo lives in Kamiah, Idaho, where he is a conservative radio-talk-show host and land developer.

Bo's military awards and decorations include the:

Silver Star (3d Award)
Legion of Merit (2d Award)
Distinguished Flying Cross
Soldier's Medal
Bronze Star (8th Award)
Purple Heart
Air Medal (26th Award)
National Defense Service Medal
Vietnam Service Medal
Republic of Vietnam Campaign Medal
Vietnamese Cross of Gallantry
Gold Star of Cambodia
Combat Infantryman's Badge
Special Forces Tab
Ranger Tab
Master Parachutist Badge
SCUBA Badge
Pathfinder Badge
Vietnamese Parachutist Badge
Panamanian Parachutist Badge
Honduran Parachutist Badge
Colombian Parachutist Badge

Thang Kieng—Rifleman, 3d Platoon

In November, 1997, I linked up with Thang at a Buddhist temple in Lowell, Massachusetts. Over the years nothing of any importance had changed. He was still as hard as woodpecker lips and retained those soldierly qualities that I had admired when we served together in the Mobile Guerrilla Force.

Over dinner that night, Thang told me that he suffered serious gunshot wounds to the head and shoulder during an October 1967 battle near Ton Le Chon. When he recovered from his wounds, he returned to Long Hai to serve with Project Rapid Fire and later the 3d Mobile Strike Force.

Following the overthrow of Prince Norodom Sihanouk in the spring of 1970, Thang was assigned to the Cambodian Army's 1st Infantry Division in Phnom Penh. He soon became a company commander and was again seriously wounded in a 6 February 1972 battle at Viheur Sour. Thang was evacuated to the 701st Military Hospital in Phnom Penh and returned to his unit following his recovery.

Thang's wife was murdered by the Khmer Rouge in 1975, and he and his son and daughter escaped to Pursat Province where he continued to fight as a guerrilla. He and his children made it to the *Khao-Y-Dang* Refugee Camp in Thailand in November 1979. In August 1981, they immigrated to the United States. Thang and his wife now live in Providence, Rhode Island.

Son—Machine Gunner, 3d Platoon
    Son was killed in Cambodia.

Suol—Rifleman, 3d Platoon
    Suol recovered from his wounds, but was later killed in Cambodia.

Huong—Rifleman, 3d Platoon
    Huong was killed in Cambodia.

Frank Hagey, Deputy Commander, 2d Platoon
    Locating the third American member of the team was sheer luck. When I called the Vietnam Veterans' Outreach Center in Queens, New York, in April, 1982, a familiar

voice answered the phone. It was Frank. The last time I had
heard his voice was on a hot summer day in August 1967.
Early in the morning on that particular day we boarded
boats at the Special Forces camp at Ben Soi for an operation called "Picnic."

After motoring down the Vam Co Dong River, we off-
loaded on the north bank of the river eight and a half klicks
northwest of Ben Soi. Moving northeast for a few hundred
meters, we entered a fortified Viet Cong base area and
immediately made heavy contact with an undetermined
number of Viet Cong. While attempting to move one of the
wounded Americans to safety, Frank was hit on the right
side of his head by an exploding rocket-propelled grenade,
which caused extensive skull damage and left him criti-
cally wounded.

During our telephone conversation, Frank told me that
after we loaded him on a medevac chopper, he received
emergency medical treatment in Saigon and was then sent
to Japan and ultimately to Walter Reed Army Hospital.
Once at Walter Reed, they found that he had complete loss
of hearing in one ear and partial loss in the other; he also
had suffered paralysis of the left arm. While recovering
from his wounds, he learned to read lips. When some of his
hearing returned, he was issued hearing aids for both ears.

When he was released from the hospital, Frank returned
to Fort Bragg and the 3d Special Forces Group (Airborne)
to continue physical therapy at Womack Army Hospital.
After a year of therapy, he went back to Walter Reed to
have a plastic plate attached over the hole in his skull.
When he was reassigned to Bragg's 6th Special Forces
Group (Airborne), he received the traumatic news that
he would no longer be allowed to remain a Green Beret.
Because of his medical problems, he was told that he
was being transferred to the XVIII Airborne Corps's 50th

Signal Battalion at Fort Bragg. Listening to Frank talk about the transfer, I could sense that it hurt him more than anything that had happened to him in the war. It was a wound that would take many years to heal.

Frank retired from the army as a first sergeant in July 1973. As a retiree, he worked in a drug and alcohol counseling program in Korea and later as a volunteer at the VA's Vietnam Veteran's Outreach Center in Queens, New York.

Frank and his wife now live on a farm near Fort Drum.

Frank's military awards and decorations include the:

> Silver Star
> Purple Heart (5th Award)
> Good Conduct Medal (3d Award)
> National Defense Service Medal
> Vietnam Service Medal
> Republic of Vietnam Campaign Medal
> Vietnamese Cross of Gallantry
> Combat Infantryman's Badge
> Special Forces Tab
> Master Parachutist Badge
> Glider Badge

Dien—Headquarters Section Interpreter

Dien was last seen at a classified site in Thailand in 1972. He was a major at the time. He was later killed in Cambodia.

Hoi—Rifleman, 3d Platoon

Hoi was killed in Cambodia.

Ernest "Duke" Snider, Commander, 1st Platoon

Three months after making contact with Frank Hagey, I located the fourth American member of the team. I was manning a veteran's information table at the July 1982 Special Forces Association convention in Atlantic City, New Jersey, when I spotted someone wearing a cowboy hat in the hotel lobby. When his voice bellowed across the room, I knew that it was the Duke.

That night, we sat in my hotel room talking, and he brought me up to date on what he'd been doing since 1967. During our conversation, I could tell that it was difficult for him to recall things he had been trying for so many years to forget. His wife Elizabeth later told me she was surprised that he would sit down and talk about it at all; he never had done so before.

As we reminisced into the early morning hours, Duke told me that when he completed his tour with the Mobile Guerrilla Force, he was reassigned to the Special Forces Training Group (Airborne) at the John F. Kennedy Center for Special Warfare at Fort Bragg. In 1970, he again left for Vietnam and that time was stationed with the B Team at An Loc. Later that year he returned to working with Cambodians when he was assigned to Forces Armees Nationales Khmer in Bien Hoa.

Duke told me that while he was in Bien Hoa, he ran into his old friend, Chote. The 1st Platoon's interpreter had become a captain in the Cambodian Army and at that time was operating out of one of the camps in the Seven Mountains area of South Vietnam. After his tour with Forces Armees Nationales Khmer, Duke received orders to report to the 75th Rangers at Fort Hood, Texas, and in 1973 was assigned to the Joint Casualty Resolution Center in Nakhon Phanom, Thailand.

Following the war in Southeast Asia, Duke returned to the States to serve at Fort Stewart, Georgia, and to attend the Sergeants Major Academy at Fort Bliss, Texas. After graduating from the academy, he reported to Fort Lewis, Washington, and then to the 10th Special Forces Group (Airborne) at Fort Devens, Massachusetts. Duke told me that the high point of his tour with the 10th was a nine-month mission to Liberia, Africa.

Duke retired from the army in 1983 as the Command Sergeant Major of the 2d Battalion, 10th Special Forces Group (Airborne). At present, he works as an immigration examiner at Point Roberts, Washington, and lives in nearby Sumas. Duke has three grown children and, in his spare time, enjoys fishing for salmon and gardening.

Duke's military awards and decorations include the:

Silver Star
Bronze Star (2d Award)
Meritorious Service Medal
Purple Heart
Joint Service Commendation Medal
Army Commendation Medal (6th Award)
Good Conduct Medal (6th Award)
National Defense Service Medal
Vietnam Service Medal
Army Service Ribbon
Overseas Service Ribbon
Republic of Vietnam Campaign Medal
NCO Professional Development Ribbon (5th Award)
Vietnamese Cross of Gallantry (2d Award)
Combat Infantryman's Badge
Special Forces Tab
Master Parachutist Badge
Vietnamese Parachutist Badge

Chote—Interpreter, 1st Platoon
Chote was killed in Cambodia.

Luc—Platoon Sergeant, 3d Platoon

When Luc recovered from his abdominal wound, he was released from the 24th Evacuation Hospital in Long Binh and returned to Trang Sup. He remained with the Mobile Guerrilla Force, Project Rapid Fire, and the Third Mobile Strike Force, and was later killed in Cambodia.

Phone—Rifleman, 3d Platoon

Phone was killed in Cambodia.

Nair—Rifleman, 3d Platoon

Nair was killed in Cambodia.

Roger Smith—Radio Operator, Headquarters Section

On a cold November day in 1982, I was at my desk working on a report when the phone rang. It was Roger, calling from California. After joking about Buffalo's weather, he told me that, through the "old boy" network, word had filtered down to him that I was putting together a book on the Mobile Guerrilla Force. Roger was very excited about the project because he felt that a good nonfiction book could do a lot for the image of Vietnam veterans in general and Special Forces in particular. He also told me that he would send me copies of his Mobile Guerrilla Force photographs and would make a tape recording of everything he could remember about the Quan Loi operation.

During our conversation, Roger informed me that he returned to the States in 1968 to serve as a radio operator with the 3d and 6th Special Forces Groups (Airborne) at Fort Bragg. Later that year, he volunteered to return to Vietnam, and served a year with Detachment A-235 at Nhon Co. In 1970, he was transferred to the 1st Special Forces Group (Airborne) on Okinawa, and in 1971, he again volunteered to return to Vietnam. During that tour, he served with MACV-SOG's Command and Control Central and operated out of Kontum with Recon Team Hawaii.

Roger was transferred to the 46th Special Forces Company (Airborne) in Thailand in 1972 and, while there, crossed paths with one of the Bodes who had fought with him and Jim Condon at Quan Loi. The Bode had received a commission as a third lieutenant in the Cambodian Army and told Roger that he was on his way back to the war in Cambodia.

Roger received orders to report to Fort Bragg and the 7th Special Forces Group (Airborne) in 1974, and in 1975, he was transferred to the Special Forces Detachment in Korea. While in Korea, he served as the HALO adviser to the Korean Special Forces.

In 1980, he returned to the States to become an infantry first sergeant at Ford Ord, California. After graduating from the Sergeants Major Academy in 1983, he applied for an appointment as a warrant officer and reassignment back into Special Forces. Roger was appointed as a warrant officer in 1984. He was assigned to Operational Detachment A-175, 3d Battalion, 1st Special Forces Group (Airborne), Fort Lewis, Washington. While assigned to the 1st Group, he served as the executive officer of the SCUBA team.

In January 1988, Roger received orders to the 1st Special Forces Group (Airborne) on Okinawa, where he served as the team leader of the SCUBA team.

Roger retired as a chief warrant officer in February 1992. He and his wife live in Las Vegas, Nevada, where he is a security supervisor at the Nevada test site. In his spare time, Roger enjoys working on his Corvette.

Roger's military awards and decorations include the:

Bronze Star
Meritorious Service Medal
Army Commendation Medal
Air Medal
Good Conduct Medal
National Defense Service Medal
Vietnam Service Medal (7th Award)
Republic of Vietnam Campaign Medal
Armed Forces Expeditionary Medal
NCO Professional Development Ribbon
   (5th Award)
Army Service Ribbon
Overseas Service Ribbon (6th Award)
Vietnamese Cross of Gallantry
Combat Infantryman's Badge
Master Parachutist Badge
Special Forces Tab
Ranger Tab
Pathfinder Badge
SCUBA Badge
German Parachutist Badge
Republic of China Parachutist Badge
Thai Parachutist Badge
Republic of Korea Parachutist Badge
Vietnamese Parachutist Badge

Truong—Rifleman, 3d Platoon
   Truong was killed in Cambodia.

Hoa—Rifleman, 3d Platoon
   Hoa was killed in Cambodia.

Larry "Stik" Rader—Commander, Reconnaissance
Platoon

In February 1983, I put together a team of Vietnam veterans to make a parachute jump and a seven-day, one-
hundred-mile run across Death Valley, California. One
of the first to volunteer was Stik Rader. He was as skinny as ever and looked every inch the long-distance run-
ner. During the run, we passed places with names like
Ubehebe Crater, Hell's Gate, Furnace Creek, and Bad-
water, and talked about Dong Xoai, Song Be, Trang Sup,
and Quan Loi.

As we ran, Stik told me that when he returned to the
States in October 1967 he became a foreign weapons instructor at the John F. Kennedy Center at Fort Bragg. In
1968, he volunteered to return to Vietnam and was assigned to MACV-SOG at Da Nang and later at Long
Thanh. Upon completion of his tour, he volunteered for
duty with the 46th Special Forces Company (Airborne) in
Thailand, where he worked on a classified project with the
Thai Special Forces at Phitsanulok.

Stik was transferred to the 1st Special Forces Group
(Airborne) on Okinawa in 1970. In 1971, he again volunteered to return to Vietnam. During that tour, he was
assigned to MACV-SOG's Command and Control Central
as a team leader with Recon Team Texas. In 1972, he returned to working with Cambodians when he was transferred to the Forces Armees Nationales Khmer Training
Center in Phouc Tuy Province.

After completing his last tour in Vietnam in 1973, Stik
returned to the 5th Special Forces Group (Airborne) at
Fort Bragg. In 1974, he left again for Southeast Asia and
the Military Advisory Assistance Group Laos. In 1975, he
returned to Thailand to work with the Thai Advisory

Group in Bangkok. While in Bangkok, he ran into one of the Cambodians from the Recon Platoon at a bar on Pat Pong Street. He told Stik that some of the Bodes from the Mobile Guerrilla Force had survived the Vietnamese, Prince Sihanouk, Lon Nol, and the Khmer Rouge, and that they were pressing on from camps located along the Thai-Cambodian border.

Stik completed his assignment in Thailand in 1976, and again returned to the 5th Special Forces Group (Airborne) at Fort Bragg. In 1977, he became an instructor and operations sergeant with the Georgetown University Army ROTC. In 1978, he attended the Sergeants Major Academy at Fort Bliss, Texas. After graduating from the academy, he attended the army's Korean Language School in Monterey, California. When he completed language training, he was assigned to the Eighth Army Headquarters in Korea. In 1981, he became the first sergeant of the Honor Guard Company of the United Nations Command in Yongsan.

Stik left Korea in 1982 and was assigned as the detachment sergeant major of the San Diego State College Army ROTC. In 1985, he asked to return to Special Forces and was assigned as the sergeant major of A Company, 3d Battalion, 1st Special Forces Group (Airborne) at Fort Lewis, Washington.

Stik retired from the army in February, 1986, and was last sighted at the Maharajah Hotel in the Republic of the Philippines.

Stik's military awards and decorations include the:

Distinguished Flying Cross
Bronze Star (5th Award)
Army Commendation Medal (3d Award)
Purple Heart

Air Medal
Defense Meritorious Service Medal
Joint Service Commendation Medal
Good Conduct Medal (8th Award)
National Defense Service Medal
Vietnam Service Medal
Republic of Vietnam Campaign Medal
Vietnamese Cross of Gallantry
Combat Infantryman's Badge
Special Forces Tab
Master Parachutist Badge
Thai Parachutist Badge
Korean Parachutist Badge

Suong—Rifleman, 3d Platoon
Suong was killed in Cambodia.

Huon—Rifleman, 3d Platoon
Huon survived the war and is believed to be living in Arizona.

Dung—Rifleman, 3d Platoon
Dung was killed in Cambodia.

Chem—Rifleman, 3d Platoon
Chem survived the war and is believed to be living in Texas.

Jim Donahue—Deputy Commander, 3d Platoon
On 10 August 1967, I was released from the 24th Evacuation Hospital in Long Binh and returned to our base of operations at Trang Sup Special Forces Camp. With constant ringing in my left ear, devastating head-

aches, and what appeared to be a permanent partial loss of hearing, I knew that at some point I would be found unfit for Special Forces duty. It was then that I made the difficult decision to leave the army and return to Buffalo to attend college. It was my intention to study anthropology and one day return to Vietnam as a civilian to help the montagnards and Cambodians.

Following our 13 August 1967 raid on the Viet Cong base complex north of Ben Soi Special Forces Camp, I returned to my home in Buffalo and registered as a student at the State University of New York at Buffalo. In September 1970, I received a bachelor's degree in anthropology, and in February 1974, a master of science degree. By the time I finished college, there were few employment opportunities in Vietnam, so I went to work for the United States Department of Labor's Veterans Employment & Training Service.

In 1996, my second book—*Mobile Guerrilla Force*—was published by the Naval Institute Press, Saint Martin's Press, and in Chinese by the Qunzhong Publishing Company in the Peoples Republic of China. My third book—*Blackjack-33*—was published by Ballantine Books in September 1999.

I live in Glenwood, New York, with my wife, Sandi, and have two grown children.

My military awards and decorations include the:

> Silver Star
> Bronze Star (3d Award)
> Purple Heart
> Air Medal (2d Award)
> Good Conduct Medal (Army and Marine Corps)
> National Defense Service Medal

Armed Forces Expeditionary Medal
Marine Corps Expeditionary Medal (Cuba)
Vietnam Service Medal
Republic of Vietnam Campaign Ribbon
Vietnamese Cross of Gallantry
Combat Medical Badge
Special Forces Tab
Parachutist Badge
Vietnamese Parachutist Badge
Cross of the Netherlands
German Performance Badge
German Sports Ribbon
German Shooting Badge
Thai Marine Amphibious Reconnaissance Badge
Thai Marine SCUBA Badge
Thai Marine Parachutist Badge
Union of Myanmar Parachutist Badge
New York State Conspicuous Service Cross
New York State Military Commendation Medal
New York Guard Service Medal

Nuong—Grenadier, 3d Platoon
Nuong was killed in Cambodia.

Binh—Squad Leader, 3d Platoon
Binh suffered a chest wound on Operation Picnic—the August 1967 raid on the Viet Cong base complex north of Ben Soi Special Forces camp. When he recovered from his wounds, he returned to Project Rapid fire and the 3d Mobile Strike Force. Binh was killed in Cambodia.

Kim Lai—Platoon Sergeant, 2d Platoon
Following his tour with the Mobile Guerrilla Force, Kim served as a company commander with MACV-SOG's

Command and Control South at Ban Me Thuot. In the spring of 1970, Kim returned to the 3d Mobile Strike Force at Long Hai to participate in the coup d'état in Cambodia. Following the installation of Gen. Lon Nol, he became a captain in the Cambodian Army. When Phnom Penh fell to the Khmer Rouge on 17 April 1975, Kim was captured but escaped execution by concealing his identity. He was sent to a Khmer Rouge reeducation camp where he was beaten and tortured regularly. A year after his capture, he escaped and walked back to his home in Soc Trang, Vietnam.

When Kim arrived in Soc Trang, he was arrested and imprisoned by the Vietnamese Communists. He escaped from the Vietnamese prison in 1979, and after making it back to Cambodia on foot, he joined a Cambodian guerrilla group that was fighting the Khmer Rouge along the Thai-Cambodian border. In August 1982, he was wounded for the ninth time and was treated by the Thai Red Cross at a refugee camp in Thailand. Kim and his wife and two daughters immigrated to Lowell, Massachusetts, in May 1984.

A week before Thanksgiving 1997, I attended a Khmer-Kampuchea-Krom Federation meeting in Cherry Hill, New Jersey, and linked up with Kim for the first time in over thirty years. It was a reunion that I will never forget.

While enjoying a Cambodian feast at Son Thai Hien's home, we talked about the wars in Vietnam and Cambodia and the men we had fought with. As Kim and I talked, he never let go of my hand, and I found it difficult to believe that a man who had suffered so much could retain his monklike qualities.

After dinner Kim lay down on the couch and died.

Bill "Fergy" Ferguson, Commander, 2d Platoon

The only American member of the team who didn't make it home from the war in Southeast Asia was Bill Ferguson. Fergy was killed in action near Ben Soi Special Forces Camp in August 1967. For the heroism exhibited on that fatal mission, he was posthumously awarded the Distinguished Service Cross, our nation's second highest award for valor. The citation reads as follows:

For extraordinary heroism in connection with military operations involving conflict with an armed hostile force in the Republic of Vietnam: Sergeant First Class Ferguson distinguished himself by exceptionally valorous actions on 13 August 1967 while serving as platoon leader of a Mobile Guerrilla Task Force on a combat mission deep in hostile territory. When another company of the same unit came under attack from a numerically superior Viet Cong force, Sergeant Ferguson immediately volunteered to lead his men to their aid. Upon reaching the scene of the battle, he moved freely among his men directing their assault although exposed to withering automatic weapons fire. An enemy grenade seriously wounded him as he attacked a hostile position, but he refused medical aid and continued to press the offensive. With complete disregard for his own safety, Sergeant Ferguson directed deadly fire on the insurgents and hurled numerous grenades into their positions. He moved openly through the bullet-swept area time after time to inspire his men to greater efforts. He was mortally wounded while leading his men with dauntless courage in the face of grave danger. Sergeant First Class Ferguson's extraordinary heroism and devotion to duty, at the cost of his life, were in keeping with the highest traditions of the military service and reflect great credit upon himself, his unit, and the United States Army.

De Oppresso Liber

GLOSSARY

Ace bandage   Elastic bandage used to cover and add pressure to dressings and splints.

Air America   CIA proprietary airline.

AK-47   Standard automatic infantry rifle used by the Viet Cong and North Vietnamese Army.

ALO   Air liaison officer.

AO   Area of operations.

A-1E Skyraider   Single-engine, propeller-driven fighter-bomber.

APC   Armored personnel carrier or aspirin, phenacetin, and caffeine.

ARVN   Army of the Republic of Vietnam.

A Team   Special Forces operational detachment that normally consisted of twelve men.

azimuth   A compass direction.

bac-si   Doctor.

BAR belt   Japanese-made ammunition belt and pouches intended to hold magazines for the Browning automatic rifle. The MGF used them to hold M-16 magazines. Each pouch held five magazines.

BA-386   Magnesium battery for the PRC-25 radio.

beaucoup   French for many. Often used by Vietnamese and Cambodian troops.

Benadryl   A strong antihistamine used to counter an allergic reaction.

betel nut   An opiate chewed by many people in Southeast Asia. It stains the user's lips red and teeth black.

B-52 Heavy American bomber.

Biere la Rue Vietnamese-brewed beer.

Biere 33 Vietnamese-brewed beer.

Big Red One 1st Infantry Division (American).

black box Top secret electronic equipment carried onboard U-2 spy plane. Unlike those electronic countermeasure systems that filled enemy radar screens with clutter, the System 13A device gave no indication to the enemy that the information displayed on his screen was false.

bo-chi-huy Headquarters.

Bode An abbreviation for Cambodian.

body bag Rubberized bag with a zipper and carrying handles that was used to carry the dead from the battlefield.

break contact The tactic of disengaging from contact with an enemy force.

B Team Exercised operational control over subordinate Special Forces A Teams.

bush The field areas where infantry units operated.

canister round 40mm M-79 grenade launcher round that is similar to, but larger than, a buckshot round that is fired from a shotgun.

CBU Antipersonnel Cluster Bomb Unit.

cc Cubic centimeter.

CCC Command & Control Central at Kontum. Coordinated SOG missions in Cambodia and Laos.

CCN Command & Control North at Da Nang. Coordinated SOG missions in Laos, Vietnam's demilitarized zone, and North Vietnam.

CCS Command & Control South at Ban Me Thuot. Coordinated SOG missions in Cambodia.

C-4 High explosive puttylike material. Small pieces would burn at a high temperature and could be used to heat water and rations.

CG Commanding general.

chao ong Hello (male).

Charlie Viet Cong.

chey-yo Victory. Cambodian battle cry.

CH-47 Large American helicopter used to transport troops and equipment.

Chicom Chinese Communist.

Chinese Nungs Mike Force troops who were of Chinese ancestry.

chloroquine Drug used to prevent and treat malaria.

Cholon Chinese section of Saigon.

chopper Helicopter.

CIDG Civilian Irregular Defense Group.

Citroen French-made automobile.

claymore mine Mine packed with explosive plastic and rigged to spray hundreds of steel pellets.

Clyde Viet Cong.

codeine Narcotic analgesic used to treat moderate to severe pain.

Col. Colonel.

commo check Radio check.

commo pad Contained a list of code names of American members of the Mobile Guerrilla Force and the primary and secondary radio frequencies of MGF and supporting units.

COMUSMACV Commander, U.S. Military Assistance Command, Vietnam.

C-130 Four-engine, medium-sized combat assault aircraft capable of landing on improvised air strips.

C-123 Two-engine, medium-sized, combat assault aircraft capable of landing on unimproved air strips.

COSVN Abbreviation for Central Office of the Communist Party of South Vietnam.

CP Command post.

CS gas grenade Used by the MGF to assist in breaking contact with the enemy.

C Team Exercised operational control over subordinate Special Forces B Teams.

C-3 Special Forces C Team in Bien Hoa.

CTZ Corps tactical zone.

cut down Making an incision over a vein so that it could be elevated and an IV needle inserted. This procedure was used when the patient's blood vessels had collapsed due to shock.

cyclo Three-wheeled bicycle taxi with a large seat used to transport one or two passengers.

dai-uy Captain.

DASC Direct air support center.

debride To surgically remove dead and devitalized tissue from a wound.

Demerol Analgesic used to relieve moderate to severe pain.

detonator cord Detonation cord for explosive charges.

deuce-and-a-half Two-and-a-half-ton truck.

Dianna one-time pad Used by radio operators to encode and decode messages.

Dien Bien Phu Major battle where the French were defeated by the Viet Minh.

Dong Nai Valley Formed by the Dong Nai River as it flows through War Zone D.

Dong Xoai Special Forces camp in Phuoc Long Province.

Duc Phong Special Forces camp in Phuoc Long Province.

dung-lai Don't move.

Dustoff A medical evacuation helicopter.

DZ Drop zone.

eight-digit fix When a forward air controller provided a MGF unit with his estimate of their location—within ten meters.

emesis basin A sterile basin used in the suture process. It also fit under the patient's chin and was used to collect vomit.

ENT Ear, nose, and throat.

epinephrine Injectable hormone that increases blood pressure by constricting blood vessels and stimulating the heart.

FAC Forward air controller.

FANK Forces Armees Nationales Khmeres.

fast mover Jet aircraft.

F-4 Phantom Twin-engine, supersonic fighter-bomber.

5th Special Forces Group (Airborne) headquarters Located in Nha Trang. Provided leadership and support to four C Teams and other special operations detachments located in South Vietnam.

fifty-one Fifty-one-caliber machine gun.

fire team An infantry unit that consisted of three to five men.

five by five Indicated that you were receiving a radio transmission loud and clear.

fix When the forward air controller provided an MGF unit with his estimate of their coordinates.

FOB Forward operations base.

Fox Control Radio call sign used by Lt. James Condon.

Fox Four Radio call sign used by the Recon Platoon.

Fox One Radio call sign used by the 1st Platoon.

Fox Three Radio call sign used by the 3d Platoon.

Fox Two Radio call sign used by the 2d Platoon.

Gen. General.

grazing fire When bullets pass through an enemy formation at a level never higher than their chests or lower than their hips—the most deadly form of fire.

greased A slang expression for "killed."

grunt Infantry.

gunship A Huey helicopter armed with machine guns and rockets that was used to provide close air support to troops engaged in ground combat.

GWOA Guerrilla warfare operational area.

halazone tablet Water purification tablet.

HALO High altitude–low opening. A technique of infiltrating an enemy-controlled area by parachute.

HE High explosive.

hematocrit A test that measures the percentage of red blood cells in whole blood.

hemostat clamp Surgical instrument used to stop bleeding by clamping tissue or blood vessels. Also used to hold a suture needle when sewing up a wound.

Ho Chi Minh trail A complex system of trails and roads that ran south from North Vietnam through Laos and Cambodia. The system was used to transport men, equipment, and supplies into South Vietnam.

Ho Ngoc Tao Special Forces camp north of Saigon.

hootch Small house or structure constructed of bamboo, straw, and thatch.

hop To hitch a ride on a helicopter or airplane.

HT-1 radio Walkie-talkie–type radio used by MGF platoon sergeants and squad leaders.

Huey UH-1 helicopter. Used to transport troops and equipment and to provide close air support.

Immediate-action drill Practicing a preplanned reaction to contact with an enemy force.

indig Abbreviation for indigenous personnel—Cambodians, Chinese Nungs, montagnards, and Vietnamese.

instant detonation To remove the four-second, time-delay section from a hand grenade so that it will explode instantly when its safety pin is removed and safety lever released.

intel Abbreviation for intelligence information.

IV Intravenous injection of blood replacements such as normal saline, or blood plasma expanders such as serum albumin.

JCRC Joint Casualty Resolution Center.

K-bar Marine Corps knife.

Kampuchea Cambodia.

Khmer Cambodian.

Khmer Krom Cambodians who live in what is now Vietnam.

Khmer Rouge Cambodian Communists.

Khmer Serei Free Cambodians.

KIA Killed in action.

kilometer One-thousand meters.

klick Short for kilometer.

Kuomintang The ruling party of the government on Taiwan, and until 1949, on the Chinese Mainland; Anti-Communist Chinese forces commanded by Chiang Kai-shek during World War II. After the Communist victory in China, many of the Kuomintang forces retreated to Southeast Asia.

lidocaine hydrochloride An injectable local anesthetic.

listening post A one-, two-, or three-man post set up on the most likely avenues of approach to a base camp. Their mission was to observe and report on enemy activity.

Lon Nol   Cambodian general who, with U.S. assistance, overthrew and replaced Prince Norodum Sihanouk as the leader of Cambodia.

Luc Luong Dac Biet   Vietnamese Special Forces.

LZ   Landing zone.

MAAG-Laos   Military Advisory Assistance Group-Laos.

MACV-SOG   Military Assistance Command, Vietnam Studies and Observation Group. Conducted reconnaissance and intelligence operations in South Vietnam, North Vietnam, Cambodia, and Laos.

mags   Short for magazines. An M-16 magazine held twenty rounds.

Maj.   Major.

MASH   Mobile army surgical hospital.

medevac   Helicopter extraction of the sick, wounded, and dead from the battlefield.

meprobamate   A mild tranquilizer that was used to relax muscles.

M-5 medical kit   Large medical kit carried by MGF company and platoon medics.

MGF   Mobile Guerrilla Force.

MIA/POW   Missing in action/prisoner of war.

Mike Force   Multipurpose reaction force whose primary mission was to come to the assistance of Special Forces units that were under attack or the threat of attack by larger enemy forces.

Mister Charles   Viet Cong.

MK-II British Sten gun   Silencer-equipped 9mm submachine gun that the MGF used when the silent killing or wounding of an enemy soldier was required.

Mobile Guerrilla Force   A Special Forces commanded unit that was assigned the mission of conducting guerrilla operations against Viet Cong and North Vietnamese forces.

moleskin   A cotton fabric used to cover blisters or areas of the skin that have been rubbed raw.

montagnards   Hill people of Vietnam.

morphine   Injectable, high-potency narcotic pain reliever.

Morse code   A coded communications system invented by S.F.B. Morse that was used by the MGF when secret transmissions were necessary.

M-79   40mm grenade launcher.

M.Sgt.   Master sergeant.

MS-1   Wire tap device.

M-3 medical kit   Small medical kit carried by MGF squad medics.

naval flare   Pen-size signal flare used to signal aircraft.

NCO   Noncommissioned officer.

normal saline IV   A sterile salt water IV that was used to treat or prevent shock. Also used to treat serious cases of heat exhaustion or sunstroke.

numba one   Very good.

numba ten   Very bad.

Nui Ba Den   Black Virgin Mountain.

nuoc mam   Strong-smelling fish extract used by Southeast Asians to add flavor to rice.

NVA   North Vietnamese Army.

O-1E   Small, single-engine, propeller-driven, forward air control aircraft.

105   105mm artillery.

175   175mm artillery.

OP   Observation post.

orange ground panel   Reflective panel that was used to signal aircraft.

pallet   a wooden platform on which fifty cases of beer or soft drinks were stacked and banded together.

penicillin   An antibiotic made from molds that is effective against certain classes of bacteria.

pHisoHex   Surgical soap.

pith helmet   Helmet worn by some NVA and Viet Cong units.

point   Lead man in an infantry column.

policed   Term for "cleaning up."

porked   Killed.

POW   Prisoner of war.

PRC-74   Radio used by the MGF to communicate by voice or Morse code with someone beyond the range of the PRC-25 Radio.

Project Delta   Special Forces unit that conducted secret reconnaissance and intelligence gathering missions.

Project Omega   Special Forces unit that conducted secret reconnaissance and intelligence gathering missions.

pull device   A wire that, if pulled, would detonate a booby trap.

pungi pit   A camouflaged hole containing sharpened bamboo stakes.

PX   Post exchange.

recon   Reconnaissance.

Recondo School   Special Forces school in Nha Trang that trained personnel for long-range patrol and other special operations.

ROTC   Reserve Officer Training Corps.

RP   A reference point on the map where two grid lines cross.

RPG   Rocket-propelled grenade.

RPM   Revolutions per minute.

rucksack   The backpack carried in the field by MGF troops.

sak-sa-bai?   How are you?

sau lam   Not good.

SCUBA   Self-contained underwater breathing apparatus.

scuttlebutt   Marine Corps/navy term for rumors.

serum albumin   A blood-volume expander that increases blood volume by absorbing fluids from the area surrounding the vessels.

SF   Special Forces.

SFC   Sergeant first class.

Sgt. Maj.   Sergeant major.

shock   A state of acute circulatory insufficiency of blood. Usually caused by injury, burns, or hemorrhage.

Sihanouk, Prince Norodom   Leader of Cambodia.

six-digit fix   When a Forward Air Controller provided an MGF unit with his estimate of their coordinates—within 100 meters.

Sky Spot   Computer-controlled air strike that could be called in on known coordinates at night or during bad weather.

slope   A derogatory term for an Asian.

SMAG   Special Missions Advisory Group.

soc-mow   Bloody nose.

SOG   Studies & Observations Group.

SOI   Signal operating instructions.

SOP   Standard operating procedure.

Special Forces   American soldiers trained in unconventional operations. Activated at Fort Bragg, North Carolina, on June 20, 1952. They were first deployed to Vietnam in 1957.

S.Sgt.   Staff sergeant.

sterile technique   To perform a medical procedure without contaminating the wound.

Stieng tribe   A montagnard tribe that lived in the northern part of the III Corps Tactical Zone of South Vietnam.

S-2   Intelligence officer.

subdural hematoma   Blood clot between the skull and brain.

Swamp Fox   Radio call sign used by Maj. James Gritz.

Swedish-K   9mm submachine gun that was manufactured in Sweden.

systolic pressure   A measurement of blood pressure.

TAC   Tactical Air Command.

tail gunner   Three- or four-man stay-behind ambush whose mission it was to booby-trap the trail left by the MGF and to ambush enemy trackers.

terpin hydrate   Liquid cough medicine.

tetanus toxoid   An immunization against tetanus (lockjaw).

Third Herd   The 3d Platoon.

III Corps Tactical Zone   Included the city of Saigon and extended from the northern Mekong Delta to the southern highlands.

time pencil   A time-delay device that could be attached to grenades or claymore mines. Once attached, it would delay the explosion for a fixed period of time.

toe popper   Small pressure-detonated booby trap intended to disable the enemy.

Tan Son Nhut   Large Vietnamese/American Air Force base located on the outskirts of Saigon.

tracer   A bullet with a phosphorus coating designed to burn and provide a visual indication of the bullet's trajectory.

trung si   Sergeant.

Trung si Camau   Sergeant Black.

Viet Cong or **VC**   South Vietnamese Communists.

Viet Cong province committee   Provided leadership at the province level.

Viet Cong secret zone   A well-defended enemy base area about which allied forces knew little or nothing.

Viet Minh   Short for Viet Nam Doc Lap Dong Minh or League for the Independence of Vietnam. Organized by Communist and Nationalist forces during the Japanese occupation of Vietnam.

Wetsu   Short for "we eat this shit up." Used as a password by the MGF.

White Dot signal mirror   U.S. Air Force issue signal mirror that was used by the MGF to signal aircraft.

white phosphorous round   Gave off a thick white smoke. Used by the forward air controller to pinpoint the location of enemy targets when he was directing air strikes.

WIA   Wounded in action.

xin-loi   Sorry.

Xylocaine   Injectable local anesthetic.

ORGANIZATIONS

Khmers-Kampuchea-Krom Federation
c/o Kim Thong
P.O. Box 2639
Lakewood, CA 90714-6239
(562) 598-5431
E-mail: kkfed@yahoo.com

Special Forces Association
c/o Jimmy Dean
P.O. Box 41436
Fayetteville, NC 28309-1436
(910) 485-5433
FAX (910) 485-1041
www.sfahq.org
E-mail: SFAHQ@aol.com

United Cambodian-American Association
c/o Son Thai Hien
5402 B Street
Philadelphia, PA 19120
(215) 455-2216
FAX (215) 455-8794

INDEX

BLACKJACK-33
With Special Forces in the Viet Cong Forbidden Zone

by James C. Donahue

In Vietnam, Mobile Guerrilla Force was the only American unit that truly carried out guerrilla-style hit-and-run operations. Its soldiers roamed for weeks at a time through steamy triple-canopy jungle in areas owned by the NVA and VC, destroying base camps, ambushing enemy forces, and gathering the intelligence Saigon desperately needed.

In 1967, James Donahue was a Special Forces medic and an assistant platoon leader for the Mobile Guerrilla Force's fiercely anti-Vietnamese Cambodian irregulars. On mission Blackjack-33, the Mobile Guerrilla Force was to act as bait, luring VC and NVA regiments into decisive engagements so that the Communists could be engaged and destroyed by the 1st Infantry Division. Well, the MGF did its job, but the 1st Infantry Division didn't show up. . . .

Published by The Ballantine Publishing Group.
Available in bookstores everywhere.